THE
EVENING GARDEN

∽ THE ∽

EVENING GARDEN

WRITTEN AND ILLUSTRATED BY
PETER LOEWER

Macmillan Publishing Company
NEW YORK

Maxwell Macmillan Canada
TORONTO

Maxwell Macmillan International
NEW YORK · OXFORD · SINGAPORE · SYDNEY

Macmillan Publishing Company
866 Third Avenue
New York, NY 10022

Maxwell Macmillan Canada, Inc.
1200 Eglinton Avenue East
Suite 200
Don Mills, Ontario M3C 3N1

Macmillan Publishing Company is part of the Maxwell Communication Group of Companies.

The lines from "The Air Plant" are reprinted from *The Complete Poems and Selected Letters and Prose of Hart Crane*, edited by Brom Weber, by permission of Liveright Publishing Corporation. ©1933, © 1958, © 1966 by Liveright Publishing Corporation.

Excerpt from "There at Dusk I found You" by Edna St. Vincent Millay. From *Collected Poems*, HarperCollins. © 1928, © 1955 by Edna St. Vincent Millay and Norma Millay Ellis. Reprinted by permission of Elizabeth Barnett, Literary Executor.

"The Evening Primrose," © 1931, renewed © 1959 by Dorothy Parker, from *The Portable Dorothy Parker* by Dorothy Parker, Introduction by Brendan Gill. Used by permission of Viking Penguin, a Division of Penguin Books USA, Inc.

"Planning the Garden" by Amy Lowell is reprinted by permission of Houghton Mifflin Company.

"The Fountain" by Sara Teasdale is from *Collected Poems of Sarah Teasdale* (New York: Macmillan, 1937).

Library of Congress Cataloging-in-Publication Data

Loewer, H. Peter.
The evening garden / Peter Loewer.
p.   cm.
Includes bibliographical references and index.
ISBN 0-02-574041-5
1. Night gardens.   2. Night flowering plants.   3. Night-fragrant flowers.
I. Title.
SB433.6.L64   1992
635.9′53—dc20   92-20499
CIP

Book design by Jennifer Dossin

10 9 8 7 6 5 4 3 2 1

Printed in the United States of America

TO JEAN

✺ CONTENTS ✺

❧ ACKNOWLEDGMENTS ❧

The Evening Garden was a long time in the writing and even longer in collecting all the needed information—in fact the project began about eleven years ago. Over those years a number of people have listened to my fixations on the evening garden (an idea that I think first belonged to Nyx, the original goddess of night, who was the daughter of Chaos and the mother of Day and the Light), and mention must go to them all.

In the world of publishing, thanks must go to my agent Dominick Abel for sticking with the initial idea and my editor at Macmillan, Pam Hoenig, for not only giving me the support needed to finish *The Evening Garden,* but for understanding the value of such a book. Then my wife, Jean, gets heartfelt thanks for putting up with the long hours and the occasional moods that go hand in hand with this kind of project.

Then thanks are not only necessary but obligatory to all the gardeners, botanists, and horticultural experts who gave me advice and answered my endless questions. They include: Fred Berry of the Tropical Flowering Tree Society; Phelan Bright of the Magnolia Society; Christine M. Burton, The Hoya Society International; Dennis Cathcart, Tropiflora; Elizabeth Clark, a Texas flower; Keith Crotz, The Amerian Botanist; Ara Das, Daylily Discounters; Ken Durio of the Louisiana Nursery; Kathleen Fisher of the American Horticultural Society; Alfred Byrd Graf, Roehrs Company; Fred Hillerman, The Angraecum House; Ursula Herz, Coastal Gardens; William Hoenig, Joyce Owens, Alec Pridgeon, and Lee C. Soule, The American Orchid Society; L. A. Jackson, *Carolina Gardener;* John A. Kafka for the daturas; W. John Kress and Warren L. Wagner, Associate Curators of Botany at the National Museum of Natural History; Myron Kimnach, Huntington Botanical Garden; Harry Logan, Western Carolina Botanical Club; Jan MacDougal, Oak Manor Press; Julia F. Morton, Director of the Morton Collectanea; Ed Rasmussen, The Fragrant Path; Robert Rolfe, Alpine Garden Society; R. Donald Spencer, Nocturnal Round Robin; Larry M. Schokman of the Kampong; Charles B. Thomas, Lilypons Water Gardens; Michael Vassar, International Geranium Society; Hans Wiehler, Gesneriad Research Foundation; and finally, The Missouri Botanical Garden, including Marshall Crosby, Assistant Director, John M. MacDougal, Conservatory Manager, James E. Henrich, Acting Director of Horticulture, Marilyn LeDoux, Senior Horticulturist, Orchid Collection, and Charlotte M. Taylor, Assistant Curator.

ℭHINGS THAT GO BUMP
IN THE NIGHT

―――――――

From ghoulies and ghosties and long-leggety beasties
And things that go bump in the night,
Good Lord, deliver us!

An old Cornish prayer

Why make an evening garden, a garden that doesn't awake until the twilight hours and, in many cases, is at its best long after the sun has set?

The answer to that can be prefaced with another question: What's left of your day after you've met your commitments to family, home, job, and community? Those hours of leisure that were promised to all after the end of World War II seemed to exist for a while during the 1950s, but with each succeeding decade, they've decreased, leading to today's cry: "What's happened to my free time?"

I can't turn back history's clock, but when it comes to gardening, I can suggest a way to make the most of the time you do have, and that is turning your garden—or part of your garden—into an activity center that begins to swing into action when most of the day's responsibilities have been met, after the sun has sunk below the horizon.

The evening garden is a great spot for entertaining. From a terrace in the city, to a deck or patio in the country, it's not only the perfect site for both relaxing and thinking about the day that's passed, it's just a very comfortable place to be, especially if your garden contains plants that either bloom at night or choose that time to waft their subtle fragrances on the air.

My wife and I have had parties that revolved around the opening of the moonflower vine on a summer evening. I've actually taken visitors on a moonlight walk in the garden, and many are the nights we've stood next to a blooming evening primrose and watched the endless stream of moths that flock to these blossoms after the sun goes down. Other times we have sat alone in the garden and enjoyed the soft lights of the moon and stars (or the lights we have installed around the garden's edges) and listened to the wonderful sounds of the evening. Without the distractions of the day, the night gives us a better chance to think and perhaps philosophize a bit about our place, if not in the grand scheme of things, at least in the world of the garden.

My interest in things nocturnal began when I was very young and my fascination with strange and sometimes evil plants began at a Saturday matinee in 1943 with a showing of *Tarzan's Desert Mystery*. Johnny Weismuller as Tarzan was forced to swing through the lianas to rescue Boy or Jane from a number of backlot threats, one of which was a colossal man-eating plant that threatened to devour a very young Nancy Kelly in the role of Jane. The tentacles looped about and whipped hither, thither, and yon, while sharp and greedy jaws gnashed about like a chlorophyllic meat grinder. Luckily Tarzan was stronger and Jane survived.

What began one year was clasped to my bosom the next, when I shivered in my theater seat and watched as *Sherlock Holmes and the Spider Woman* pitted Basil Rathbone against Gale Sondergaard. She grew night-blooming plants in a hot and dank basement south of Soho in order to feed a poison-producing spider of such venom that death was instantaneous (the spider was called the *Lycosa carnivora* and it came from the upper reaches of the Obongo River). But she didn't hit her stride until the 1946 sequel *The Spider Woman Strikes Back*. In this film, the plants moved about a lot but any clue to their real botanical nature was effectively hidden by mists that swirled in the underground hothouse.

It was twenty years later when I finally caught the 1935 movie *Werewolf of London* on Zacherly's television horror movie show in the 1960s. In this case a botanist, Dr. Wilfred Glendon, is bitten by another botanist, Dr. Yorgami (who is also a werewolf), while both are searching the mountains of Tibet for the rare plant that is the one effective antidote to the curse of lycanthropy. This fanciful flower, known as *Mariphasa lumena lupina*, will only unfold its stop-action petals for the two nights out of every twenty-seven when the full moon floats high. That's the only time the chemical cure is available.

Under the light of Wilfred's moon machine—an effective-looking apparatus with a large lens about three feet wide surrounded by four smaller lenses, looking like the top to the Chrysler Building—a moonvine flowers.

"But this is a human plant," remarks Wilfred's assistant. "Of course it would open. But this other plant is a plant of the devil—"

And with those telling words, the mariphasa opens.

When I saw the 1931 *Dracula* on television I learned about the values of garlic but it wasn't until I caught up with the 1935 *Mark of the Vampire* that I found out about bat thorn, a plant that vampires really dislike.

When the second or third body was discovered in the library, the police inspector asks the local doctor why he did nothing to stop the murders. The professor stands by.

"But it was night and I realized there was nothing I could do," said the doctor.

"You're no moon flower, you're a morning glory," replies the inspector.

"There's a certain thorny weed that grows in these parts?" asks the professor.

"Yes, bat thorn," answers the inspector.

"But there's a catch. The head must be severed from the body and bat thorn placed in the open wound."

There have been other movies that have used nocturnal flowers in their plots. In the 1951 *The Thing*, the creature (described as a giant carrot) leaves behind strange pods that grow under artificial light and feed on human plasma; in the 1963 *The Day of the Triffids*, seeds from another world arrive in a meteor shower and germinate in the greenhouses of Kew Gardens after the sun sets and the visitors have all gone home; and in the 1978 *Dinner for Adele*, a carnivorous plant named Adele chooses her victims with care and dispatches them in the dark.

The Beginnings of This Book

Back in the late 1970s, when I really became interested in writing about gardens on a full-time basis, I remembered some of the early movies that I had enjoyed and began to wonder just how many nocturnal flowers there really were. And I began to wonder about what really happens in the evening garden: not about monsters but about real living things that decided millions of years ago that the world of the night could be just as valuable as the world of the day.

Literature, of course, painted a more romantic view of the evening garden. In the 1922 mystery *The Red Redmaynes* (published by Macmillan), Eden Phillpots wrote the following:

> She was in his arms now and he sought to soothe her, sustain her and bring her mind to regard a future wherein peace, happiness and content might still be her portion. Another hour passed, the fireflies danced over their heads; sweet scents stole through the garden; lights twinkled from the house; on the lake in the silence that now fell between them they heard the gentle thud of a steamer's propeller.

I became so enamoured of the garden at night that visitors to our home would be taken on moonlight walks. I can remember one Christmas weekend with a full moon overhead when fifteen people, bundled up and breathing hard, were taken on a tour around the winter garden, the snow sparkling in the moonlight, the trees and shrubs in sharp silhouette—and everyone enjoyed the experience.

By 1985 I began work on a book entitled *Gardens by Design* (Rodale Press). In its pages I designed and wrote about twelve different theme gardens, including one called "The Night Garden."

Then I really became consumed with the subject. I called the late Elisabeth Woodburn, who had one of the most complete selections of rare garden books in the country and was herself a very knowledgeable gardener and a very intelligent observer.

"Elisabeth," I asked, "do you know of any books ever written about nocturnal flowers or about evening gardens or gardening at night?"

She thought for a moment and asked: "How about *The After Dinner Garden Book*?"

"No," I answered, "I know that one and it's about gardening with seeds from the various foods at the dinner table."

"I'll call you back."

The next day she called and said: "Not a one."

So I began to search old books for information on plants with nocturnal habits. But it's easier said than done. Most authors assumed that readers were not interested in such things and never used the heading of nocturnal (or night blooming, crepuscular, or vespertine for that matter*) in their indexes. That meant that the usual reference book had to be checked from front to back for any floral or scent information.

But I continued in the search: Plants came from far and wide and I joined an inordinate number of seed exchanges in my continual hunt for flowers of the night. My tropical collections grew to include bromeliads and orchids, especially those with fragrance, and other delightfully unusual blossoms of the evening—and the search goes on today.

The Plants in This Book

Most gardeners in America live in parts of the country where winter temperatures fall below

---

*There are three words used in the study of night-blooming and night-fragrant flowers. *Vespertine* means of or done in the evening and refers to flowers that open at that time. The word is derived from the Latin for the evening star. *Crepuscular* means activity at dusk or twilight and comes from the Latin word for twilight. *Nocturnal* means only blooming at night, from the Latin *nox* or *noctis* for night. And of course *diurnal* means opening only during the day, its roots being the Latin for day.

freezing for vast stretches of time. Since the majority of nocturnal plants are tropical in origin—and unwilling to adapt to frozen ground—plants for the evening garden must be chosen from cold-hardy perennials and annuals, with tropicals limited to those flowers that winter either in the greenhouse or a sunny window and summer in the backyard. Since a large number of fragrant plants, daylilies, water lilies, cactuses, evening primroses, and even wildflowers are nocturnal, they each have a chapter of their own.

A WORD ABOUT CLIMATE ZONES

For decades, the United States Department of Agriculture (USDA) published a map showing ten climate zones based on average minimum temperatures found in various parts of the United States and Canada. The Arnold Arboretum (AA) also published a map depicting ten zones. The maps did not match. The USDA listed Zone 5 as −20°F to −10°F while the AA has Zone 5 between −5°F and −10°F. Various books and nursery catalogs would use one map or the other, often not pointing out to the reader which was being quoted. Then to further confuse the issue, in January 1990 the USDA issued a new map that depicted eleven zones. Zone 11 has a minimum temperature above 40°F and in the continental limits of our country is found in two tiny parts of California and the Florida Keys.

Be sure to keep in mind that the first ten zones on the new map do not match the old map. Take North Carolina, for example. In the old USDA map, that state was in Zone 7 (except for a tiny spot in the upper northwest corner) and Zone 8, with the coldest minimum temperatures ranging from 0°F up to 10°F. In the new map it is in Zone 6 and Zone 7. The coldest temperatures are now −10°F to 10°F. This is the result of averaging in some colder than usual winter temperatures over the past few years and possibly a belief by the government that there is no warming trend.

Unfortunately, it will be decades before all the garden reference books, nursery catalogs, and commercial plant lists are reprinted to align with the new 1990 USDA map. Therefore in the interests of clarity, this book uses the old USDA map (see page 245).

And microclimates should be mentioned. These are areas that are sheltered from the worst of the winter winds or receive protection from a small hill or enjoy extra warmth from a southern exposure. Such areas help marginally hardy plants to survive. One of the marvelous adventures of gardening is experimenting with plant placement and therefore succeeding with a rare specimen that everyone else in the neighborhood has lost because they did not provide that extra margin of protection.

Flower Pollinators

Flowers are often grouped into those pollinated by animals and those pollinated by insects. The first group contains the birds and the bats, the birds working during the day and the bats at night. The second group includes bees, beetles, flies, butterflies, and moths (and, of all things, slugs, those noxious insects of the garden that pollinate the aspidistra when it grows in its native China). Moths are mentioned throughout the book while bat-pollinated flowers are mentioned in the chapters on cactuses and flowering tropical trees. A number of night-blooming and night-fragrant flowers including the occasional lily and most of the magnolias that are visited by beetles are covered, too. As to the flies, they pollinate by day, reserving their services for flowers like the desert stapeliads with their odor of rotted meat or the giant amorphophallus, those exotic flowers of the steaming jungles, and these are mentioned in a chapter devoted to plants that look like they should bloom at night—but don't.

I've also included a chapter about other denizens of the night, including fireflies and glowworms, the singing insects, and even frogs. Finally there is a chapter on the light of the eve-

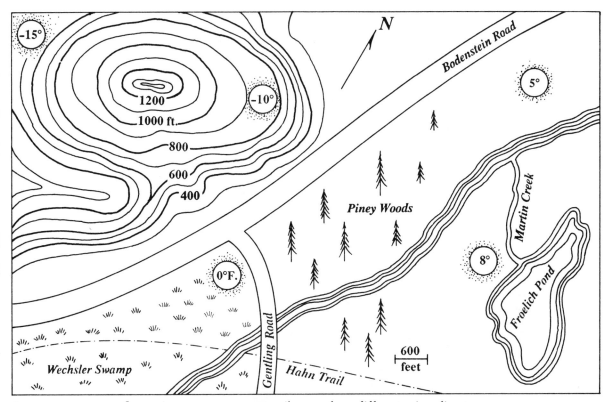

January temperature fluctuations over one square mile area show different microclimates.

ning skies including the moon and the stars plus a chapter on planning your own light system if you wish to outshine the skies above.

So what began with Saturday afternoons at the movies turned into a life with plants. I've grown hundreds and lost hundreds of flowers; I've also read hundreds of gardening books, both old and new; I've broken fingernails and torn the knees out of countless pairs of pants; and I've suffered the outrageous stings of black flies and mosquitoes; and as a result of my imaginary travels, I've gardened the regular way and I've gardened for the night. This book is the result of taking the second path through the garden.

The fragrant blossoms of the *Lilium formosanum* attract a virgin tiger moth, *Apantesis virgo*, to the evening garden.

CHAPTER ONE

𝒯HE BEAUTY OF THE NIGHT

———

And from the phlox and mignonette
    Rich attars drift on every hand;
And when star-vestured twilight comes
    The pale moths weave a saraband.
And crickets in the aisles of grass
    With their clear fifing pierce the hush;
And somewhere you may hear anear
    The passion of the hermit thrush.

CLINTON SCOLLARD, *A Midsummer Garden*

𝓛et me tell you about the night. It often begins in late afternoon when the sun is low on the horizon. The blue of the sky begins to darken and suddenly has a different quality. On the American prairie the day continues until the sun is suddenly sliced off at the bottom. In the mountains night comes faster and we see the light still reflected on the far-off peaks while we ourselves are in darkness. At the shore, we watch the sun dissolve into the sea and those in the know wait for the green flash,* a second or two of unexpected color before the sky turns rusty red and Venus as the evening star begins to shine.

*As the sun nears the horizon it becomes an overlapping set of colors in the order of red, orange, yellow, green, blue, and indigo, with red on the bottom. Blue, indigo, and violet are scattered by the atmosphere and we never see them. Orange and yellow are soaked up by the water vapor in the earth's atmosphere. So only red and green are left. When the red image of the sun sets, we see a brief flash of green.

Birds sing just as they do in the morning but somehow it all seems louder at dusk. Bees that have become so drunk with honey and pollen that the lengthening afternoon has passed them by, settle down within a flower and wait for the heat and directional beacon of the morning sun to waken them and lead the way back to the hive. Wasps cease their buzzing, bumblebees go back to their abandoned mouseholes, butterflies fold their wings, dragonflies find a perch, and a silver-spotted ghost moth begins to dance up and down in the fading light.

It's time for the evening primroses in the wild garden to begin to unfold their sulfur yellow petals and the hawkmoths to respond to the blossoms' sweetness that is wafted on the cooling air. The moths suddenly leave their daytime hiding places and, like phantom shuttlecocks, zero in on the luminous flowers.

But as the sky turns to purple and the Milky

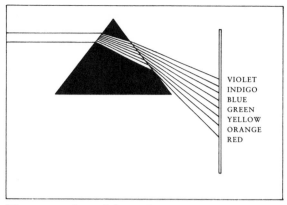

The seven colors of the sun's spectrum.

VIOLET
INDIGO
BLUE
GREEN
YELLOW
ORANGE
RED

Way streams across the heavens, many other insects come out: the fireflies send their Morse codes to other fireflies; beetles of every description appear from nowhere to climb about the garden lilies; and the night-fragrant plants begin to send their Lorelei perfumes out on the evening air.

By the Light of the Moon

The light of the full moon equals the light of 100,000 stars of the brightness of Arcturus in the constellation of Boötes (itself about zero magnitude and the third brightest star in the sky) and it is 1/600,000th part of the sun's light. Amazingly, the moon only reflects about one tenth of the sunlight that falls upon it, the rest being absorbed by the lunar surface. In turn, the earth reflects to the moon about fourteen times as much light as the moon sends to earth because of the light reflected from the oceans and the clouds of the world. (Around the time of the new moon, if you know where to look, the lunar disk is easily seen basking in the somewhat reddish light provided by the earth. Leonardo da Vinci was the first scientist to explain this phenomenon.)

The rumor is that it's easy to read a book or a newspaper by the light of the full moon, but go out and try to read under these conditions and you'll find it's not that simple.

Garden Colors at Night

According to the 1935 *Murder in the Madhouse* by Jonathan Latimer (Curtis Brown Ltd.), the garden at night was a place without color:

> In the moonlight the garden was a photographic negative, all blacks and grays and whites, without depth and without relation to each other, as if they had been pieces of dark paper pasted on a blackboard. A savage slash of chalk was the path, while the shadows of shrubs and flowers were substantial blocks of black, and the vegetation itself was gray and unreal. Overhead there was the cry of night birds, sometimes angry and sometimes alarmed.

Tradescant, writing in the June 1991 issue of *The Garden*, reports that well-printed black and white photographs have a power that is denied to color "by scanning the profile of a garden scene and the tones that comprise it with a relentless undistracted eye." So he took advantage of a full moon and went out to inspect his own garden. There he saw all his mistakes including spotty planting and ugly outlines and admits that the garden in black and white is a tough test to pass.

Just as red, and that sometime touch of green, are the last colors to be seen when the sun dips below the horizon, red is the first color to fade in the evening garden. After the sun has set go out on a moonlit night and stand near some bright red geraniums. Look at their color as they stand out against the dark green of a shrubbery background or the green of the grass. Soon those reds turn gray and if you stand patiently, you will see them finally fade to black. Some purples brighten up for a few moments thanks to the loss of red but they soon fade. Then the yellows and whites begin to stand like beacons in the growing dark. And finally the world is all in shades of gray and even with a full moon above, there are no colors to be seen. The world becomes a black-and-white movie. But why?

The Eyes at Night

In normal light our eyes see with the cells in the retina. The long cells are called rods and the short cells, cones. They are shaped like wooden kitchen matches and a box full of such matches makes a good model of the retina. Originally animal eyes were made entirely of rods and the eyes of all nocturnal animals have only rods. But animals that see by the light of the day need better eyesight and since the cones are much more efficient, the ratio increases—in fact, the eyes of birds are composed entirely of cones. With man, the area around the center of the retina consists of cones, then, as you move out to the periphery of the retina, the rods take over and eventually at the outer margins, only rods are present. The eye of man gets the best of both worlds.

Those readers who have been in the armed services will no doubt remember the special training received for the night firing of a rifle or how to walk along a pathway in the dark. If an observer stands in front of, let's say, a used-car lot with a building in the center, during the day the eye sees the building and the immediate cars with great clarity and is usually unaware of objects at the outer limits of the lot. But at night, the building itself becomes blurred but to the right (or the left), we see a small area with greater clarity. This is why the first sergeant would tell you to look out of the side of each eye.

You can test this out by placing two three-by-three-inch Post-its on a wall about ten inches apart. Then darken the room until the papers can just be seen. If you fix your eyes on the left paper, it will not be visible but you will see the paper on the right. If you look at the paper on the right, only the left will be seen. Some scientists claim that this peripheral vision is responsible for the sighting of most ghosts. In the twilight you will see something out of the corner of your eye that will disappear when you look directly at it.

There is a special chemical in the rod cells of the eye called rhodopsin, or visual purple, and this chemical is bleached out by bright light. Without rhodopsin, the rods in the retina are unable to sense light. But when you enter a dark room, visual purple begins to form and before too long there is enough present to detect light. (One of the primary ingredients of rhodopsin is vitamin A, so carrots and squash are good for your eyes.) Soon your eyes begin to be aware of their surroundings. After fifteen minutes there is enough visual purple present to boost the eye to two thousand times its original efficiency.

Another way to try this out is to go to the movies. As you buy your ticket, close one eye (and ignore any looks you get from theater personnel), and keep it closed until you enter the darkened auditorium. Then open that eye and close the other, and you will be amazed to find that finding a seat will be easy as pie.

So to really enjoy the garden at night, remember to give your eyes the chance to adjust themselves to the dark.

THE PURKINJE EFFECT

Johannes Evangelista Purkinje was born in Libochovice, Bohemia (now Czechoslovakia), on December 17, 1787, and died in Prague, Bohemia, in 1869. He's remembered for many scientific findings including the Purkinje fibers in the heart and the Purkinje cells in the cerebellum, but for the evening garden the most important discovery was the understanding of the Purkinje phenomenon, the shift in the relative apparent brightness of red and green as compared to yellow and blue in dim light.

Only the cones in our eyes can distinguish color; the rods located within the periphery of the retina are colorblind. The rest of the eye can see blue and yellow while the fields for red and green are restricted to the eye's center section. Purkinje demonstrated that in dim light the ability to see red and green disappears and we are left with blue and yellow plus black, white, and shades of gray. As the light continues to dim, yellow fades—though it seems to glow just before it passes from our sight—but our eyes are still capable of discerning brightness and can easily see white light. Finally only white light remains in the evening garden, and though studded with stars, the deep blue of the night sky has quickly changed to black.

Even though the moon above looks brilliant and the garden is spread before us in its glowing light, the intensity of that light is not enough to stimulate the cones and we are left with the black and white vision of the rods.

NOCTURNAL EYES

If you could see the pupils of your eyes in the dark, they would be huge circles of black, the irises widened to their ultimate, allowing the maximum amount of light possible to fall on the rods in the retina. But the human eye must take a backseat when compared to the eye of the cat or the owl, or for that matter, the moth. Although a cat's eyes are well adapted to seeing in daylight, you will note that in bright sunlight the pupil is a mere black slit. But comes the night, that slit expands until most of the creature's eye is black.

The great family of the birds, for example, has daytime members like chickens, and nocturnal members like the owl. Chicken retinas contain only cones and these birds are entirely blind at night—hence their docile return to the roost. Owls (and bats) have retinas that contain only rods, and because these rods occur in clusters, they have a sensitivity far stronger than man's. The eye of a cat has two thousand times as many rods as man, and because it hunts in the water at night, a dolphin has seven thousand times as many such cells.

Nocturnal animals have another unique ability. If they possessed eyes like man or other diurnal animals, a certain amount of light would escape detection by the rods and simply be absorbed by surrounding tissues to no effect. But night-wanderers have a tapetum, a layer of spe-

cialized cells that act like mirrors, reflecting light back through the retina where it has a second chance at stimulating the sense of sight. This structure is quite visible when night-prowling animals like rabbits, dogs, cats, skunks, and deer are caught in the headlights of a car or stare back at a flashlight. In some animals it creates a red glow while in others it is yellow or green.

Starlight and Skylight

Even without the moon above, there is light. Starlight alone produces enough light to be able to walk a garden pathway, once the eyes are accustomed to the dark. And if it's a cloudy night and you live anywhere near a concentration of civilization, there will still be light, causing a glow on the horizon. Jules Verne once said: "On earth, even on the darkest night, light never abdicates its rights. It may be subtle and diffuse, but however little light there may be, the eye finally perceives it."

Our galaxy is called the Milky Way and contains about a trillion stars. That band of stars that stretches far overhead is the result of looking either toward the edge or the center of our galaxy. The sun is located about 27,000 light-years from the center of our galaxy, and about 13,000 light-years from its edge. The Milky Way is disk-shaped, about 80,000 light-years across and averages some 10,000 light-years thick. Luckily for gardeners in the northern hemisphere, because of earth's orbit, the Milky Way is far more spectacular in the summer than the winter.

VENUS AND THE
TEN BRIGHTEST STARS

Why should planets and stars be included in a talk about the evening garden? Because they are there, clear and sparkling in the black sky above. Once we decide the weather for the day and how it will affect our gardening, we immediately ignore the daylight sky. But the overwhelming presence of that night sky is difficult to ignore.

The planets roam the evening skies, sometimes bright and sometimes dim, but one planet should be mentioned in any talk about evening gardens—Venus. Depending on the earth's place in its orbit and its relation to Venus, this cloud-cloaked sister planet is either an evening star or a morning star. When Venus shines in the evening, she is very bright indeed, easily visible in the western sky, while the twilight sky is still flushed with the waning light of the setting sun.

At certain times Venus can be the brightest object in the sky after the sun and the moon. It can be brighter than the magnitude − 4, and can even cast shadows in the garden.

Magnitude is the method astronomers use to measure the brightness of a star. It's obvious that some stars are brighter than others. The term magnitude, when applied to stars, has no relation to size but instead to brilliancy as seen from earth. Stars are classified as first magnitude, second magnitude, on up to the twentieth magnitude—the higher the number, the weaker the star's light. Each magnitude is two and a half times brighter than the preceding number. Thus a first magnitude star is two and a half times brighter than one of the second magnitude, while a second magnitude star is six and a quarter times brighter than a third magnitude star. A star of the sixth magnitude can just about be detected by the human eye. Since a few stars are brighter than true first magnitude, they get a minus sign. The star Sirius is so bright, its magnitude is − 1.46.

The following are the ten brightest stars in the evening sky of the northern hemisphere (excluding the sun):

Sirius, the dog star and the brightest in the heavens, is located in the constellation Canis Major, the Big Dog. Sirius was worshipped by the ancient Egyptians and temples were built in its honor because its rising in the eastern sky warned of the rising of the River Nile.

Arcturus is a red star with a magnitude of

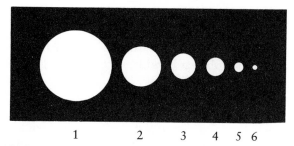

Stellar magnitudes.

− 0.04. It lies at the foot of the kite-shaped constellation of Boötes, the Herdsman. This group of stars was among the first constellations recorded and Homer referred to it in the Odyssey. Twelve centuries ago, the Arabs called this star the "Keeper of Heaven."

On an evening in late summer, if you look high up and over your head, along the Milky Way, then a little to your left, you will see Vega, with a magnitude of 0.03. It lies in the constellation Lyra, the Lyre.

At dusk on a winter evening, the Big Dipper is low in the northern sky and almost overhead, the Milky Way running from east to west. Within the band of these million stars lies the constellation Auriga, the Charioteer. There you will see Capella, with a magnitude of 0.08.

Rigel is a bluish star with a magnitude of 0.12 and marks the heel of Orion, the Hunter. Orion is the most brilliant of the constellations and is found in the southern skies in winter. Rigel is estimated to be 14,000 times brighter than our own sun and is 460 light-years away from earth.

Procyon, with a magnitude of 0.38, is in the constellation Canis Minor, the Little Dog, to the east of Orion and Auriga in the winter sky.

Betelgeuse is a giant red star with a magnitude of 0.50 that sits on Orion's shoulder. This was the first star ever measured, back in 1920. Its width is 215 million miles and it's 240 light-years from earth.

Altair is the key star in the constellation of Aquila, the Eagle, a feature of the summer sky, located just at the edge of the Milky Way. It has a magnitude of 0.77. Those of you who saw the science-fiction film *Forbidden Planet* will remember that this retelling of Shakespeare's *Tempest* took place on a planet circling Altair.

Just beyond Orion's shield in the winter sky, you will see the beautiful star cluster, the Hyades, called the "little she camels" by the Arabs. Aldebaran is a reddish star of a magnitude of 0.85, and its name in Arabic means "the follower."

Finally Pollux is a reddish star with the magnitude of 1.14. In spring, this star will be almost overhead to the left of the Milky Way. Pollux is assocated with the star Castor, almost as bright with a magnitude of 1.58. They are found in the constellation of Gemini, the Twins.

OTHER LIGHTS IN THE SKY

On a moonless but star-filled evening there is plenty of light to enjoy a garden. But the sky glows for other reasons; auroras, for example.

The closer you live to the North Pole, the more likely you will see the auroral glow light the evening sky. If you live at the latitude of Washington, D.C., the auroras will be visible about five to ten nights a year. Gardeners in upstate New York and New England get to see the auroral glow some thirty nights a year while in Alaska the glow lights the sky one hundred nights a year.

The colors are shades of red, pink, chartreuse, yellow, and blue, and flicker and undulate like transparent rolls of crepe paper in the northern sky. Nobody knows precisely what causes these lights shows, but most scientists belive they are the result of protons and electrons streaming out from the sun and striking the gasses in the earth's upper atmosphere, causing them to glow.

Then there is the zodiacal light, a dim, wedge- or cone-shaped glow that appears above the western horizon usually about ninety minutes after sunset. It can also be seen ninety minutes before sunrise in the eastern sky. The name refers to the constellations of the zodiac since this faint light appears in their domain.

I've only seen it a few times and then only when we lived in the country and on moonless nights, the best time being, unfortunately, in February and March in the northern hemisphere.

As to the cause, most astronomers believe that tiny dust particles spread out in a huge disk on the same plane as the earth's orbit, and the zodiacal light is the reflection of sunlight on these tiny bits of matter.

The *gegenschein*, or counterglow, is even fainter than the zodiacal light. It's a rounded, nebulalike glow, the result of the light concentrated at the tip of the cone of light produced by the zodiacal light. It's best seen in October, looking east into the constellation of Pisces.

CHAPTER TWO

NIGHT FRAGRANCE AND NIGHT-FRAGRANT FLOWERS

There is continual spring and harvest there,
For all the plants do scented blossoms bear;
Among the shady leaves, their sweet delight
Throw forth such dainty odors day and night.

ANONYMOUS

The flowers that keep
Their odor to themselves all day;
But when the sunlight dies away,
Let the delicious secret out
To every breeze that roams about.

ANONYMOUS

Fragrances can reach across the decades like a physical link, reminding us of an eventful time that is now long forgotten. And often it is a floral scent that triggers memory: the faint odor of orange that recalls the mock orange bush that grew next to grandmother's front porch; the sweet but cloying scent of tuberoses that my Aunt Ida would force into bloom for Thanksgiving dinner; and the light and citric smell of the evening primrose as it opens its sulfur yellow flowers to the darkening sky.

In May 1978 I had the opportunity to interview Nigel Nicolson at Sissinghurst Castle. After a tour of the garden we went back to the living room for tea and upon a table piled with books and an overflowing ashtray, sat a glass bowl full of white tree peonies (*Paeonia suffruticosa*). To this day when I smell the clean, light fragrance of our newly opened tree peonies, I remember that early afternoon, the sweet pungency of the blackberry tea, and the murmurings of the nearby visitors to the castle.

"A garden full of sweet odours is a garden full of charm," wrote Louise Beebe Wilder in her 1932 book *The Fragrant Garden* (The Macmillan Company),

a most precious kind of charm not to be implanted by mere skill in horticulture or power of purse, and which is beyond explaining. It is born of sensitive and very personal preferences yet its appeal is almost universal. Fragrance speaks to many to whom color and

The fragrant flowers of the Chinese wisteria, *Wisteria sinensis*.

form say little, and it can bring as irresistibly as music emotions of all sorts to the mind. Besides the plants visible to the eye there will be in such a garden other comely growths, plain to that other sense, such as faith, romance, the lore of old unhurried times. These are infinitely well worth cultivating among the rest. These are an added joy in happy times and gently remedial when life seems warped and tired.

Miss Wilder knew her way about the garden and if she could write about the importance of fragrance in such a way in the mid-1930s, you can just imagine what she would write about today's world of high-speed drama.

Many flowers need more than a glowing nighttime color to generate an outside interest in their pollination, and that additional push is likely to be fragrance. That fragrance is usually sweet (though occasionally a flower will produce a sweet-sour smell reminiscent of stale beer, or in the case of blossoms pollinated by bats, a distinctly musty odor that is much like that of the animals themselves).

Anyone who ever had a dog or cat will know how important smell is to the animal's everyday activities. Most physiologists and psychologists believe that mankind's ability to recognize and remember an odor was far more pronounced thousands of years ago than today; we have lost the ability to recognize and catalog literally thousands of smells. But even our weakened olfactory senses can recognize minute differences in a formula for perfume or the subtle changes in an ageing bottle of wine.

Faegri and van der Pijl in their book, *The Principles of Pollination Ecology* (Pergamon Press, 1971), note that odors are especially prominent in primitive plants and are especially strong in blossoms that are pollinated by beetles. Tropical nights, they write, are filled, almost beyond belief, with the fragrance of beetle-pollinated blossoms, including the powerful scent of the great Victoria

water lily, the sweet smell of the magnolia, and the rich odor of the nutmeg tree (*Myristica fragrans*). The rhythm of odor production, especially in night-flowering plants, points to the fact that even those pollinators with keen eyesight depend on the flower's fragrance as an olfactory road map, especially if the flower is small or drab in appearance. In essence, odors can work as the catalyst that in turn triggers the release of instinctive reactions in animals, and especially in insects.

Floral Fragrance of Yesterday

Since fragrance is such an important ingredient of the flower, Dr. Robert Brown, an English botanist of the last century, devised three classifications for floral odor: superodorants, subodorants, and nidorants. *Superodorants* include the perfumes which are agreeable to man, bird, and insect, the sweetest being the odors of the pinks, the orange, roses, the vanilla orchid, daffodils and narcissus, many of the lilies, violets, tuberoses, wallflowers, and the stocks.

Subodorants are flower smells a bit less bright and sweet, but still agreeable. Brown picked flowers like the jessamine, acacias, and the flowers of the almond.

Brown's classification of *nidorant* included the fragrance of the rues, garlics, a number of wildflowers that were simply called foxy (in a salute to the strong odor associated with that animal's personal aura and often to its den) and, of course, noted that the aforementioned stapelia—and especially the amorphophallus—smelled so strongly of carrion that their presence soon made a room unbearable to be in. These were flowers of such a noxious quality that when first smelled in eighteenth-century English greenhouses, they caused strong men to weep and stout British women to faint.

Happily the evening-fragrant flowers that are described in this chapter are either superodorant or subodorant, or a combination of both. The nidorant have been left by the wayside.

Floral Fragrance of Today

We can divide the floral scents that most of us find pleasant in the evening garden into four categories.

1. *Heavy* is a fragrance classification that describes those sweet-smelling flowers that can be overpowering at close range. Mock orange (*Philadelphus* spp.), tuberoses, osmanthus, some lilies, and honeysuckles come to mind. Gerard in his 1597 *Herbal* called mock orange "too sweet, troubling and molesting the head in a strange manner." For those with a chemical bent, these scents contain benzyl acetate, indole, and methyl anthranilate. Indole is found in the excrement of animals, including humans, and points to the fact that life has always been a strange mix.

2. *Aromatic* represents those flowers possessing a spicy fragrance like garden pinks. The chemicals, among others, that conspire to create this odor include cinnamic alcohol, eugenol, and vanilla. Many aromatic flowers in Group 2, especially nocturnals, often contain some of the chemicals found in Group 1—night-scented stock, nicotiana, many tropical orchids, heliotropes, and *Gladiolus tristis*, for instance. Surprisingly, while many of the orchids do have powerful scents, none of the plants in this group contain indole, so even if the flowers that produce these fragrances can be strange or even bizarre, their odor is never overpowering.

3. *Lemon* contains citral, a chemical found in oil of lemon, oil of orange, and bay leaves. While not being that common in the typical garden flower, lemon scent is very noticeable in magnolias, water lilies, nocturnal daylilies, and four-o'clocks.

4. The last category is termed *foxy*. This refers to plants or flowers that have a ferine odor, slightly musky but certainly not equal to the odor of a caveful of stegosauruses and not enough to lead to the defenestration of the offending plant. Outside of some night-flowering tropical trees pollinated by bats or one or two perennials, I can't think of any nocturnal flowers that fit the description.

FRAGRANCES OF THE EVENING

Horace Walpole was born in 1717 and is famous as the author of the first true English Gothic novel of horror, *The Castle of Otranto*. Thanks to a healthy income, Walpole bought a small villa in Twickenham, a country cottage that he "Gothicized" by adding battlements and armor to such an extent that he was eventually forced to sell tickets to an overenthusiastic public. He called his home Strawberry Hill.

On June 10, 1795, Walpole came in from his garden after a late-evening stroll and wrote:

> I am just come out of the garden on the most oriental of all evenings, and from breathing odours beyond those of Araby. The Acacias, which the Arabians have the sense to worship, are covered with blossoms, the Honeysuckles dangle from every tree in festoons, the Seringas* are thickets of sweets, and the new cut hay in the field tempers the balmy gales with simple freshness.

Strawberry Hill has always been at the back of my mind and one day I always hoped to create an evening garden of fragrance worthy of Walpole's memory. But except for a few of the more common night-fragrant flowers and some tropical residents of our greenhouse, the climate of the Catskill Mountains or upstate New York seemed to preclude any heavy doses of garden romanticism.

Yet I continued to collect information. For example, almost ten years ago, I bought a copy of what has become one of my favorite garden

---

*Seringas belong to the genus *Seringia*, and comprise three species of shrubs, two from Australia and one from the Mascarene Islands. They can reach a greenhouse height of eight feet and are often covered with night-fragrant, white tubular flowers.

books. The book was copy number 214 of 350 copies of a special printing of *Old-Time Gardens* by Alice Morse Earle, published in 1901 by The Macmillan Company. The paper was specially made and ninety years later is as good as new. The front board contains a bookplate proclaiming the book as belonging to Ida Dudley Dale. The last page was initially blank but someone, perhaps Miss Dale, had written the following in what is today pale blue ink:

"The Fragrant White Garden"
White callas; Peruvian daffodils; nicotiana; moon flowers; and double tuberoses. It is for evening enjoyment and has a mystic beauty; attracts moths and has a wonderful fragrance. Article in "These Times" (March '54) Another fragrant garden recommends a white petunia border; Wabash white bearded iris; and a shrub Viburnum said to smell like carnations and mint.

This year, with the warmer outlook of USDA Zone 7, I tried a small border of callas, Peruvian daffodils (*Hymenocallis narcissiflora*), and white nicotianas, backed with a trellis of moonflowers and edged with white petunias. The tuberoses were left out of the plan since I find their scent when mixed with other fragrant flowers somewhat overpowering. The result was everything the book's original owner thought it would be. An evening's walk, especially on a moonlit night, became a wonderful mix of fragrance—and attracted a surprising variety of moths.

In answer to my request for more night-fragrant flowers, Ursula Herz of Coastal Gardens and Nursery in Myrtle Beach, South Carolina, wrote the following:

"There are a number of evening-fragrant flowers in my garden: the perfumed fairy lily (*Chlidanthus fragrans*), lily-of-the-valley (*Convallaria majalis*), *Holboellia grandiflora* from China, a number of honeysuckles including the Japanese (*Lonicera japonica*), the very fragrant *L. fragrantissima*, and the Italian woodbine (*L. capri-*

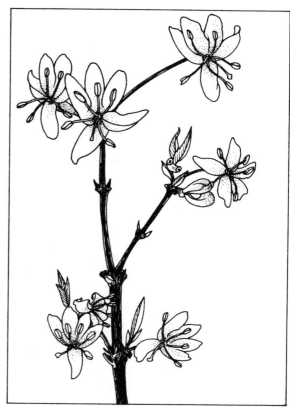

A fragrant honeysuckle, *Lonicera fragrantissima*.

folium) all perfume the night air. All the wisterias are sweet, the chocolate vine (*Akebia quinata*) is also very sweet while the confederate jasmine (*Trachelospermum jasminoides*) and *T. asiaticum* from Korea are the same.

"The same holds true for petunias, the white, pink, and lavender to purple ones being the most fragrant but a caveat imposes itself: One has to select the new hybrids in the afternoon to make sure that in the effort to produce a new flower, the fragrance has not been lost.

"The February daphne (*Daphne mezereum*) and the winter daphne (*D. odora*) are definitely fragrant in the evening while gardenias can fill a room or garden space with their perfume. While sweet William (*Phlox divaricata*) have a nice sweet scent especially the light blues, and *P. pilosa* is fragrant. My daughters called my attention to the sweet scent of the liriopes when blooming *en masse.*

"Some more ephemeral favorites of mine are the weeping willows with their light sweet fragrance after a late-afternoon spring rain. *Hypericum patulum* releases a particular fragrance of balm after a rain and *Populus balsamifera* and some other species and their hybrids can also fill a warm moist spring evening with the clean smell of balm. The hay-scented fern (*Dennstaedtia punctilobula*) smells stronger in the later part of the day. The blossoms of the different honeysuckle azaleas—the parents to the Exbury hybrids—keep their fragrance until late in the evening. And last but not least, the oak-leaved hydrangea (*Hydrangea quercifolia*), and to a lesser degree *H. mariesii*, produce a clean sweet smell that attracts insects to their small blossoms.

"Having lived in Southern France, my olfactory nerves have registered forever the strange fragrance of a hillside of mimosa (*Acacia* spp.) in bloom. There again the heat of the pre-spring days brings out the full volume of the esoteric oils in the latter part of the day."

SEX AND THE
NIGHT-FRAGRANT GARDEN

Even though I grew up in the 1950s, lived in Greenwich Village in the 1960s, attended Woodstock in 1969, and have watched moths flocking to the flowers of the night for years, the last thing I ever thought of when dealing with the evening-fragrant garden was the concept of sex. It was Norman Taylor, he of that staid and traditional tome *Practical Encyclopedia of Gardening*, who in his 1953 book, *Fragrance in the Garden* (D. Van Nostrand Company, Inc.), suggested that before planning a night garden devoted to fragrance, "No one . . . can escape the implications of an atmosphere redolent with the fragrance of sex."

He urged his readers to consider whether their night gardens of fragrance should "reflect the mature scents of the middle-aged" or whether it should be "a thing of haunting beauty, sex-charged with the mystery of night and perfumed with the intoxicating fragrance which drove Sappho in her ode to Aphrodite" to write the following around the year 600 B.C.:

> "Its beauties charm the gods above;
> Its fragrance is the breath of love;
> Its foliage wantons in the air;
> Luxuriant, like the flowing hair."

Needless to say, while never expecting a saronged Dorothy Lamour to walk into my garden on a moonlit night, I believe that regardless of the gardener's age, I would tend to think in terms of the mysteries of the night rather than choosing the mature scents of the middle-aged—whatever they may be.

PLANNING THE
NIGHT-FRAGRANT GARDEN

One person's favorite perfume is another person's stink. This is because the sense of smell is a far more personal—and emotional—thing than those esthetic sensibilities one develops over a lifetime.

So when it comes to choosing plants for the evening-fragrant garden, let your nose be your guide and remember the line of Terence, "Moderation in all things." To me a whiff here of jasmine and a whiff there of heliotrope makes more sense than to be bowled over by a cacophony of honeysuckle, evening stock, and mock orange, all mixed together.

Flowers That Have a Pronounced Fragrance at Night

The following plants all produce flowers that are fragrant during the evening hours. Some produce the most perfume at dusk while others wait until

The peacock orchid, *Acidanthera bicolor*.

the dark of night before making their presence known. Some are tropical and will only summer in the garden, being moved to the conservatory, greenhouse, or an enclosed porch for the worst of the winter months. Others are perennial and are so noted. The common name, when available, is given along with the scientific name. In addition to the following plants, bromeliads and orchids have chapters of their own and many other night-fragrant and night-blooming plants are found in other chapters throughout this book.

There are, no doubt, many, many more flowers that are still fragrant at night after pumping out perfume for most of the daylight hours. Lilacs, peonies, and roses come to mind. And there are many plants described in various books, plants like *Martynia fragrans*, an annual from Australia that is reported to have a marvelous evening scent but has never graced my garden since in all the years of collecting seed from around the world, I've never found a source.

HARDY AND TENDER BULBS

The peacock orchid or the magpie gladiolus, *Acidanthera bicolor* (syn. *Gladiolus callianthus*), is a member of the iris family that is often lumped with the gladiolus but differs in slight botanical details. The sword-leaved plants—originally from Ethiopia—arise from corms that produce about six flowers atop eighteen-inch stalks. The blossoms are creamy white, about three inches across, and have a rich chocolate-maroon center, but they scent the evening air with a sweet, violetlike perfume. The fibrous-coated corms are not frostproof but will sometimes survive in northern areas if they are well mulched and the ground does not freeze. They need a night temperature of not less than 50°F and will usually bloom in late July from plantings made in mid-April. After flowering, allow the foliage to die back, then let the corms dry, brush them clean of earth, and store over the winter in a cool, dry place.

The perfumed fairy lily, *Chlidanthus fragrans*.

The perfumed fairy lily or the delicate lily, *Chlidanthus fragrans*, and the fact that it was fragrant at night, came to my attention when corresponding with Ursula Herz. Then I found that Louise Beebe Wilder wrote all about it in her 1936 book, *Adventures with Hardy Bulbs* (The Macmillan Company). This lily belongs to a small genus of bulbous plants from the Andes of Peru, and only *C. fragrans* is in general cultivation. Three or four yellow, funnel-shaped flowers about four inches long are carried in clusters on stems up to a foot high. They are rich with the fragrance of lilies at night.

Rex D. Pierce in the 1934 edition of the *Year Book of the Amaryllis Society* suggests that the bulbs be stored in a dry, cool cellar and should be planted out in the garden as soon as the ground has stopped freezing to a crust in spring. Only well-grown and fairly large bulbs will flower, and they need very fertile soil and ample moisture. They can be left in the ground as long as they are kept free from freezes.

The Amazon lily, *Eucharis grandiflora*, is a beautiful tropical bulbous plant belonging to the amaryllis family, first collected along the Rio Magdalena in Colombia. The glossy green leaves resemble those of a large hosta, about ten inches long, and would be an attractive garden subject in their own right. Its beautiful clusters of white, starlike flowers, each over three inches across, are superb especially since they are accompanied by a glorious perfume. As long as the bulbs are given good soil, an occasional helping of fertilizer, partial shade, and temperatures above 60°F, the plant will thrive. You can force flowering by letting the plants dry out for a few weeks, then adding water again. By resting the bulbs in March or August, Amazon lilies will bloom in May or late fall.

Gladiolus callianthus is an unusual member of the glads, a native of the mountains of East Africa where it grows in grasslands on wet rocks and cliffs. When the corms are grown in the northern hemisphere, they bloom in July. The white flowers have a deep purple blotch in their throat and are intensely fragrant at night, emitting their perfume from a tube that is over seven inches long. They are pollinated by a particular hawkmoth with a very long tongue. Grow them like *G. tristis*, described below.

The night gladiolus, *Gladiolus tristis*, is found growing wild in South Africa, usually along ditches and the borders of swampy areas. The creamy yellow blossoms are intensely fragrant at night with a spicy-sweet perfume, and rise above very unusual leaves that have a most peculiar structure—they look like a pinwheel when cut in half. As I write this in mid-February, a small pot of these flowers are in full bloom on a table in our living room and as soon as the sky darkens and the city lights come on, their fragrance fills the air. There is a cultivar called 'Christabel' with

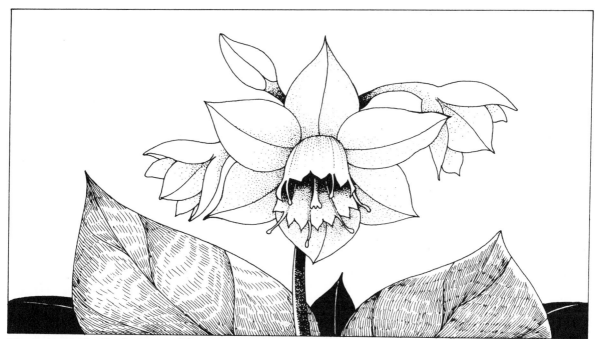

The Amazon lily, *Eucharis grandiflora*.

a deeper yellow color. The frost-tender corms are small and six or more will do quite well in a six-inch pot. Allow the corms to completely dry by withholding water after the flowers and leaves fade. Let them rest for about three months before bringing them into flower again.

The garden liles, *Lilium* spp., represent a large genus of bulbous plants that are easy to grow, both in the garden and in pots, the majority of blossoms producing a rich and marvelous scent.

The Madonna lilies (*Lilium candidum*) have been used in gardens since the Minoan culture flourished, fifteen hundred years before the birth of Christ. Medieval gardens had whole corners dedicated to these symbols of purity. The immaculate white fragrant flowers perch on top of stems up to six feet tall, with up to fifteen flowers per stem. Unlike the other lilies mentioned, these should be planted with only an inch or two of

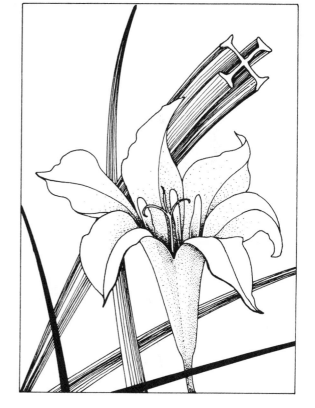

The night gladiolus, *Gladiolus tristis*.

soil over the top of the bulb. They should be mulched in areas of cold winters that lack snow cover.

Beverly Nichols, writing in his book *A Thatched Roof* (Jonathan Cape, 1933), wrote of the fragrance of Madonna lilies:

> Then a little further on you come to a delicious white cottage on the right, which belongs to the Professor. I always associate the Professor with Madonna lilies, because a bed of them runs all round his walls. I see them beginning to hoist their green belfries above the earth in spring; I watch their spires ascend through April and May; I see the bells being hung in June; and on quiet evenings I wander past, night after night, waiting for the bells to open and chime their scented praise to God. . . . First one bell opens, and rings a hesitant note, then another . . . till there comes a day, towards the end of the month, when they are all pealing their chorus in the breeze and the whole village is drunk with a perfumed melody.

The lilies, as a genus, are certainly not designed to be pollinated by bees, and although marvelously fragrant by day, their wondrous scent at night would seem to indicate a different insect is involved in fertilization.

Last summer in early September, I went out into the garden well after midnight to check the fragrance of a large clump of the gold-banded lily (*Lilium auratum*), blooming at the edge of the fern garden. A katydid and two earwigs were there gorging themselves on pollen. The earwigs ignored my flashlight but the katydid looked up for a moment, glanced at the light, then brushed some specks of the bright blushing orange pollen from its dull greenish brown antennae, and went back to its meal.

The most important thing to remember about lilies is that, unlike other bulbs, they are never dormant and the scales that surround the bulb have no protective covering and are easily broken. Handle with care is the rule when planting.

A few lilies, like the Madonna lily, want shallow planting with the top of the bulb only an inch below the soil. But most of the other species and cultivars have flowering stems that produce roots as they grow up to the surface and depth must be allowed for this growth habit. This means setting them four to eight inches deep and ten to eighteen inches apart, depending on the ultimate height and type of lily. Plant the bulbs out as soon as you receive them. If your soil is heavy, dig the hole an inch or so deep and put in a layer of sand, scumble a teaspoon of bonemeal in the bottom of each hole, and, after inserting the bulb, add some more sand before covering them up.

For bloom in mid- to late September, use the fine *Lilium formosanum* with its elegant, six-inch-long white blossoms on top of four- to six-foot stems. 'Little Snow White' is a cultivar from Taiwan with a large flower on a nine-inch stem. If grown from seed sown in September, this lily will bloom the following summer. It also makes an excellent pot plant. The scent, like most lilies, is profound when your nose is close to the flower, but becomes pleasantly sweet when you back away a few paces.

Pamianthe peruviana is another member of the amaryllis family, a single-species genus from Peru, resembling the genus *Hymenocallis*. The straplike leaves are about a foot long and the flower stem bears several sweet-scented, white flowers that bear a yellow-green strip on the other segments; the scent is especially powerful at night. They are about four inches long. The plants need evenly moist soil, temperatures above 60°F, and partial shade. Like many members of this family of bulbous plants, it is not necessary to dry them out completely at the end of the season—just withhold most of the water during the cold and dark winter months.

The tuberose, *Polianthes tuberosa*, was said by Shelly to be "the sweetest flower for scent that blows," and the Victorians delighted in its sweet and heady fragrance. William Robinson called it

The tuberose, *Polianthes tuberosa.*

"this deliciously fragrant plant," and noted that it often lived through London winters. German ladies called it *Nachtliebste* and, just as with the gas plant, there were reports about the flowers giving off sparks of light.

George Moore wrote:

> The tuberose, with her silvery light,
> That in the gardens of Malay
> Is called the Mistress of the Night,
> So like a bride, scented and bright,
> She comes out when the sun's away.

Unfortunately, the tuberose became so popular as a funeral flower, that it fell out of the public's favor. Today we can forget the past and once again plant a few bulbs in the summer border or underneath the dining-room window, so that at night the rich odor can penetrate an interior dulled by room deodorants.

There are two varieties: 'Mexican Everblooming', which reaches a height of four feet and bears two-inch-long waxy white, extremely fragrant flowers, and 'The Pearl', which is a short sixteen inches high and bears two-inch double flowers. The bulblike bases are really rhizomes, as these plants are in the same family as yuccas and agaves. Unless you live in an area where the ground never freezes, store the roots in a warm, dry place over winter. In the north, start the plants indoors about four weeks before the last frost of spring, since they take a long season to bloom. Tuberoses can also be forced for November bloom.

HARDY SHRUBS AND TREES

The silk tree or mimosa, *Albizia julibrissin*, is a glorious plant to some people and a noxious weed to others, since it does have the ability to "seed about" and those seedlings, when they take root, are difficult to remove. But the waving leaves, made up of small leaflets, are tropical and attractive and the flowers, packed with threadlike stamens, are very beautiful. As a tree, it is hardier than many people realize and I know of trees in upstate New York that survive temperatures well below freezing. The powder-puff flowers are very fragrant during the day but they also produce their sweet smell for the evening garden. They prefer a well-drained soil and flower best if planted in full sun.

The common boxwood, *Buxus sempervirens*, fits the description of a compact shrub to a T. After all, it takes hundreds of years to reach thirty feet; like the oak, this is not a tree to plant for instant gratification. We have a boxwood *allée* that is now about thirty-five years old. The two rows of plants are now some three feet high and border an open pathway three feet wide. The evergreen leaves are dark green ovals about a half an inch long and the brushes are hardy to USDA Zone 6.

Boxwood leaves give off a strange fragrance,

The silk tree, *Albizia julibrissin*.

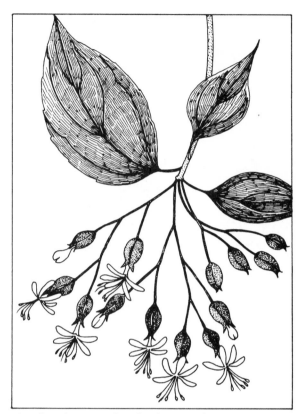

The glory-bower, *Clerodendrum trichotomum*.

slightly foxy and penetrating, but quite distinctive—liked by some and abhorred by others. The odor is especially noticeable after a summer shower when the air is warm. Our *allée* is lit by night with uplighters hidden in the lower branches of the boxwoods and while the leaves give off their fragrance day or night, it is in late evening after a rainfall that the effect is the best.

Oliver Wendell Holmes wrote about the box:

"They walked over the crackling leaves in the garden, between the lines of box, breathing its fragrance of eternity; for this is one of the odors which carry us out of time into the abysses of the unbeginning past."

And Louise Beebe Wilder wrote in *Adventures in My Garden and Rock Garden* (Doubleday, Page & Company, 1923): "The pungent smell of the leaves is to me highly refreshing and stimu-

lating, but all do not like it. Near me is a cottage half surrounded by a fine boxwood hedge, but of it the woman who dwells therein said, 'It's gloomy and I don't like the smell all through the day and night.' "

The glory-bower, *Clerodendrum trichotomum*, is a shrub that reaches a height of about ten feet in the Botanical Gardens at Asheville, where I was first introduced to its honeysuckle fragrance. The starry white flowers are produced in late summer or early autumn and are followed by bright blue berries. Originally from China, if given a protected spot these bushes are often hardy in USDA Zone 5—although killed to the ground, the crown, if protected, will send out new shoots in spring.

There are a number of species of *Clerondendron*, and most have been described as having evil-smelling leaves when crushed. This has never been a particular problem in my garden since we don't rush about crushing leaves at every opportunity, but if you are so inclined, *C. trichotomum* is just mildly foxy.

The rose daphne, *Daphne cneorum*, is the one of the few of these evergreen shrubs to be reliably hardy in USDA Zone 5. It makes an elegant edging for a flower or shrub border, and in early spring is covered with small four-lobed, tubular flowers that bloom in early spring and are wonderfully fragrant. These plants like an alkaline soil, so be sure and mix in some lime if your pH is low.

John Creech, the well-known explorer, told me about the wonderful qualities of daphne, especially their elusive but sweet fragrance that, in early evening, can filter into a dining-room window and brighten up the entire room. Since the flowers are pollinated by moths, it is always amazing to me that when some species bloom in mid- to late February, there are enough insects about to fertilize the flowers.

The spurge laurel, *Daphne laureola*, presents its greenish yellow flowers in early spring. E. A. Bowles (1865–1954), one of the greatest of English gardeners, said of this plant: "It is strongest just after dark but sometimes one catches its fragrance at dusk. It is one of the scents that is borne on the air many yards from the plant and it is rather elusive, I mean you suddenly smell it and take a long breath to get more and lo! it has vanished. You go nearer the bushes but you cannot pick it up, then you pass them suddenly and get another whiff of it." It is only hardy to USDA Zone 7, but with protection could probably survive a colder spot. Give these three-foot shrubs a well-drained spot in full sun or partial shade—and add some lime to the soil.

Daphne tangutica has been observed by Robert Rolfe (he authors the Euphrasia column in the *Quarterly Bulletin of the Alpine Garden Society*) to be another species entirely pollinated by moths, which is why the sweet fragrance is only released in the evening. The species seeds easily,

forms a three-foot-high shrub in five years, and flowers reliably in England at least twice a year, in April and July. On still nights the scent can be detected over twenty yards away.

The Russian olive, *Elaeagnus angustifolia*, is a shrub or small tree of the first order, not only because of its silver foliage and beautiful gray bark, but its spring-blooming flowers. When we first began our country garden, we planted a long row of bare-root Russian olives about twenty-five feet long and six to eight feet wide. The line was initially used as a windbreak, both for the house some fifty feet away and for a bed of what I hoped would be unusual, but not always hardy, wildflowers.

The shrubs began to bloom by mid-June of the second year, their small flowers giving off a delightfully sweet odor that was evident over a very wide range. Both night and day, visitors to the garden would stand for minutes, enjoying the perfume, but their joy was nothing compared to the ravenous appetites of flocks of birds that turned up in late summer to devour the berries produced by those fragrant flowers.

In the winter, when the leaves had fallen, the gray bark of the Russian olive provided more interest to the garden. These shrubs age quickly, and before ten years have passed their trunks are gnarled and wrinkled with the look that others take decades to acheive. Provide ordinary, but light, garden soil in full sun.

The cherry elaeagnus, *Elaeagnus multiflora*, is hardy to the southern range of USDA Zone 4, and grown for the red, cherrylike berries that appear in summer. The dark green leaves are silvery underneath, about two and a half inches long, and the flowers are extremely fragrant. Some authorities credit Commodore Perry with the introduction of this plant from Japan in 1862.

The thorny elaeagnus, *Elaeagnus pungens*, is not reliably hardy north of USDA Zone 7 but in the South it's used to plant median strips along highways, where the gardenialike fragrance of the flowers, which bloom in October, can confound the motorist driving with windows open on a lovely autumn day or night. Introduced from Japan in 1830, this shrub with evergreen leaves grows about twelve feet high and can be sheared to make an effective hedge.

The mock oranges, *Philadelphus* spp., are shrubs said to have such fragrant flowers that people in the vicinity often get headaches from the odor. *Philadelphus coronarius* is often recommended as the species with the best—and the most powerful—fragrance. These shrubs have been grown in English gardens since the sixteenth century. *Philadelphus coronarius* was the shrub that grew in front of my grandmother's front porch and almost every other home that I visited as a child had these shrubs growing in the border. The blossoms resemble orange blossoms borne in terminal clusters and have a very sweet scent that is not easily forgotten. A vase of mock orange at the dining room table would allow the host or hostess to serve almost any wine but convince the diners that it was great, so pungent is the smell— it's best to move the flowers to the living room when dining. The cultivar 'Aureus' has the same flowers, but has leaves tinted a bright golden yellow that slowly turns to greenish yelow as the heat of the summer advances but the flowers are the same.

The best soil for mock orange is well-drained with a spot in full sun but they will adapt to partial shade, especially in the South. New flowers appear on new wood so the tangled thicket of branches that make up the clumps of mock orange should be thinned after flowering but other than that effort, these shrubs are trouble-free. They're hardy to USDA Zone 5.

There are a number of mock orange cultivars and hybrids. *Philadelphus* × *lemoinei* is a medium-size shrub with two-inch leaves that are slightly hairy beneath; the white flowers are an inch and a half across. *Philadelphus* × *virginalis* also has a number of cultivars, including 'Minnesota Snowflake', reportedly hardy to −30°F and 'Dwarf Snowflake', a dwarf shrub about four feet high with fragrant double white flowers.

The sweet azalea, *Rhododendron arborescens*, is a native of the east, growing from New York to Kentucky, and south to Georgia and Alabama. The shrub first came to our attention after a late afternoon walk at Bent Creek near the North Carolina Arboretum. The clouds were riding low and there had been a light rain. As we walked, my wife and I could smell a sweet fragrance coming from the bushes lining a nearby stream. It turned out to be the sweet azalea—and the fragrance continues on into evening. This deciduous shrub reaches a height of ten feet if left unpruned and the white flowers appear after the leaves. The flowers bloom in groups of three to eight, and have stamens that stick out beyond the petals, with a long style tipped with a dot of gleaming black. The dried leaves give off the odor of coumarin, and smell of vanilla, a dead giveaway to its identity. This is probably the most beautiful of our native azaleas, so it's a wonder why more gardens do not feature it, especially since it's hardy to USDA Zone 5.

The hammock-sweet azalea, *Rhododendron serrulatum*, bears clove-scented blossoms that are more fragrant at night, and *R. viscosum*, the swamp azalea, has white flowers that smell of spice. I assume that most of these flowers are pollinated in late afternoon or evening by moths but have found no suggestions to their habits so far—but the search is on.

Salix spp. represent the large willow family. Many writers on fragrant plants have mentioned the honeylike smell of the white willow blossom (*Salix alba*) or the smell of balsam that is evident after a spring rain when willows are about. But last year I saw mention of a particular species by Euphrasia, appearing in the "Alpine Anthology" column of the June 1991 (Vol. 59, No. 2) issue of the *Quarterly Bulletin of the Alpine Garden Society*. He reported on the experiences of R. W. Collingwood of Shropshire, England, with an attractive species of *Salix* that hails from the Himalayas ranging from Uttar Pradesh in the west to Bhutan in the east. Wrote Mr. Collingwood:

> On a fine October evening, whilst admiring the sunset across the valley, a delightful fragrance of honey distracted my attention: it was eventually traced to a large mat of *Salix hylematica*. This prostrate willow, which attracts the eye in spring and summer with its glistening green leaves and contasting red stems and catkins, is engaged in a last fling before the onset of winter. Over a period of several weeks the leaves yellow and fall (all of two inches) and during this time the scent given off is both powerful and pervasive. This attractive feature, which is omitted from all accounts I have read, is especially valuable in that it occurs when many a garden is at its least fragrant. The plant received an Award of Merit in 1981—a rather more open specimen than the five-year-old plant I possess. Even this relatively youthful mat has already spread to cover a couple of square yards and both autumn- and spring-flowering bulbs seem to thrive within its embrace.

The fragrant snowball, *Viburnum × carlcephalum*, is a wonderfully fragrant shrub that over the years turns into a small tree. In the spring, the clusters of blossoms—often six inches across—bloom and throw their perfume out across the yard and into the street. People who walk by will often ask what the sweet fragrance is. The bonus is that at dusk, and on into evening, the flowers continue to produce their fragrance. Give plants good garden soil, plenty of water if rains are scarce, and full sun. The plant is hardy to USDA Zone 6.

My good friend, Harry Logan of Hendersonville, North Carolina, wrote me a long letter about viburnums and their odor, pointing out the fact that many of the deciduous clan have a decidedly unpleasant and strong scent when they lose their leaves in autumn. Harry noted that Peter Van Melle in his book *Shrubs and Trees for the Small Place* (The American Garden Guild, 1943) advised against putting viburnums too close to home because of the ill-smelling qualities of flower, foliage, or fruit—especially on warm moist days in autumn. Despite these warnings, *Viburnum × carlcephalum* has been one of the good things to happen to our garden over the past thirty years.

TROPICAL TREES AND SHRUBS

The sweet bouvardia, *Bouvardia longiflora*, belongs to a genus of shrublike plants from Mexico and Central America. Although they will summer outside, winters must be spent with temperatures above 50°F and with as much sun as possible. Use a good, well-drained soil and let the soil dry out between waterings. Plants reach a height of three feet and have glossy, medium green leaves, and toward the tip, produce white waxy flowers with four petals at the end of a three-inch tube. When evening approaches they become intensely fragrant with a perfume that is a blend of honey and jasmine. Bouvardias usually bloom in late spring; in summer they can be pruned back for a second bloom in midwinter.

Brugmansia spp. are tropical plants that belong to the nightshade family, along with the potato and tomato. Some references include these plants in the genus *Datura* but they are beautiful enough to warrant their own niche. I first saw these flowers at Logee's Greenhouses where the nodding, white bell-like flowers of *Brugmansia suaveolens* reached a length of over ten inches. In a tropical or greenhouse atmosphere, the plants can attain a height of over ten feet, but with pruning they can be kept to within more reasonable bounds.

Brugmansias want evenly moist, well-composted soil in a spot with as much sun as possible, and never let the temperature fall much below 60°F or they will go into a snit. Although the flowers are open during the day, as evening approaches the blossoms actually swell a bit and the heady sweet scent will quickly fill the greenhouse or garden. Although nobody knows why, the brugmansias seem to peak their blossoming in conjunction with a full moon, a habit that makes them even more desirable as potted plants for the evening garden in summer or as outdoor perennials if you live in southern Florida or Texas near the Gulf.

Mai-koa, *Brugmansia arborea*, is a shrub or small tree reaching a height of fifteen feet and found growing only in the Andes of central Ecuador at an elevation of ten thousand feet, or above. Most plants found growing in gardens are really *B. × candida*, a hybrid between *B. aurea* and *B. versicolor*.

Brugmansia aurea is really a small tree, growing to thirty-five feet in central Colombia. The flowers are over eight inches long and are white or golden yellow.

Brugmansia × 'Betty Marshall' is the compact angel's-trumpet, a smaller bush about three feet high with very fragrant white flowers.

The hybrid *Brugmansia × candida* is a six- to eight-foot-high shrub or small tree with large foot-long leaves and foot-long white flowers with an incredible fragrance.

Brugmansia × insignis (*B. suaveolens × B. versicolor*) has led to a new group of cultivars, these offering many colors. 'Frost Pink' bears flowers of a light silvery pink; 'Jean Pasco' has orange-yellow flowers; 'Orange' bears blossoms of a golden orange; 'Pink' has extra-large pink bells and is especially fragrant at night; and 'U.S.L. Special' has flowers of a deep salmon-pink color.

Brugmansia suaveolens is another angel's-trumpet, only the foot-long white flowers are shaped like those of a campanula rather than a trumpet, with their edges flared out instead of recurved. 'Jamaica Yellow' bears ten- to twelve-inch yellow bells.

Brugmansia sanguinea originally came from the Andes in Chile and can reach a height of thirty-five feet in its native environment. Accord-

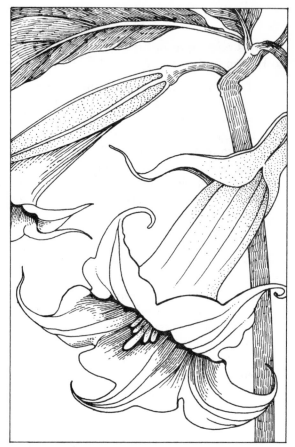

An angel's-trumpet, *Brugmansia suaveolens*.

ing to John Kafka, a life-long grower of these plants, the blossoms are pollinated by hummingbirds. He cautions that the seedpods, which are five inches long, are extremely poisonous and can cause lung, heart, and skin problems. Since Mr. Kafka grows plants to a height of eight feet with as may as fifty blossoms each—and lives in Toronto, Canada—I thought his advice on growing these plants would be the best available.

"I cut my *Brugmansia sanguinea* back in March," writes Mr. Kafka, "leaving only one inch of the annual old growth. They are repotted in eighteen-inch plastic pots with a soil mixture of manure, topsoil, sand, and peat moss. Then I place them under fluorescent lights in the garage at a temperature of 70°F, keeping the soil moist at all times.

"When the frost is over—here in Toronto that's approximately May 25, I set the pots directly in the ground, in full sun. Every few weeks, I fertilize the plants with 20-20-20. They bloom as often as three times during the summer months, and before the frost hits, the plants go into the basement, uncut, with no light and occasional watering—they never should dry out."

Brugmansia versicolor can become a small tree, eventually reaching eight feet in greenhouse conditions, so it's best grown in a tub or kept to the more tropical parts of the country. The flowers are cream upon opening but change to a rich apricot-peach color with age. 'Apricot' has appropriately colored flowers and 'Ecuador Pink' bears large pink trumpets, the cultivar originating from Ecuador.

The lady-of-the-night or *dama-de-la-noche, Brunfelsia americana,* is another member of the nightshade family that produces flowers seemingly meant for walks under a full moon on warm tropical nights, with a perfume that is sweet and spicy. It eventually grows into a large shrub up to eight feet high, bearing oval, leathery leaves. The white flowers resemble bouvardias, except there are five petals at the end of a two-inch tube. They fade to yellow with age. Follow the same cultivation routine as with brugmansias.

Brunfelsia jamaicensis is new to the market, with creamy white to pure white flowers that are very fragrant at night. This plant will not tolerate any frost at all, so unless you live in USDA Zone 10, treat it to a summer in the garden but when winter comes, bring it inside and place it in a window with full sun.

The night jessamine, *Cestrum nocturnum,*

Above: One of the tropical brunfelsias, *Brunfelsia pilosa.*

Right: The night jessamine, *Cestrum nocturnum.*

grows to a twelve-foot shrub in its native West Indies but kept in a twelve-inch pot, the plant rarely reaches six feet. Although the flower's trumpet flares slightly at dusk, there is so little difference between an open or closed blossom, I've included them in this chapter, especially since the fragrance is so spectacular. As a shrub it's not much to speak about but when the tubular green flowers open to the night air, it produces a perfume that is intensely fragrant—a mix of musk and heliotrope—that is so strong it can be sensed twenty feet from the plant. As with *Brunfelsia americana*, the odor is at times so strong that one popular name for jessamine is *dama-de-la-noche*, or in Sudanese, *sundel malam*, meaning nightwhore: it is unobtrusive during the day, agreeable at night, and disgusting in the morning. Prune jessamine either after blooming or in early spring. Plants generally bloom all summer into autumn. If it's burned by a slight frost it will recover, but north of USDA Zone 9 plants must be kept inside over the winter. *Cestrum nocturnum* × *diurnum* bears clusters of evening-scented yellow flowers throughout the year. If plants get to be ungainly, trim them back. It should be noted that the eventual fruits, if any, and the plant sap are both poisonous, containing traces of nicotine and other dangerous alkaloids.

Cestrum 'Day × Night' is a hybrid of *C. nocturnum* and the day-blooming jessamine, *C. diurnum*. The result is the best of both worlds since the plants are almost everblooming and quite hardy in USDA Zones 8 through 10, and while having some scent during the day, are most fragrant in the evening.

The willow-leaved jessamine, *Cestrum parqui*, is a deciduous shrub that originally came from southern South America. The flowers are greenish white and bloom in terminal clusters, emitting its characteristic sweet and spicy perfume at night. It is also more attractive than *C. nocturnum*.

The Mexican orange, *Choisya ternata*, is an evergreen shrub reaching a height of ten feet,

The Mexican orange, *Choisya ternata*.

bearing three-part glossy green leaves that smell like eucalyptus leaves when crushed. The five-petaled, one-inch-wide flowers resemble orange blossoms, blooming from spring into summer, and are intensely fragrant both day and night. The soil should be kept evenly moist, with winter temperatures dipping no lower than 50°F, and full sun. From a hardiness standpoint, it's interesting to note that Louise Beebe Wilder, quoting from the *National Horticultural Magazine* for January 1931, mentions a photograph of a Mexican orange taken in the Philadelphia garden of one Mr. Furness, definitely in USDA Zone 6. Mr. Furness says his plant "has come through four winters fresh and green with only the unripened growth cut back." Rosemary Verey calls this one of her favorite garden shrubs and advises gardeners that while young growth can succumb to winter winds, the damaged wood can be trimmed back and will soon sprout again.

The Arabian coffee plant, *Coffea arabica*, first came to my attention many years ago after I constructed a window greenhouse in our country house in order to grow a few tropical plants to brighten up the bleak Catskill winters. Along with my first orchid and some lovely ferns, I purchased a rather large coffee tree from a local greenhouse. Coffee trees are beautiful evergreen shrubs with shiny leaves about four inches long and are covered with clusters of white, waxy, starlike flowers usually appearing in midsummer. The blossoms are very fragrant during the day, but at night they increase the amount of perfume wafted on the air, an odor that is light and sweet and not at all heavy or dark like many evening scents become. The flowers are short-lived and, on mature plants, they fall away, soon giving way to round green balls that, if left to ripen, eventually bcome cherry red berries that contain two seeds. These are the beans that Juan Valdez picks in coffee commercials. The plants need temperatures above 55°F, evenly moist soil, and as much sun as possible during the winter months but partial shade in the summer.

The cornstalk plant, *Dracaena fragrans* 'Massangeana', is a fairly common houseplant often found in plant collections sent up to the Northeast from Florida nurseries and sold out of tents at malls and in supermarkets. They are small when they start out but soon grow into small trees, often reaching the ceiling of home or office. In addition to being attractive, if given plenty of water in a well-drained soil, temperatures above 60°F, plenty of sun in the winter with partial shade in the summer, mature plants will sometimes bloom. The flowers appear in many individual clusters, each composed of tiny white flowers with long stamens, and hang down from the top of the tree. They are also very, very fragrant in the evening and soon fill the house with

The Cape jasmine, *Gardenia jasminoides*.

an odor that reminds many gardeners of scented bath soaps. According to the *Exotic Plant Manual* (Roehrs Company, 1970) by Alfred Byrd Graf, flowering usually begins after there is a drop in the 60°F that the plants require.

The Cape jasmine, *Gardenia jasminoides*, has always been a favorite night flower of mine even though few if any references ever mention their nocturnal scent. I corresponded with Dr. Charlotte Taylor at the Missouri Botanical Garden about this seeming omission and she replied:

There is a notable absence of information about the pollination and blooming periods of gardenias. My general impression is the cultivated gardenias will flower on a seasonal basis or several times during the year, depending on the water and temperature regime. Certainly the odor is produced in the late evening and at night. As for pollination, I assume that they are pollinated by moths, probably hawkmoths as the flowers are large with relatively long tubes.

Gardenias originally came from China. They require a great deal of sun, the only proviso being to protect potted plants from the fierce summer sun of early afternoon. They also need an evenly moist soil and warm temperatures for maximum growth but bud growth is initiated at temperatures below 65°F—and if the light is not strong enough, the buds will drop. The best temperature for winter growth is between 60°F and 65°F and between 65°F and 85°F during the summer. Remember to feed every few weeks when the buds are developing.

My garden friend in Cochection, Marie Benedum, always fed her gardenia Knox gelatin and kept an iron coathanger in the soil behind the bush. The plant flowered all year long.

Many of the plants now sold in garden centers and greenhouses are the *Gardenia jasminoides* 'Veitchii', producing double flowers up to three inches in diameter. If given warmth, moisture, and light, they will often bloom from January on into summer.

Scented cups, *Gardenia rothmannia* (synonym, *Rothmannia capensis*), make excellent houseplants and are easily grown from seed, often flowering the second year from seed. The foliage is glossy and attractive and the flowers are two inches wide and flare from a two-inch tube. They are ivory white and spotted with maroon dots in the throat. Eventually they bear hard, round fruits like small apples. When dried, the flowers retain their fragrance, and are often used for potpourri.

The stompdoorn or hip gardenia, *Gardenia thunbergia*, is a shrub from South Africa that reaches a height of five to seven feet, with shiny oval leaves and bearing very night-fragrant white

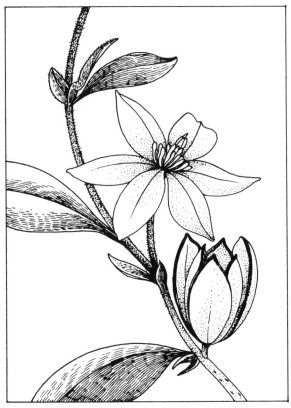

Michelia figo.

gardenias. The flowers soon become leathery; the fruits remain on the shrub and are eventually eaten—in its natural habitat—by antelopes, which, in turn, digest the seeds and spread them about. Seeds are often available and it makes an excellent houseplant.

Michelia figo was once classified as a magnolia because of a strong resemblance between the flowers of the two genuses. These broad-leaved evergreen shrubs, called banana shrubs, can become small trees over the years. They were hardy in eastern North Carolina up until the infamous winter of 1985 when the cold killed twenty-foot specimens to the ground. The flowers have six creamy yellow petals (really tepals) edged with purple surrounding many carpels on a long stipe and about thirty anthers. In the spring when the flowers open, the scent of bananas is sometimes overpowering. The cultivar 'Port Wine' has flowers of a pale purple color and less fragrance, but their compact growth makes them excellent plants for pots or tubs.

Murraya paniculata (synonym, *M. exotica*), the orange jasmine, bears clusters of three-quarter-inch, bell-shaped flowers that bloom several times a year. The sweet fragrance of jasmine is especially heavy (and heady) in the evening. The blossoms are followed by half-inch, vivid red berries. In the tropics, orange jasmines can reach the size of a small tree but they are usually smaller when confined to a pot. They prefer partial shade in the hot summer, and a moist soil laced with humus or compost. Outside of USDA Zone 9 or 10, keep orange jasmines in the greenhouse or sunporch. Temperatures can fall to 50°F in the winter months without causing damage.

The Victorian box, *Pittosporum undulatum*, came to me as seed from The Fragrant Path in Nebraska. This was a popular conservatory plant in the last century. Over the years my plant could have become a thirty-foot tree but they respond well to pruning and, in warmer climates, are used as hedges. Because the small yellow-brown fruits resemble little oranges it came to be called a mock orange and confused with the *Philadelphus* genus. The half-inch-long white flowers appear in late winter and last well into spring, are borne in terminal clusters, and have an orangelike odor at night. If growing in pots or tubs, keep the soil evenly moist, maintain temperatures around 50°F, and provide full sun, especially in the winter, although they will adapt to partial shade.

Plumerias were first described in 1522 by a Spanish priest, Francisco de Mendoza, exploring southern Mexico. Although revered in India as the temple or pagoda tree, all plants originally came from the Caribbean and were shipped about by the Spanish. Their common name of frangipani is from the French word, *frangipanier*, for coagulated milk and refers to its sticky white latex sap. Most of the flowers in this genus are from the species *Plumeria rubra*. The five-petaled flowers are twisted in such a way as to resemble pinwheels. They have been used for generations in Hawaii for leis. The white-blooming varieties, including 'Singapore' and 'Cindy Moragne', are not only effective during the day, but the sweet scent intensifies at night when the white blossoms are particularly effective in the moonlight.

Give them as much sun as possible in the summer, keep the soil on the dry side, and keep them warm in winter. In colder climates let the plants go dormant for winter and store them in a protected place where they will not freeze. Once the threat of frost is past, bring them outdoors, resume watering, and they will soon flower.

Rondeletia odorata is a tropical shrub first imported from Panama and Cuba in 1836 and

Rondeletia odorata.

named in honor of William Rondelet (1507–1566), a physician and student of fishes and algae. Mature plants reach a height of three feet and have two-inch-long spear-shaped leaves that are attractive enough to warrant its use even without flowers. The cinnabar-red flowers have a yellow eye, grow in terminal clusters, and are long, thin tubes that flare out in into five lobes. During the day there is little or no perfume, but when the sun begins to set and the first stars appear, the blossoms begin to produce a sweet odor redolent of honey. Our plant spends summer hanging from a branch of our viburnum tree and begins to bloom in late summer, continuing on into fall. The soil should be evenly moist and plants need as much sun as possible. Temperatures should be above 50°F.

The crape jasmine, Clavel de la India, or moonbeam *Tabernaemontana divaricata* (synonym, *Ervatamia coronaria*), is an evergreen shrub with milky sap that grows to a height of eight feet bearing glossy green, oval leaves about five inches long and waxy white flowers about two inches wide, the tube divided into five crisped lobes. At night, the fragrance is sweet. Keep it in a warm room in winter with the soil evenly moist and as much sun as possible; summers can be spent in the garden, where they will bloom when night temperatures rise above 60°F.

The crape jasmine, *Tabernaemontana divaricata*.

TROPICAL PLANTS

The water hawthorn or Cape pondweed, *Aponogeton distachyus*, originally came from the Cape of Good Hope. This is an aquatic plant that does well in a tub or small garden pond but must come inside where temperatures fall much below 20°F, overwintering in tubs or buckets of water. The lance-shaped leaves lie flat upon the water and in late summer the plant produces spikes of small waxy white flowers that smell of vanilla in the evening air. The plants should be potted and kept under about two feet of water. There is a cultivar with larger flowers called 'Giganteus'.

Anemarrhena asphodeloides is the only species in this genus, a member of the lily family native to northern China. The rhizomatous root produces grasslike leaves fifteen to thirty inches long. In summer, a three-foot-long raceme appears with many three-eighth-inch, rosy purple flowers, lightly lined with brown. The flowers are fragrant at night, with a rather sweet, honeylike scent, and somewhat resemble the flowers of a snake plant (*Sansevieria trifasciata*). Unfortunately they quickly succumb to freezing, so are best brought indoors for a northern winter.

The Cape pondweed, *Aponogeton distachyus.*

The Kahili ginger, *Hedychium gardneranum*, belongs to the genus of flowers used for the leis tossed at tourists in Hawaii. This particular plant bears canes to six feet high and eighteen-inch-long leaves that are powdery white when young. The yellow flowers have conspicuous bright red filaments and an incredible sweet perfume that is produced both day and night. Keep the soil evenly moist, give partial shade, and keep temperatures above 60°F.

Helichrysum angustifolium is not to everyone's liking because the leaves smell of curry when they are pinched. But on warm, summer nights, when heat lightning streaks across the sky, you can smell its unusual odor on the evening air. The foot-high plant belongs to an Australian family of everlasting flowers called immortelles, and as such is not hardy below 28°F, but will do

wonderfully on a sunny window over the winter. Small terminal clusters of tiny flowers with yellow bracts appear in late summer.

Heliotropium arborescens (synonym, *H. peruvianum*) was first called *herbe d'amour* when it was introduced to Paris after being discovered in Peru in 1740. The English called it cherry-pie but the flowers really smell more like vanilla. This is a semishrubby plant and, in warm climates, a herbaceous perennial. The fragrance is powerful both day and night, but in the evening when the dew begins to form along the garden pathways, the flowers are at their best. American gardeners usually treat it as an annual and the cultivars 'Marine' and 'Mini-Marine' are offered by many of the seed houses, easily flowering in your garden from seed sown in late winter or early spring. They are advertised as being "very fragrant," but to have some idea of the perfume available before hybridizers gave fragrance away in favor of flower size and color, buy a rooted cutting from a greenhouse plant that hopefully goes back a few years.

Humea elegans is a biennial member of the daisy family from Australia. I first found mention of it in *The Contemplative Gardener.* In this wonderful book, Jason Hill notes that the plant is tender but worth growing because it "pours out at night a powerful scent of incense." According to *Hortus Third* (Macmillan Publishing Company, 1975), the tiny seeds—which must be fresh—should be sown from the first of July to September, covering them lightly with a sterile medium and using a heating cable set for 60°F or 65°F. Germination takes about a month. The young plants should be kept nearly dry and in a cool greenhouse during the winter. Plant them out in the garden after all danger of frost is past. Plants reach a height of four to six feet and produce one-sided panicles of feathery flowers of varying colors of purple, rose, or pink, and shades in between.

Pelargonium spp. represents the florist's geranium, not the common wildflower and garden

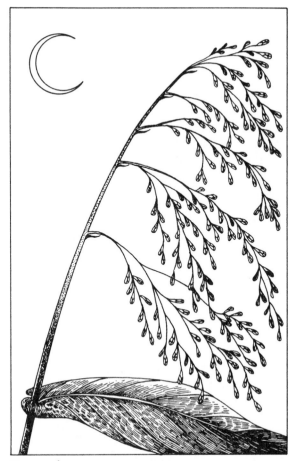

Humea elegans.

perennials belonging to the species *Geranium*. Most gardeners would probably be very surprised to find that at least four species are fragrant at night. Claire Powell in *The Meaning of Flowers* (Shambhala, 1979), calls the night-smelling geranium melancholy. "Like those who suffer from melancholy, this charming plant, also called the dark geranium, flies the light of day, but its delicious perfume delights those who cultivate it."

The flowers are certainly nothing to write home about. They are small and a dull yellow-brown with five petals, appearing in clusters, each blossom on a toothpick stalk. The plant stems are corky like other geraniums, the leaves finely cut, and everything begins with tuberous roots.

But when you walk into a room at night, their sweet fragrance is delightful. These plants are thought to be the first geraniums to be cultivated in Europe, arriving in England before 1632.

Michael Vassar of the International Geranium Society (see Sources for address), sent me plants of *Pelargonium triste* and *P. lobatum*, the two species with the most scent.

"The best planting mixture," he said, "is a coarse sandy mix that does not have a lot of organic matter. Water the plants well and then let them become slightly dry before soaking again. Give them full sun and keep above freezing. These are tough plants that resent pampering—the harder they are grown, the better they flower. Both produce large tuber systems, so a rather large planting container is best, starting with a six-inch pot, then on to a ten- or twelve-inch container. They go dormant in late spring or early summer, with growth beginning again in September."

Other powerfully night-scented species are the yellow-green flowered *Pelargonium gibbosum* and *P. × glaucifolium*, the black-flowered geranium, a hybrid of *P. gibbosum* and *P. lobatum*.

The snakeplant or mother-in-law's-tongue, *Sansevieria trifasciata*, is a stalwart houseplant often found growing between the back of a luncheonette booth and the steamy window to the outside world. Another common name, bowstring hemp refers to the use of the tough fibers that run along its leather leaves for making hats, mats, and rope. Sansevierias are members of the lily family, a fact that is evidenced immediately when they bloom. The blossoms have six pale green petals and long, curving stamens, opening in late afternoon and at evening, that exude a penetrating but sweet fragrance which quickly fills a greenhouse or plant room. Where the flower base meets the stem, they drip with crystal beads of a sugary nectar with a sharp undertaste. Giving cultivation instructions for sansevierias is unnecessary since they survive just about anything, but give them a summer outside in partial shade.

Sinningia tubiflora is a gesneriad, one of a genus of South American flowers that have long been favorites of houseplant aficionados. Some are very small plants; *S. pusilla* can be grown in a thimble, while others have flowering stems up to four feet long. The blossoms of red, orange, and other bright colors are probably pollinated by hummingbirds but according to Dr. Hans Wiehler, Director of Research for the Gesneriad Research Foundation, *S. tubiflora*, native to Paraguay is night-fragrant. It has a three-inch-long, funnel-shaped white corolla with snapdragonlike lips, is pollinated by sphinx moths, and has a beautiful spicy fragrance in the evening. These plants like to be kept warm in evenly moist soil in partial shade.

Pelargonium × glaucifolium.

HARDY ANNUALS AND PERENNIALS

The hay-scented fern, *Dennstaedtia punctilobula*, does not flower but it is beautifully fragrant when the leaves are crushed. In our evening garden there is a patch of this fern surrounding one of the larger lights that illuminate a star magnolia (*Magnolia tomentosa*), its branches hung with a number of tropical plants. I often pinch a leaf on evening walks. The leaves are endowed with coumarin, a chemical with a vanillalike fragrance that is especially pronounced in the fall when the fronds are touched with frost and begin to yellow and dry. Thoreau said of this, his favorite fern:

". . . Nature perfumes her garments with this [plant]. She gives it to those who go a-berrying and on dark autumnal walks. The very scent of it, if you have a decayed frond in your chamber, will take you far up country in a twinkling."

Dianthus alpinus 'Albus' is the white form of the alpine pink, a rounded plant about eight inches high that produces some of the most fragrant flowers around. The sweet and spicy odor, touched with cloves, makes most of the pinks desirable members of the evening garden, especially since the flowers produce the fragrance both day and night—butterflies visit by day and moths by night. Give them full sun and perfectly drained soil. They are all at their best as edging plants in a rock garden or along an old stone wall.

Dianthus petraeus is a pink that forms mats of growth, producing dozens of small white pinks with a very sweet scent.

Dianthus squarrosus grows about six inches high and produces lovely little white blossoms with fringed edges that are so fragrant that butterflies and moths will pass over other pinks to drink the nectar of these flowers.

The meadowsweet, *Filipendula ulmaria* (synonym, *Spiraea ulmaria*), bears plumes of fluffy white flowers. It is a naturalized plant throughout the Northeast, having arrived in ships that sailed from England empty of cargo, but full of dirt for

The meadowsweet, *Filipendula ulmaria.*

ballast (and went back *sans* dirt but loaded to the gills with merchandise). Louise Beebe Wilder quotes one Richard Jefferies as saying: "Where ever the scythe has not reached, the meadowsweet rears its pale flowers. At evening if it be sultry, on some days especially before a thunder storm, the whole mead is full of the fragrance of this plant. So heavy and powerful is its odour that the still motionless air between the thick hedges becomes oppressive and it is a relief to issue forth into the open fields away from the perfume and the brooding heat. But by day it is pleasant to linger in the meadow and inhale its sweetness." We had a few plants that appeared at the edge of our meadow when we lived in New York State.

The fragrance at night was heavier than during the day, with more of the undertone of pollen, but decidedly attractive. I never smelled it just before a thunderstorm because in the Catskill mountains when one heard a distant roar of thunder, one went for cover immediately.

Hebe cupressoides (synonym, *Veronica cupressoides*) is often listed in books on fragrant plants for the balmy odor of cedarwood touched with violet that emanates from its tiny scalelike leaves. Plants reach a height of four feet and are perfect in a rock garden setting. Clusters of one-eighth-inch pale purple or sometimes white flowers appear in summer. According to Jason Hill in *The Contemplative Gardener*, this plant tells the gardener when the dew is on the grass by giving off its scent, which he describes as cedarwood and orrisroot, perfect for a small garden designed for sitting out in on sumer nights. Unfortunately hebes are not reliably hardy north of USDA Zone 8.

The saw-toothed sunflower, *Helianthus grosseserratus*, would seem to be a strange choice for an evening garden since these flowers, more than any you could choose, epitomize bright sun and blue sky. Like its relative in the annual garden, this perennial plant can reach a height of thirteen feet when in a happy situation of average soil and full sun. The golden yellow blossoms are over two inches in diameter and up to twenty of them can top a stem. Blooming early in October, they are easily grown from seed. So why are they listed here? Because the blossoms smell of chocolate—both by day and night. Nothing can surprise a visitor more that to take a deep whiff of these flowers and be reminded of all things good and chocolate.

Dame's rocket or sweet rocket, *Hesperis matronalis*, performs as an annual, biennial, or perennial, depending on luck and well-drained garden soil, performing best as a biennial. It earned it genus name, which means "evening" in Greek, because it releases its sweet fragrance at dusk. The species name in Latin refers to the

The saw-toothed sunflower, *Helianthus grosseserratus*.

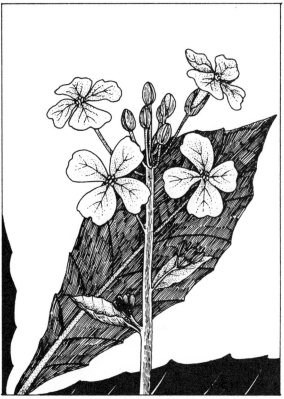

Dame's rocket, *Hesperis matronalis*.

Roman festival of matrons, though the reasoning behind this is obscure.

The plant was introduced into England in the 1500s, and it's been a popular garden subject ever since. Miss Jekyll always recommended planting dame's rocket at the edge of a woodland or in clumps within the wild garden. The term rocket is derived from the French *roquette* and has nothing to do with artillery or distress signals but refers instead to a resemblance between this plant and an old European green, *Eruca vesicaria* subsp. *sativa*, or rugula. The height is about three feet and the half-inch flowers resemble those of phlox but have four petals rather than five. The colors are usually lilac and shades of purple but there are cultivars with double flowers and in white, and the whites are the best choice for the evening garden. The odor has a touch of violet,

and one of its older common names is dame's violets.

Two more rockets are occasionally found in *Index seminums*—the fancy name for the seed lists published by botanical gardens—and rock garden seed exchanges. The cut-leaved dame's violet, *Hesperis laciniata*, is a southern European wildflower from the Mediterranean region. The leaves are deeply lobed and the flowers are reddish violet or yellow. *H. tristis* hails from central Europe and bears brownish red or dark purple flowers. The fragrance is said to be the best of the three and plants are especially happy when growing and seeding in old walls or rock outcrops.

The twinflower, *Linnaea borealis*, represents one species in a genus first named in honor of the great Linnaeus, the founder of modern botanical

The twinflower, *Linnaea borealis*.

The pineapple weed, *Matricaria matricarioides*, is an annual plant, originally from Europe, that is strongly aromatic with an odor reminiscent of sweet fruity pineapple. The plant is similar to wild chamomile, *M. chamomilla*, but the flowers lack the white daisylike rays. The leaves are finely cut and plants rarely reach above a foot in height, since they often sprawl. We first noticed the plant in the gravel area where we parked cars next to a field at our home in upstate New York. When we got in and out of a car, the leaves would be crushed and the pineapple odor immediately apparent. Save the seeds and plant them somewhere along the pathways of the evening garden for a special treat on a moonlight stroll.

The great sea stock, *Matthiola sinuata*, is a member of the genus that includes the annual evening stock. This species is biennial with white wooly leaves that grow along Mediterranean beaches in the perfect drainage of sand and rock.

nomenclature. It's a member of the honeysuckle family and as a result the flowers give forth a lovely sweet fragrance with a hint of almonds, especially at night. The twin flowers are nodding, bell-like tubes of a delicate pink or sometimes white, their edges making five lobes. The plants stand about five inches tall and are really a trailing evergreen subshrub that wanders through the cooler woods of North America and the circumpolar regions. It is hardy to USDA Zone 2. Twinflowers need a light, moist garden soil in partial shade.

Mr. Edward St. John of New Hampshire wrote to Louise Beebe Wilder about this flower:

> Just now our forests are richly perfumed with the odour of the *Linnaea*. A few days ago I noticed it along the trails before I could find a single blossom. . . . I noticed and recognized the odour as I was wandering through a swampy forest and following it up the breeze traced it to a large colony which was fully fifteen rods [about 248 feet] away from the point where I first noticed the odour.

The pineapple weed, *Matricaria matricarioides*.

The great sea stock, *Matthiola sinuata*.

Mentzelia lindleyi.

The flowers are a bright reddish purple or sometimes white and are extremely fragrant at night. Look for seeds for this and the following stocks in rock garden seed exchanges.

I only saw the sad stock (what a wonderful name) once, at a rock garden adjoining a delightful bed and breakfast at Rottingdean on the White Cliffs of Dover. The botanical name is *Matthiola fruticulosa*. The plant has very narrow leaves that are covered with white wool and the flowers are green to reddish purple and have a marvelous fragrance. *M. odoratissima* is an evergreen subshrub, a native of Persia mentioned by Louise Beebe Wilder as having dirty cream-colored flowers that deepen to purple with age. The flowers are very fragrant at night.

Mentzelia lindleyi (called *Bartonia* in older books) is a beautiful annual from the deserts of central California. For years I saw reference after reference mention its night-blooming habits. Finally I obtained seed from one of the rock garden seed exchanges, planted the seedlings in a spot in full sun with well-drained, sandy soil, and waited for the show. Buds swelled and opened to reveal golden yellow flowers two and a half inches across with a beautiful satin texture to the petals, but the time was early afternoon. By accident I happened to smell its sweet fragrant scent in the evening air, so all was not lost. (There are other members of the genus that do bloom in late afternoon and on into evening including *M. decapetala*, a biennial or short-lived perennial that is also delightfully fragrant but is described in Chapter Seven as a night-bloomer.)

I've searched for years to find seeds for the first and original petunia, a plant from Argentina called *Petunia axillaris* (synonym, *P. nyctaginiflora*). The white flowers of this species are about two inches wide and more than two inches long— and they are especially fragrant at night. In fact, old botanical records mention that nocturnal moths visit the flowers all night long. (The name petunia is derived from Latinizing *petun*, the word used by Brazilian natives for describing *Nicotiana*, a flower that belongs to the same family as and resembles petunias.)

Most modern petunias that grace summer borders, planters, and window boxes are derived from hybridizing three species, *Petunia axillaris*, *P. inflata*, and *P. violacea* (although many botanists think all three are variations on the first). Some of today's cultivars are still fragrant at night, but many more are not. Mrs. Wilder writes that the "scent of petunia is not altogether pleasant, save at night when it loses a certain coarseness of quality and becomes lighter and more transparent."

Here is a case where gardeners must do their own detective work. A number of whites are perfect for the evening garden, including 'Celebrity White', 'Ultra White', and 'Apollo', but none of these are guaranteed to be especially fragrant.

Although petunias are perennials in warmer climates (we have had plants survive our USDA Zone 7 winter, but not every year), they are usually treated as annuals. Most of today's hybrids will bloom from seed after seven weeks of growth. Just make sure the plants get plenty of sun—although they will take partial shade in the South—and plenty of water.

One problem with most petunias is the excessive length of their stems. Since the blossoms are usually terminal, the plants become rather messy by midseason. To remedy this, take a long stem about halfway up and roll it gently between your fingers, just enough to squeeze and soften the tissue. Then bend the stem gently backward so the upper part is now pointing to the ground. This action prevents a hormone produced in the growing tip from reaching the side buds and inhibiting bloom. Now the side shoots will develop and flower, while the top will continue to bloom

and hide the growing process. Then you can pinch off the top stem for a more compact plant.

The perennial garden phlox, *Phlox paniculata*, is a stalwart member of the white garden but it also has a marvelous fragrance both day and night. By day swallowtail butterflies will hover over its blossoms, unwinding their watch-coil tongues to the nectar in the bottom of the flower's tube; in the afternoon and before dusk, the hawkmoths dart in and out like the hummingbirds they resemble, and at night, the other moths take over. The scent is rich and sweet but too much of it at one time and one detects faint overtones of an odor more animal than vegetable.

The best cultivars are the whites and light pinks. Give these plants well-drained but good garden soil, with organic matter added, and full sun to partial shade. Remember to deadhead the flowers to prevent the seeding of unwanted colors. Look for 'Everest', white flowers with a light rose-colored eye; 'Mt. Fuji' (although the correct name is 'Fujiyama'), with large heads of pure white flowers on three-foot stems; and 'World Peace', with white flowers that bloom from August into September on forty-inch stems.

There are other phloxes with scent but the wild blue phlox (*Phlox divaricata*) and creeping phlox (*P. stolonifera*) are too low to the ground to effectively scent the evening garden. When their lighter and whiter forms are used, they become elegant edges to the moonlight garden.

The Caucasian crosswort, *Phuopsis stylosa*, came to our garden with seed from the Alpine Garden Society. This single-species genus is often suggested for rock gardens where it grows about eight inches high, and according to many authorities, can quickly become rampant. In late spring, flat-topped clusters of pink, tubular, starlike flowers appear. Like many tubular flowers, they give off a penetrating odor after the dew begins to collect in the evening. Some people find it musky, but pleasant, others resort to the term "foxy." I straddle the fence and call it interesting.

The Himalayan cowslip, *Primula sikkimensis*,

The Caucasian crosswort, *Phuopsis stylosa*.

The California tree poppy, *Romneya coulteri*.

comes from Tibet, discovered at a height of nearly twenty thousand feet. I learned of its fragrance from Roy Genders in his book *Perfume in the Garden* (The Garden Book Club, London, n.d.), published in the mid-1950s. The leaves are pale green and finely toothed and in late spring, pale yellow funnel-shaped blossoms over one inch across appear in umbels atop eighteen-inch stems. Genders suggests growing these primroses in a mass and since they are very easy to cultivate and come easily from seed, this is no problem. The perfume is very sweet but light and not cloying. The soil should be rich in compost, moist, and in dappled shade.

Other evening-fragrant primroses include *Primula florindae* bearing drooping sulfur yellow flowers with a sweet perfume and *P. helodoxa*, the glory of the marsh, a Chinese species not hardy north of USDA Zone 7, but worth every effort at cultivation. Genders says that this second plant, while not richly fragrant, is a sight to behold when seen growing by the waterside in the evening twilight.

Finally, the old double French primrose 'Marie Crousse' is described as having an especially fine fragrance at night, reminding one of honeysuckle.

The California tree poppy or Matilija poppy, *Romneya coulteri*, is probably the only flower in the world that I will wish for at odd hours of the day or night. This is an American wildflower of great beauty: the white flowers are six inches wide, have six petals that resemble white satin, all surrounding a golden ball of stamens—and they are sublimely fragrant in the evening. Unfortunately, it's not hardy north of USDA Zone 8, though stories filter down of dedicated northeastern gardeners keeping a plant going for a while. The problem is that seedlings will not flower for several years and they resent transplanting. Since a mature plant can reach a height of eight feet, once they settle in they become a garden highlight, but getting there requires a great deal of patience—and work.

Schizopetalon walkeri has no common name—at least none that I ever learned about. It's an annual plant from Chile that is worth growing if only for its delightfully lovely white flowers. The four petals have fringed edges that look as though they were cut by a Chinese scissors artist. The flowers are about three quarters of an inch wide and appear in racemes on one-foot stems. Come the dusk, these small blossoms start to produce an extraordinary sweet fragrance, compounded of an almond odor as sweet as marzipan mixed with vanilla. The plants resent being moved, so start the seeds in peat pots to prevent root disturbance. Grow the plants either in pots or in the front of the border, planting out after

Schizopetalon walkeri.

frost. Keep deadheading to prolong bloom. They also will do well in a winter greenhouse, flowering in early spring from seed sown in the fall.

Stackhousia pulvinaise, from the Australian Alps and parts of Tasmania, is hardly ever cultivated but has been noted by the late Professor Otto Schwarz for its "delightful nocturnal scent." The five-petaled flowers are small, about a quarter inch long. I have never grown these flowers but continue to look in the various seed exchanges of the rock garden societies and eventually they will come my way.

Verbascum phlomoides is a biennial from central and southern Europe that has naturalized over parts of the eastern United States. It resembles the great common mullein or flannel plant (*V. thapsus*) but in this case the bright yellow flowers crowd the top of the stem and the leaves line up along the bottom. While not a great plant for the formal border, it's wonderful in the wild part of the evening garden, especially since the yellow flowers are especially luminous at dusk and it is then (and on cloudy afternoons) that the flowers produce a faint, but slightly sweet odor attractive to moths.

PERENNIAL VINES

The chocolate vine, *Akebia quinata*, if well-grown, can become invasive where winters are usually warm. I first encountered it growing on a trellis in John Cram's next-store garden, where in late April the branches are covered with small, purple-brown flowers about an inch long, each with three sepals, the male flowers above and the female flowers below. As the afternoon warms they produce a sweet and spicy scent that becomes stronger as evening approaches. The vines can reach a length of twenty feet and will ultimately crowd out anything else on the trellis. But on a hot summer day, the semievergreen leaves, each with five leaflets, give a wonderful, filtered shade. They need a reasonably good soil and a spot in full sun to flower well.

The chocolate vine, *Akebia quinata*.

Louise Beebe Wilder mentions a raisin vine in her book *The Fragrant Garden*, and I think this is the plant she is talking about. She mentions the vine growing about the library windows of her Maryland home and recalled its "spicy breath" appearing at night and mingling with the smell of dust and old leather, an odor characteristic of rooms where old books are piled upon wooden shelves.

There are a number of fragrant clematises, but *Clematis rehderana*, a deciduous climber from China, is the only one I know of that chooses the evening hours to produce its scent. The twenty-foot-long vines have three-inch leaves that closely resemble those of a hop vine, and are especially valuable for clambering over a wall. In the summer clusters of pale primrose yellow, bell-like flowers appear and, as evening approaches, they produce the scent of cowslips. Although a rare item from the nursery point of view, this clematis is often available from seed exchanges.

The honeysuckles, *Lonicera* spp., are clambering vines that have flowers with a wonderful fragrance that is especially pungent at night. Having spent the better part of a year fighting the up

to now uncontrolled ravages of Japanese honeysuckle (*Lonicera japonica*), I write the following with the warning that this beautiful but tough vine can be a problem if left to its own resources—and that includes abandonment. But if kept under a semblance of control, it's worth having for the glory of the flowers, especially fragrant in the early morning and at dusk and on into the evening. From the number of moths that I've seen flying about the flowers, it is obviously best pollinated at night.

The Japanese honeysuckle can reach thirty feet and is an evergreen or partly evergreen vine, depending on the climate. The eighteen-inch fragrant white flowers are often tinged with purple, turning yellow with age, and appear from summer and on into fall. They are very easy to grow but, as noted above, can become a nuisance if not kept under control. In fact, in various woodland areas of the North and Southeast, this particular honeysuckle rates second only to kudzu in running amok. Ordinary moist garden soil is best and as shade deepens flowering decreases.

Hall's honeysuckle, *Lonicera japonica* 'Halliana', bears two-inch white flowers that turn creamy yellow on the second day and is not quite as invasive. *L. periclymenum* var. *belgica*, the Dutch woodbine, has lovely flowers that grow in whorls, white inside and flushed with purple-pink on the outside.

One of the more colorful trellises that have been suggested to hold honeysuckles is described by William Robinson: "A good plan is to plant some in good soil against wooden posts at distances of twelve feet apart, and when they have reached the top of the posts to connect them by festooning chains from post to post, as roses and clematises are often done."

The wisterias, *Wisteria* spp., are vines that always excite comment when they are in bloom. They possibly have more cachet than any other vine in the garden. As a child, I often played beneath a large trellis in my mother's garden that held an ancient wisteria vine. When I tried to think of the flowers' fragrance, my mind's eye saw a picture of late afternoon with the garden full of flowers and I could smell its sweet perfume mixed with all those floral scents of long ago— but try as I may, I could not remember what happened at night.

I then asked Fairman Jayne of Sandy Mush Herb Nursery about wisterias at night because I remembered that the old summerhouse at their garden is crowned with an ancient wisteria vine.

"They are fragrant at night," he said. "The Japanese has the most powerful scent, the Chinese a bit less, and the American has the most delicate of all. And the white form of the flowers also has a lesser scent.

"And," he added, "they certainly are wonderful on a summer's night."

The Japanese wisteria (*Wisteria floribunba*) is a deciduous woody vine with delicate compound leaves that are very attractive, and those wonderful, large, drooping clusters of day- and night-fragrant lilac flowers appearing in spring are showstoppers. Full sun is best coupled with moist but well-drained soil with an acid pH. Plants produced from seed will often not flower for years and then the flowers will be second-rate.

The Chinese wisteria (*Wisteria sinensis*) is also a deciduous woody vine with delicate compound leaves and drooping clusters of day- and night-fragrant lilac-colored flowers in spring. Full sun is best, in moist but well-drained soil, not too rich in nitrogen, with an acid pH. Both wisterias are hardy in USDA Zone 5, but need protection from bitterly cold winds. They also need frequent pruning to keep them neat and under control; if left unchecked, they can actually warp metal poles and break through trellises.

Gardeners often have wisterias that refuse to bloom. Even plants produced from cuttings will occasionally refuse to set flowers for eight to ten years, or more. The standard advice has always been to root prune the vines, to prune those vigorous young shoots, and to feed the plants with superphosphate. If that doesn't work, remove the offending vine and buy a new plant from a reliable nursery.

The American wisteria (*Wisteria macrostachya*) has smaller flowers than its oriental cousins. It's only hardy in USDA Zone 6 and south. Not all wisterias transplant well, so buy plants propagated by cuttings and grown in containers.

TROPICAL VINES

Allamanda cathartica 'Williamsii' is a cultivar of a species of plant called the golden trumpets, clambering vines that can be trained on a trellis or allowed to wander over a greenhouse during

Allamanda cathartica 'Williamsii'.

the winter. In our garden, the plant hangs under our viburnum tree from early May until the first threat of frost, then goes into the greenhouse where it continues to flower. Unlike other members of this genus, Williams' allamanda has a delightfully sweet fragrance—often described as resembling the smell of grapes—especially at night.

The leaves are smaller than those of the original species and are not as glossy and the three-inch flowers of butter yellow, which begin to open in the afternoon, are stained with reddish-brown streaks. When buying this cultivar, make sure the one you purchase is a cutting from a plant with fragrant flowers, since every once in a while a plant will produce blossoms with no odor. Once winter comes, cut back on watering and in spring, prune back the oldest branches. Unlike many tropical plants and vines, if this plant freezes to the ground, as long as the roots are protected, it will spring forth again like a phoenix. When growing in pots, keep the soil evenly moist, the temperature above 50°F, and give it as much sun as possible.

The cruel plant, *Araujia sericifera*, comes from Brazil and Argentina and is only hardy where the ground never freezes. It does quite well in a ten-inch pot filled with a mix of commercial potting soil and composted cow manure, two parts to one. The pots should be backed by a trellis as the cruel plant is a climber. You will usually find it as seed; germination takes three to six weeks, with seedlings coming into bloom about ten months later. The plants prefer a moist soil and a spot in filtered sun or light shade, doing well hanging from a tree limb and in the greenhouse for the winter.

The blossoms are white or pale pink, and about an inch wide. The common name is apt and refers to night-flying moths and their attraction to the sweet smell of these beautiful flowers. Moths descend with their probosces on high, ready to sink them within the long floral tubes.

The cruel plant, *Araujia sericifera*.

But the pollen is very sticky and the insects are soon stuck in the glue. Then, with the morning sun, the pollen dries, and most of the moths fly away—although many die in the process.

Since cruel plants belong to the milkweed family, after the flowers fade and turn to seed, large pear-shaped pods break open and reveal a mass of silky threads. If the vines get too leggy, cut them back. Like other milkweeds, the wounds exude a white sap but will soon form a crust that prevents further bleeding.

The evening trumpet flower or Carolina jessamine, *Gelsemium sempervirens*, grows throughout the Deep South and down into Florida. There it winds its way over fence posts and up telephone poles, and, when brought to civilization, around trellises. The evergreen leaves surround sweely fragrant, bell-shaped flowers of bright yellow that are particularly sweet as evening approaches. They bloom as early as mid-February in the Deep South and later in the spring to the north. The only requirements are full sun or partial shade. It survives winters in Asheville, North Carolina, and, rumor has it, most of Vir-

The evening trumpet flower, *Gelsemium sempervirens.*

ginia, too, so I assume it is hardy throughout USDA Zone 7. The plants also do very well in a conservatory or greenhouse if the soil is kept evenly moist and the vine gets all the sun it can. It should be noted that this plant is extremely poisonous and it can cause contact dermatitis. No part should be eaten.

Hoya spp. are tropical and subtropical members of the milkweed family that have a long history as house-, greenhouse, and conservatory plants. They were named in honor of Thomas Hoy, one-time gardener to the Duke of Northumberland at Sion House in England. There are some two hundred species of this root-climbing and twining plant with fleshy and succulent leaves and clusters of exotic flowers. The seeds are connected to long silvery down, belying their family connection.

The plants usually found in most houseplant collections are *Hoya carnosa* and *H. bella.* For years I have kept an *H. carnosa* in a twelve-inch wire-mesh basket lined with a sheet of sphagnum moss. It spends summer out of doors and winter in the greenhouse. When it flowers the plant is

breathtaking—in more ways than one. First, each of the star-shaped flowers is lovely, resembling a perfect creation carved from wax, then stamped with a red star at the center. The flowers appear in bunches (or umbels) of twelve to fifteen individual blossoms, each on a slim stem, all connected to the branch at a point called the peduncle. This peduncle must never be removed, since year after year new flowers will appear at the same place. At one time the flowers were grown for buttonholes when that was the custom. As a custom it didn't last, since the flowers produce crystal beads of sweet, sticky nectar—for that reason, hoyas are usually not hung overhead in floral displays or in greenhouses.

Second, the evening fragrance can become so sweet and penetrating that often a plant with many flowers must be taken from the room. Yet from a discreet distance, it is quite lovely.

And speaking of hoya nectar, readers of the Royal Horticultural Society's magazine *The Garden* have reported that insects, including wasps and greenflies, have been observed to feed at hoya flowers then become trapped in the sticky stuff, eventually dying of thirst. It's been suggested that the nectar of hoya blossoms might contain a particular sugar called mannose. This is a substance that bees and wasps cannot metabolize properly and because their digestive enzymes become chemically locked with the sugar, they literally starve in the midst of plenty.

Christine M. Burton is editor of *The Hoyan,* the bulletin of The Hoya Society International, and gave me a great deal of information about hoyas, including the fact that most are pollinated by wasps or flies, and that one species lives in a symbiotic relationship with ants.

"It's called *Hoya imbricata,*" she said. "There is only one leaf per node and where that leaf is connected to the stem, there is a little flap where ant colonies live; the ants provide the fertilizer while the hoya gives them shelter."

When asked about fragrance, she said, "Many

The wax plant, *Hoya carnosa*.

hoyas are fragrant by day, some by day and night, but the plants that I describe all bear night-fragrant flowers." Among the hoyas she suggested for the evening garden were:

Hoya carnosa and its many cultivars.

Hoya 'USDA 354244' with pure white flowers about eighteen inches in diameter. The cultivar name refers to an acquisition assigned by the collector, in this case the United States Department of Agriculture.

Hoya fungii is closely related to *H. carnosa* and has similar flowers but its leaves are huge and often one umbel will bear up to seventy flowers, all arising from a peduncle that is so slim it looks unable to bear the weight. The species name is in honor of a Chinese botanist named Fung.

Hoya megalaster bears thirty-inch flowers with nine or ten in an umbel, but can produce up to eighteen. It is unique in appearance since the flower is deep maroon with a white center and an almost black corona.

Hoya melifluea is also very unusual since the white flowers are often stained from a pink to a deep rose because the nectar, instead of being crystal clear, is black. A true midnight flower.

Hoya imperialis (synonym, *H. sussuela*) has as many as fourteen brownish purple flowers in an umbel, each about three inches across. When introduced into Europe, it won the prize for the best new plant at the 1848 exhibition in Regent's Park Gardens. The leaves have solid edges. The variety *rauschii* has flowers mixed with white to pink to green and has wavy leaves.

Hoya odorata has a lemon or citrus smell at night and differs from most hoyas in being shrublike, but in old age, plants will tend to twine. The flowers are greenish white, about an inch wide and two or three to an umbel.

Hoya pauciflora has slim leaves and is unusual in that each peduncle bears only a single one-inch-wide flower with a very sweet odor.

Hoya shepherdii, normally sold as *H. longifolia*, has half-inch flowers, eight to ten in an umbel, that are very fragrant.

Hoya longifolia is very fragrant too, but has larger, one-inch-wide white flowers, often with twenty-five to an umbel.

"And there are always new hoyas coming along," said Mrs. Burton. "We have a new hoya, temporarily known as 'BSI-1'—it's the first unknown from the British Solomon Islands—when you walk into a room, there is a fantastic smell of Concord grapes. Then there is *Hoya latifolia* subsp. *kinabaluensis* that has leaves the size of dinner plates with palmate veins of dark green and wonderfully fragrant flowers of a cream color that are extremely fragrant at night."

The winter or pink jasmine, *Jasminum polyanthum*, is one of those plants that make a gardener wish that he or she owned a Greek island, with a stone cottage backed by a terrace overlooking the Aegean and clothed from top to bottom with jasmine. These twining plants produce hundreds of rosy pink buds that open to a three-quarter-inch tube with five pointed lobes like perfumed stars that carry the scent well into the night. Plants want an evenly moist soil, temperatures of 50°F or above, and plenty of winter sun. Use this plant for winter flowers but be sure the room is cool and there is plenty of light. After it flowers, cut the stems back to force new growth.

Chilean jasmine, *Mandevilla laxa* (synonym, *M. suaveolens*), produces clusters of white trumpet-shaped flowers over two inches long and two inches across. They are fragrant with a jasmine-like perfume, especially at night. The ovate leaves have a heart-shaped base and grow along a very woody, twining stem, but since the vine is deciduous, it always seems to be losing leaves and looking scruffy. But the flowers are worth it all. These plants are easy to reproduce from cuttings, but because of tuberous roots, difficult to transplant. Allow the soil to dry out between waterings, provide temperatures above 50°F, and provide light shade.

The *Solandra* genus encompasses about ten species of vines from tropical America of which four are in general cultivation. Most have showy flowers and most are fragrant at night. And, unlike most other plants in this chapter, they rest during the summer when water should be withheld. But these vines need plenty of water from early autumn to late spring, a minimum winter temperature of 50°F, and lots of sun. They usually bloom in December and since flowers appear on old growth, you can cut back any new twining stems to keep the plants within bounds.

Solandra grandiflora is native to the West Indies. The sweetly fragrant funnel-shaped flowers are about eight inches long, greenish white at first, and lined with purple, then turning yellow-brown on the second day. The five lobes at the trumpet's edge are crenulated. In nature the vine can reach thirty feet.

The chalice vine or cup-of-gold, *Solandra guttata*, comes from Mexico and the West Indies. This quick-growing woody climber bears large oval leaves that are thick and shiny. The ten-inch flowers are shaped like goblets, the buds being protected by a green calyx at the base. The flowers begin as a greenish white, turn to a creamy yellow as they open, and finally gold before they fall. The petals are delicately traced with purple. At night they spread a fresh coconut fragrance. Although the vines rarely climb more than thirty feet, the aerial roots require strong support. Sandy loam is best for a growing medium and young shoots can be stuck in sand.

Gabriel's trumpet or the *copa de leche*, *Solandra longiflora*, bears white flowers about ten inches long and they are powerfully fragrant at night. Like *S. grandiflora*, the flowers start out as white with five purple lines running down the throat, but soon turn yellow, then darker with age.

The *capa de oro, Solandra maxima,* has the fanciest flowers of them all. The ripe yellow cup-shaped blossoms are about seven inches long and six inches across. Five dark purple lines run down the tube from the lip (where the five edges of the cup are folded back), ready to guide a moth to the bottom of the well. As the flowers age, they take on a tint of orange. Like many of the night-fragrant tropical flowers, the *capa de oro* hits the nose with the smell of cheap toilet soap when it comes close to the gardener but mellows with increasing distances.

The Madagascar jasmine, *Stephanotis flori-*

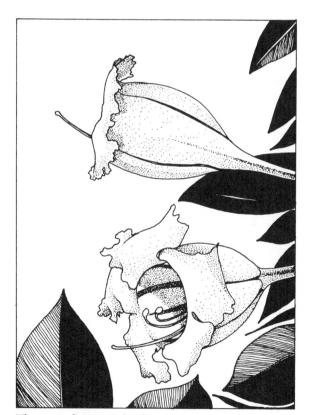

The *capa de oro, Solandra maxima.*

bunda, is a tropical climber with thick, leathery, glossy, dark green leaves about four inches long that bloom in the winter months—in the Northern Hemisphere—with clusters of lovely white, waxy, trumpet-shaped flowers that flare out to five pointed lobes. They need temperatures above 60°F, evenly moist soil, and a spot in partial shade. As a reward the plants will even bloom in a winter window garden (if kept warm), and the fragrance at night reminds many of the scent of Easter lilies, marvelous especially with snow whirling about outside. As with all tropical plants, they should summer on the terrace or in the garden, being taken inside well before the first threat of frost. Dr. Hans Wiehler reports that these flowers do exceptionally well in his Sarasota, Florida, garden.

The star or confederate jasmine, *Trachelospermum jasminoides,* is named for the Federation of Malay States where it is native and not for the Southern side during the Civil War. This is a beautiful, but tender, vine with shiny green leaves. The floral tubes of the very fragrant light yellow flowers are divided into five parts, each with a wavy edge. Blossoms appear throughout most of the year. It's a weaver, entwining itself back and forth and in and out of a trellis as it climbs. Let the soil dry out between waterings and fertilize every two months during the summer.

Strophanthus preussii has no common name but if it did, it would probably be midnight whiskers. The botanical name comes from the Greek word *strophos,* or twisted cord, and *anthos* is the Greek word for flower, referring to the twinelike extensions to the petals. The seeds are used to provide drugs valuable in the treatment of heart complaints and continuing research shows a possible use for the relief of rheumatoid arthritis symptoms.

The bizarre trumpetlike flowers have five petals, each having a long trailing whisker that extends five to twelve inches and entangles itself

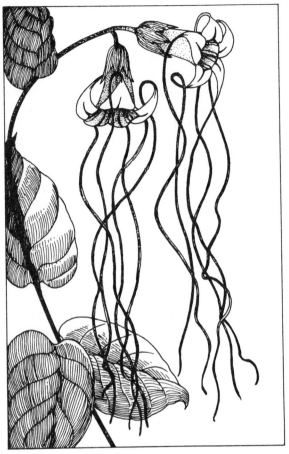

Strophanthus preussii.

with the other whiskers and, eventually, with the plant's leaves. The flowers are white when they first open, their throats stained with purple, but, with age, they gradually turn to a cream color and finally to orange. The plants are climbing shrubs and can reach a height of twelve feet in nature but in the greenhouse stay between five and eight feet high. Strophanthus grows in central and west Africa where its wood was once used to make bows. Both the sap and the seeds contain a drug called strophanthin used by Africans as one ingredient in making arrow poison.

Not only is this plant a striking addition to the evening garden, as night falls it exudes a powerful sweet fragrance—I have no idea what pollinates the flowers in the jungle and somehow, looking at this plant, one is left with the thought that it's best not to know. Temperatures must be above 60°F. Plants can summer outside but need greenhouse conditions during the winter. Use good garden soil laced with some humus. They need bright light but not full summer sun and the soil must be kept evenly moist. The species are easily propagated with cuttings stuck in sand under a glass with a little heat.

CHAPTER THREE

NIGHT-FRAGRANT ORCHIDS

Bring orchis, bring the foxglove spire,
The little speedwell's daring blue.
Deep tulips dash'd with fiery dew,
Laburnums, dropping-wells of fire.

ALFRED, LORD TENNYSON, *In Memoriam A. H. H.*

In the reader's eye, Nero Wolfe, the portly detective who lives on the west side of midtown Manhattan, has a brownstone with a glass-covered top floor that houses a world-class collection of fantastic orchids. I remember reading about his trips to that exotic greenhouse, just as I remember Brenda Starr, Reporter and her search for Basil St. John's extremely rare black orchid, and all those twitching night-blooming orchids of Basil Rathbone's Sherlock Holmes's archenemy, Gale Sondergaard as the Spider Woman.

There is a story told about a rare orchid being auctioned off at Protheroe's in London back at the turn of the century. The plant was *Dendrobium phalaenopsis* subsp. *laratensis*, collected from the Tanimbar Islands, some five hundred miles off the Australian coast. Supposedly the native tribe that first owned the orchid made it a condition of the sale that both the flower and the human skull pot that it grew in went together. Orchids have that kind of cachet.

But not everyone cares for orchids. In the 1946 movie *The Big Sleep* these flowers certainly symbolize evil. When Humphrey Bogart, as the private detective Phillip Marlowe, is ushered into the steaming greenhouse of General Sternwood, it is a place festooned with Spanish moss and blooming cattleyas.

"Too hot in here for any man who has blood in his veins," says the general, bundling a blanket around his shoulders. "I seem to exist largely on heat like a newborn spider. The orchids are an excuse for the heat. Do you like orchids?"

"Not particularly," answers Marlowe.

"Nasty things," says the general, waving his hand. "Their flesh is like the flesh of men—their perfume has the rotten sweetness of corruption."

Strong words but a bit of poetic license is allowable when describing plants that have reached the ultimate in floral evolution. Instead of opening up their sexual activities to any number of pollinating agents like the wind or rain, or run-of-the-mill bees, butterflies, moths, beetles, spi-

One of the many moth orchid hybrids, *Phaleonopsis* 'Hawaiian Clouds' × 'Round Wonder'.

ders, or even birds, many orchids have narrowed down their choices to specific insects who must operate a series of living levers (that often resemble the little bones that make up the middle ear in humans) in order to facilitate pollination. Mosquitoes, for example, pollinate certain members of the *Habernaria* genus, and two species of *Trichoceros* have flowers that so closely resemble a female insect that males attempt to copulate with the orchid blossoms, resulting in pollination. Without these aids, the plants would perish. And because pollination options are often limited, orchids produce many, many seeds, often numbering in the millions.

Orchids are perennial plants. *Terrestrials* grow either on or in the ground while *epiphytes* make their homes in trees, clinging to crevices in bark or ensconced where branches bend. Epiphytes are not parasitic but simply use other plants as anchors.

When growing, most orchids are *sympodial*, that is they produce new growth from the base of previous growth. And many sympodial orchids have thickened stems called *pseudobulbs* that store food and water. The other orchid form is *monopodial*. Here upright stems get higher every year, often producing aerial roots along the way.

The most amazing thing about many orchids is the fact that they are not weak and timid plants that cling to life, ready to topple over at the least effort; rather, if given the basics they require, they will do well in the average home.

NIGHT-FRAGRANT ORCHIDS

Years ago I, too, had a greenhouse devoted to orchids—nothing particularly rare or exotic, just a number of cymbidiums, some cattleyas, a few dendrobiums, two dancing dolls (*Oncidium* spp.), and a lovely night-fragrant orchid called the lady-of-the-night. Then one afternoon in late April 1979, we had a sleet storm that toppled powerlines all over the Catskill Mountains, including those that provided electricity to our

house and the greenhouse. That night temperatures fell to the low twenties but by using a small kerosene heater I kept the greenhouse at about 35°F, but the next night, temperatures plummeted to the teens and frost formed on the inside windows. Needless to say I lost all of the tropicals including the cattleyas, the dancing dolls, and of course, the lady-of-the-night.

I missed many of the orchid flowers but most of all I missed those with sometimes elusive, sometimes powerful, but always provocative fragrances at night. There is something profoundly enticing about most orchids.

To date, nobody has found a truly nocturnal orchid; once orchid flowers open, they remain open day and night. But a number of species are very fragrant, the various fragrances produced in glands called osmophores, located in various places on the flower or even the bud.

Those orchids pollinated by bees and butterflies are often brightly colored and only produce fragrance by day; at night and on dull days, their odors disappear. Orchids pollinated by moths have strong odors only at night, produce abundant nectar, and are usually white, off-white, or a light green in color.

"Most night-fragrant orchids," said Lee C. Soule, a member of the American Orchid Society and a specialist in night-fragrant orchids, "have a strong landing platform, which is more readily visible to moths when they follow the scent trail to the flowers. To the orchid grower, the evolution of these night-scented flowers adds a touch of mystery and delight to a hobby often graced with the unusual."

When asked about the different orchid pollinators, Mr. Soule replied: "Of all the orchids in the world that are fragrant, and that is more than fifty percent of the twenty-five thousand known species of orchids, only a tiny fraction of the pollinators have been identified.

"Some of these plants produce pheromones or chemical compounds that are nearly identical to the sexual hormones of insects, and the plant either mimics that hormone to attract the pollinator or produces a product that the insect can then eat to help it produce a sex hormone. So it's more than just attracting a pollinator to the flower for feeding; there's also the sexual thing mixed in. But very little research has been done on this subject since there is no economic advantage to knowing the outcome."

The Angraecoid Orchids

But some pollinators of the night-fragrant orchids have been studied by no less a man than Darwin. Many of the plants are from South Africa and an even larger number from the nearby islands of the western Indian Ocean, including the Seychelles, the Comoros, the Mascarene Islands of Réunion and Mauritius, and Madagascar. Here, under a wide variety of climatic conditions—and on Madagascar years of of the slash-and-burn approach to agriculture—over 250 species are still found. Over the millennia, most of these orchids have coevolved with night-flying moths in order to ensure their survival and neither will survive without the other. The following genera make up the angraecoids: *Aeranguis, Aeranthes, Angraecum, Jumellea,* and a large number of smaller genera with many consisting of only one or two species.

Of all these flowers, the one with the most fascinating background is *Angraecum sesquipedale,* the Christmas star orchid from Madagascar. It has many other common names including the vegetable starfish, the comet orchid, star of Bethlehem, the rocket orchid, the star of Malagasy, and finally, one of the most interesting names of all, Darwin's moth orchid. The seven-inch-wide, waxy white starlike flowers have a prominent lip and a spur and are exceedingly beautiful. The foot-long spur projects from the rear of the flower and only the bottom inch or so contains any nectar. The species name of *sesquipedale* is Latin for "measuring a foot and a half," referring to the spur which taken in measurement with the

flower, almost reaches that length. They are decidedly fragrant with an odor described as heavy and spicy; in fact, an almost masculine scent.

When the plant was first discovered by the French explorer and botanist Aubert-Aubert de Petit-Thouars in 1822, the spur became a topic of botanical speculation.

In 1862 Charles Darwin thought about the possibilities behind that spur and suggested that there must be a nocturnal hawkmoth in Madagascar "with proboscides capable of extension to a length of between ten and eleven inches!" and added: "This belief of mine has been ridiculed by some entomologists. . . ."

Forty years later, as predicted, a Madagascarian moth was discovered with a twelve-inch tongue. Its name is *Xanthopan morgani praedicta.*

"What happens," said Fred E. Hillerman, one of the world's experts on Angraecoid orchids, "is this: the moth lands on the flower's lip, drawn by the heavy fragrance, and with wings aflutter, inserts it springlike tongue through a cleft in the rostellum—that's the beaklike structure that separates the male anther from the female stigma—and down into the spur to partake of the nectar. After satisfying its thirst, the moth raises its head instinctively as it withdraws its tongue, and the sticky pads beneath the rostellum adhere to the insect's head or body and cause pollen masses to be withdrawn from the flower.

"As if that isn't amazing enough, once on the moth's head or antennae, an elastic cord that connects the sticky pads to the pollen masses dries, and in so doing, its angle to the moth's tongue is changed in such a way as to ensure the entrapment of the pollen within the stigma of the next flower it visits."

In 1927 John Burdon Sanderson Haldane, a professor of biometry at University College in London, wrote: "Now, my suspicion is that the universe is not only queerer than we suppose, but queerer than we *can* suppose," and the pollination of this orchid certainly bears that out.

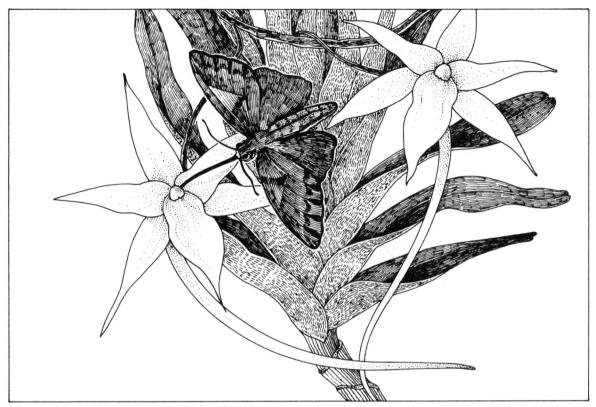

The Christmas star orchid, *Angraecum sesquipedale*, with the hawkmoth, *Xanthopan morgani praedicta*.

"The complexity of nature's planning and timing," continued Mr. Hillerman, "boggles the mind, and the mental image of this exotic orchid perfuming the tropical night air with its seductive fragrance, calling to one species of moth out of thousands, cannot fail to conjure up all kinds of hitherto unformed thoughts about the interaction of living creatures with the myriad aspects of their environment."

The following angraecoids are all night-fragrant. They have been picked for description because they are usually available from specialist orchid nurseries. There are many others but they are rare in commerce. If a reader is bitten by the angraecoid bug, membership in the American Orchid Society and letters to the suppliers listed in the Sources will surely start them on their way to being collectors.

THE GENUS *AERANGIS*

Of the *Aerangis* species listed below, all but one came from Madagascar, all enjoy intermediate temperatures, and all but two bloom in the winter.

Aerangis brachycarpa comes from Africa and blooms in the spring. In nature the plants are found at higher altitudes, growing on tree trunks usually level or only a few feet above one's head. The surprising thing about this orchid is its fondness for shade. The plant itself is a typical-looking plant with dark green leaves about eight inches long and many roots flying in all directions. The two-inch-wide flowers open as a pale green but soon become white. A sweet and heavy fragrance first appears toward dusk, then, as the night falls, the scent becomes even stronger, though it only

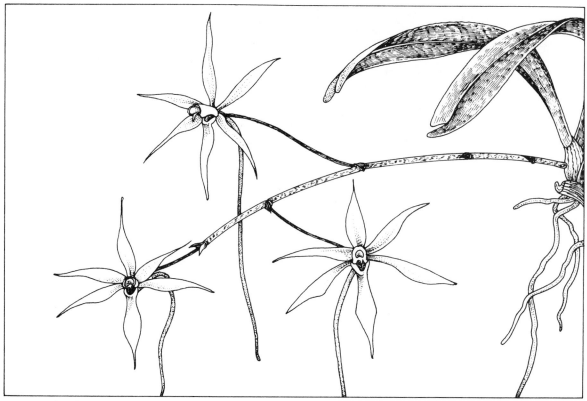

Aerangis brachycarpa.

lasts a few hours. Individual flowers last about three weeks.

Aerangis clavigera has leaves about four inches long of a dull gray-green color often with faint red margins. The small flowers are about a half-inch wide and appear on stems up to ten inches long. Each stem bears between ten and twenty-five white flowers that from a distance resemble lacework in progress. This orchid can either be potted in fir bark or mounted on a slab and needs lots of light in order to flower.

Aerangis curnowiana is a very small plant with leathery leaves less than three inches long, gray warty roots, and buff-colored flowers about two inches wide with a white lip. The spur forms a perfect circle when the flowers are in bud but upon opening becomes a half spiral, strongly resembling a flower that could dance in Walt Disney's *Fantasia*.

Aerangis ellisii has stems that reach a length of up to thirty inches and eventually become pendant. Thirteen to seventeen pure white flowers appear on sixteen-inch spikes and, like many flowers in this family, look like birds in flight. This species is very close in appearance to *A. cryptodon*.

Aerangis fastuosa blooms in spring with white flowers that resemble tight gardenias and are especially fragrant at night, smelling of tuberoses and lasting three weeks or more. The spur is about four inches long and tipped with green. The plants are very small with leaves usually less than three inches long. Plants will either grow in small clay pots or affixed to slabs. During summer months these orchids should be watered every day, especially if temperatures are warm.

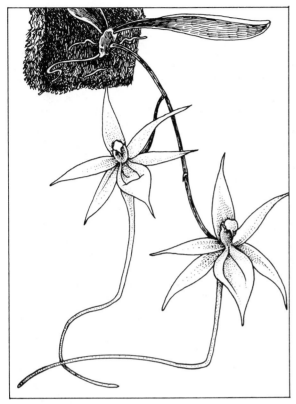

Aerangis curnowiana.

THE GENUS *ANGRAECUM*

Of the *Angraecum* species listed below, all but one are from Madagascar, they enjoy varying temperature combinations, and bloom at varying times throughout the year.

Angraecum didieri is a jewel of an orchid. There are five to seven leaves about two inches long. The flowers are a little over two inches wide with white sepals and petals having just a hint of green. The lip is pure white and has a sparkling texture and the blossoms smell of gardenias. At first the spur is coiled but later straightens to a length of over five inches long. Plants can be mounted or potted up but need a daily soaking and a well-ventilated location. Plants like intermediate temperatures (a minimum of 55°F to 60°F) and bloom from spring to summer.

Angraecum leonis is found in two forms. The first form comes from Madagascar and is the smaller of the two. Leaves are between four and five inches long and usually number between five and eight. The pure white flowers are under two inches wide and have a very pleasant scent. The Comora Islands' form has longer leaves and larger, three-inch-wide flowers that are slightly greenish as they open but soon turn white. They too, have a delightful fragrance. Both plants want warm to intermediate temperatures (above 65°F) and bloom from winter into spring.

Angraecum magdalenae received its species name in 1925 because the white flower was thought to compare to the purity of Mary Magdalene after the exorcism. This is a beautiful flower with full-petaled blossoms often up to four inches wide with an S-shaped spur about four inches long. Plants should be potted using a combination of fir bark and sphagnum moss, taking care to keep the roots damp but not wet. When in flower, the scent is termed spicy and enticing, permeating the entire area around the plant. Blossoms last up to five weeks. Plants want intermediate to cool conditions (a minimum of 45°F to 55°F) and bloom from spring into summer.

Angraecum rutenbergianum has stiff and leathery two-inch leaves, a dusty green in color. The two-inch-wide flowers are pure white, occurring singly and bearing a four-inch white spur with a green tip. This species does well either mounted on a slab or in a pot. Plants should have intermediate to cool temperatures and bloom from spring to summer.

Angraecum Sp. 70 is a small plant, less than three inches high and the leaf color is grayish, sometimes with a bluish cast. The tiny white flowers are less than an inch wide. Plants enjoy intermediate temperatures and bloom in the spring.

Angraecum superbum is a large plant with a stem up to a foot high. The leaves can reach a length of twenty inches and last for many seasons. Older plants not only branch but form basal keikis, or pups, that will bloom at an early age. Each inflorescence can be up to forty inches long and bear eight to twelve flowers. The flowers are greenish with a white lip, about four inches high and two inches wide with a two-inch spur that is bright green. Blossoms last more than four weeks and produce a sweet fragrance every night. Plants want warm to intermediate temperatures and bloom in the winter.

THE GENUS *JUMELLEA*

Most of the species of *Jumellea* are still rare and not readily available to today's market. I'm still waiting to acquire *J. fragrans*, a species from the Mascarene Islands, Mauritus, and Réunion. A special beverage called Faham tea is prepared from the dried leaves of this plant and is reputed to be very fragrant with a delicate flavor.

Jumellea densifoliata comes from Madagascar, takes intermediate to cool temperatures, and blooms from winter into spring. Its six to seven leaves are about fourteen inches long and a greenish white as they open then slowly turn white, finally changing to an apricot-yellow in their last week. The spur is five inches long. Plants should be potted and seldom outgrow a five-inch pot.

CARE OF ANGRAECOIDS

Bill Hoenig has been growing orchids for over twenty-five years in upstate New York.

"I have a humidifying system in my greenhouse that is automatically controlled by a clock to keep the humidity up, but it doesn't allow droplets of water to collect on the leaves. If I use clay pots, I knock the bottoms out and insert screening because drainage is so important. In fact, with angraecoids, I never put them in pots but mount them directly on cork oak bark slabs with a bed of New Zealand sphagnum.

"In nature these plants are bathed in a fog every morning but by afternoon the leaves have dried. So I follow the same routine when watering. In the winter, I dunk them in water, with a quarter teaspoon of fertilizer to a gallon, every two weeks, but in the summer they all go outside and I dunk them according to the amount of rain we get. But they are misted every day. And give them medium light by screening them from the direct sun.

"Finally I have fans located throughout my greenhouse to keep the air moving along and I hang Spanish moss around, not only because it looks nice as it moves in the breeze, but it also holds water and helps with the humidity. But the really important thing is: Within an hour and a half of watering or misting, the plants are again dry."

The Lady-of-the-Night

There are other orchids for the evening garden, either because they have fragrance or because like the moth orchids, their flowers when white are so delightful when washed by the light of the moon. Lady-of-the-night is called *dama-de-la-noche* in Spanish and *Brassavola nodosa* in botanical nomenclature. It's probably one of the most accessible orchids for the average home. It should be noted that botanically the correct name for the genus is *Rhyncholaelia* but most orchidologists agree that for all practical purposes the old familiar name of *Brassavola* should be retained.

The lady usually comes into bloom from late September into February and, unlike many orchids, it's an attractive plant when just in leaf. But after the four-inch blossoms appear on top of six- to eight-inch stems, she becomes a true showstopper. The flowers have a white flaring lip surrounded by greenish white sepals and petals with an average of five buds per stem. The fragrance is sweet and spicy with a touch of cloves, equally delectable when far away or when close to the source.

There are other night-fragrant members of the *Brassavola* genus. *Brassavola cucullata* has fleshy

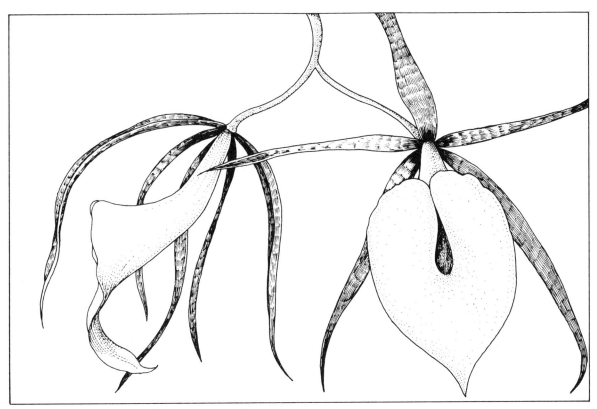

The lady-of-the-night orchid, *Brassavola nodosa*.

foot-long leaves and fragrant flowers with greenish white sepals and petals that will turn somewhat yellow with age.

Brassavola digbyana has thin pseudobulbs, each supporting one long leaf about eight inches long and producing one fantastic flower. The flower's lip is over four inches across and the edges are fringed as if a Chinese paper cutter had been at work. The color is a greenish white and the petals have a delicate satin sheen. The flowers produce a wonderful fragrance with a strong scent of citrus. They bloom in July and August, making them perfect for the summertime evening garden.

Brassavola glauca has four-inch pseudobulbs that each bear a single five-inch leaf. The single nodding flowers are yellow-green and have a two-inch lip, sometimes marked with a rose-pink spot and a few reddish stripes in the throat. They are very fragrant and bloom in late winter to early spring.

Brassavola perrinii comes from Brazil and Paraguay. It has fleshy leaves that are cylindrical in shape and reaches a height of about ten inches. The flowers are three inches long with greenish yellow sepals and petals and a white lip with a yellow throat. "This is by far and away the most fragrant," said Bill Hoenig, "and I've had people question me here on hot summer nights about the wonderful fragrance coming from the greenhouse ventilators—and it was *Brassavola perrinii.*"

There is a hybrid called 'Moonlight Perfume', the result of crossing *Brassavola nodosa* with *B. glauca.*

Brassavolas prefer temperatures between 60°F

and 80°F, with nighttime temperatures about ten degrees lower. The plants need a sunny window with sunlight for at least six hours a day. When summer comes around, hang the plants underneath a tree so they get plenty of bright light but are protected from the noonday sun.

Pot them up in clay pots with plenty of drainage holes in the bottom, using osmunda or a commerical mix for epiphytic orchids, and fertilize with an all-around liquid plant food every other watering, allowing the growing mix to dry out between applications; although they're jungle plants, they resent continually wet roots.

The Reed Orchids

The reed or buttonhole orchids make up the genus *Epidendrum*. These are easy-to-grow plants, doing well at household temperatures between 50°F and 70°F, in a growing medium of commercial fir bark, with plenty of sun during the winter months and summering out-of-doors shaded from the worst of the noonday sun. Let the growing mix dry out between watering.

Epidendrum brassavolae originally came from Guatemala where they live as epiphytes in the narrow crotches of trees. The pseudobulbs are pear-shaped and have two nine-inch-long leathery leaves. The distinctly spidery flowers have very narrow sepals and petals of a light greenish yellow and a lip of pale yellow that narrows to a purple tip. And they are especially fragrant at night. Blooming season is from April to September. *Epidendrum nocturnum* is another species from Mexico and Central America, and it's also a native in Florida. Cylindrical stems resembling canes reach a height of about three feet, and bear thick six-inch leaves and, during the summer (sometimes throughout the year), spidery flowers of greenish white with a white lip that are extremely fragrant in the evening.

The Mustache Orchids

Mystacidium venosum is a tiny epiphytic orchid from South Africa that belongs to a genus of plants so named because their rostellum resembles a little mustache. The charming and petite white flowers are only a half inch wide and have the typical long spur, but in this case it's under two inches in length. The plants are only two to three inches in width. In North America they bloom in fall and winter and, as darkness falls, they release a light and sweet perfume.

Because *Mystacidium venosum* is found growing in a number of climate situations, ranging from hot and humid to cool and misty, it's fairly easy to grow at home. The extensive root system will soon cover a fir bark slab. Water by dunking the plant or misting it, allowing the slab to dry out between waterings. Plants do best in an intermediate greenhouse with temperatures above 55°, but can be moved to a sunny window in winter to fill the room with their night perfume.

Mystacidium venosum.

The Japanese Neofinetia

Neofinetia falcata is a one-species genus of small epiphytic orchids from China and Japan. The branching plant only grows about three inches tall and its sickle-shaped leaves are under four inches long. The flowers usually bloom all summer and are over three inches wide and have a one-and-three-quarter-inch spur. They are intensely fragrant at night and, like many such orchids, they open as pure white but turn a light yellow-orange with age. Because the flowers are compressed vertically, they resemble wolf spiders. Plant in a small clay pot with plenty of drainage holes at the bottom using fir bark kept evenly moist and at temperatures between 45°F and 60°F. It does not need a greenhouse to survive.

The Moth Orchids

Except for a few aberrant members of the family, moth orchids are not fragrant. They also come in a number of colors, including two species (*Phalaenopsis aphrodite* and *P. hieroglyphica*) that are white. But the new white cultivars are, however, larger, more florific, and even more magnificent in the evening garden. So it was a toss-up between including them here with the night-fragrant orchids or in the chapter devoted to white flowers for the moonlight garden. But they are orchids and so these glorious flowers are featured here. The genus name is *Phalaenopsis* from the Greek, *phaluna,* or moth.

I am writing this section in September and on a table in our living room, a pot of a hybrid called 'Hawaiian Clouds' × 'Round Wonder' has been in bloom for weeks and will probably continue on into November. The flowers are oval in shape, slightly over four inches across, of a pure white with just a dot of red and yellow at the center. There are seven along a stem segment of over a foot. This is the second period of bloom. They began in March and spent the summer hanging in the branches of our star magnolia where their flowers would shine through the night.

These orchids do well in the average home. They should be potted in plain fir bark and repotted only when the medium begins to break down (about two years) or when the plants have lost their lower leaves and roots. Repot when new roots are developing and when flowering has finished. Temperatures should be kept between 65°F to 85°F in bright, indirect sunlight. Depending on the humidity in your home, water the plants once to twice a week but remove any standing water—although I've found that plastic pots that are set within larger decorative pots and hang a few inches above standing water do very well. Use a dilute mix of a standard houseplant fertilizer once or twice a month.

Tillandsia duratii, a night-fragrant bromeliad.

CHAPTER FOUR

NIGHT-FRAGRANT BROMELIADS

This tuft that thrives on saline nothingness,
Inverted octopus with heavenward arms
Thrust parching from a palm-bole hard by the cove—
A bird almost—of almost bird alarms,

Is pulmonary to the wind that jars
Its tentacles, horrific in their lurch.
The lizard's throat, held bloated by a fly,
Balloons but warily from this throbbing perch.

HART CRANE, *The Air Plant*

ost gardeners will probably be surprised to see an entire chapter in this book devoted to bromeliads. I knew when I began research on this project that a few of these unusual plants were nocturnal in character and that a few were night-fragrant but I had no idea how many.

But I have always known the value of bromeliads in the evening garden, especially the epiphytic members of the clan. A number of these plants always hang on wire hooks from the branches of our viburnum tree. Their curled and twisted leaves make elegant silhouettes against the circle of the moon or the diffused light from various lamps located in that part of the garden.

Like orchids, there are terrestrial bromeliads and epiphytic bromeliads. The first type are exemplified by the typical pineapple of commerce or the large, thick-leaved plants that bear brilliant flowers and are often used as floral decorations in upscale malls across the country. But most of the bromeliads are epiphytic and grow as air plants, their roots acting only as holdfasts, locking the plant to the bark of tree twigs and branches. Floridians are very familiar with these plants since they grow on just about every tree in southern Florida.

Even though they are exposed on all sides to the elements, epiphytic bromeliads do not really live on air. Just like their grounded relatives, they need light, water, and various minerals and elements in order to survive. The key to their survival are specialized cells called trichomes. Trichomes form scales or hairs on the leaf surfaces of these bromeliads and absorb moisture and water-soluble food, delivering it directly to the plant cells within the leaf. The water can be in the form of rain, fog, mist, or, in some cases, atmospheric humidity. The food consists of minerals and animal wastes dissolved in water which are in turn absorbed by the plant. It's because of trichomes that many epiphytic bromeliads need very little direct watering. On some tillandsias, the trichomes look exactly like coats of silver fur and give the plants an exotic and unworldly appearance.

A VISIT TO TROPIFLORA

Dennis Cathcart farms bromeliads in Sarasota, Florida, just outside of town. In a junglelike setting with palms, ferns, live oaks, and neat gravel pathways, greenhouses—both covered and open at the sides—hold thousands of his plants. They grow in pots, cling to bark plaques, hang on wires suspended in the open air, or recline on horizontal screens. Over three hundred named species are represented here, not including dozens of unclassified plants collected from various jungles in tropical America. In those jungles, Mr. Cathcart is only one step ahead of the developers who, in their zeal for crop and cattle land, slash and burn all the plants in their path.

Luckily Mr. Cathcart is not always busy with exploring and discovering new bromeliads and one warm and sunny day in early March, I visited him at his nursery known as Tropiflora. As we walked along he pointed with pride and knowledge to various plants and told me about bromeliads, in particular one genus called *Tillandsia*.

"My first encounter with a fragrant bromeliad flower was as a new member at a meeting of a bromeliad club. Someone brought in a sprig of *Tillandsia mallemontii*, a species from Brazil. And that sparked the interest that began a career that has spanned fifteen years.

"Now, many collectors were aware that some bromeliads had fragrant flowers but I found little real information on the subject. Much of what I've learned is due to my own observations during some seventy-five collecting trips to over fifteen countries in Latin America. Then I thought of a survey.

"Early in 1988 we distributed a flier entitled 'Fragrant-Flowered Tillandsia BSI Membership Survey' to all the members of the Bromeliad Society International. Of all the plants reported to be fragrant, most were fragrant in the daytime. A smaller percentage were said to be fragrant only at night. But the surprise was the number of tillandsias reported to have a fragrance both by day and night—and I'm sure the percentage for night fragrance would have been higher except for the likelihood that fewer people check their collections at night."

The survey asked if the fragrance of tillandsias was faint, mild, or strong and whether the plants were observed in cultivation or in the wild, the assumption being that wild conditions are more favorable for plants and any fragrance would be more evident there.

"Humidity seems to be a factor," said Mr. Cathcart, "and plants were reported to be more fragrant in the East and South than in the drier areas of the West. And one thing worth noting: all fragrant tillandsias seem to have a pleasant smell. Some were likened to other flowers like gardenias, or described as fruity or lemony or simply as sweet."

Care of Bromeliads

Most bromeliads, especially tillandsias, bloom over a period of weeks, sometimes months. Although long thought of as monocarpic plants, meaning they die after they have bloomed, today most authorities call bromeliads polycarpic. Polycarps bloom and then produce offshoots which in turn eventually bloom so the plant is not really dying, just branching out. These offshoots, or pups, cluster about the base. Since each plant usually produces a number of offsets, the result usually is an attractive plant that is continually changing its appearance. There are a few bromeliads that are truly monocarpic but none of the fragrant-flowered species fall into this category.

When pups are one third to one half the size of the parent, they may be removed by grasping them firmly at the base and twisting sideways.

Larger specimens may require a sharp clean knife or clippers. Pups may be mounted right away using wire (but never use bare copper since it is toxic to the plants), adhesive of the epoxy or liquid nail type, pins, or fishing line. Cork bark, driftwood, and tree fern slabs—usually available at orchid supply houses or craft shops—are common mounts but any material having a rough, porous surface that enables the roots to attach themselves can be used. When potting terrestrials, allow freshly cut offsets to dry for a few days, then pot in a loose, well-drained medium. A mix of one third peat, one third coarse perlite, and one third bark chips is very good.

Care of these plants is easy. Just make sure they have plenty of bright light—never use a north window unless you supplement the light with broad spectrum fluorescents—and plenty of air movement. Since the average home is low in humidity, the gardener usually will have to water. But remember, as with most houseplants, to avoid overwatering. A thorough wetting twice a week should be enough. Submerging the plants every few weeks—tree bark and all—in either the kitchen sink or bathtub filled with water and a small amount of plant food may be beneficial. Most liquid or soluble plant food should be used at one-third to one-half strength. In areas with especially low humidity, misting the plants every few days is very beneficial.

Starting from Seed

Tillandsia and other members of the Tillandsioideae subfamily have seeds provided with a silken tuft or parachute, technically called coma hairs, that allows them to fly away into the air, eventually lodging in the bark of a tree, where they germinate. Other bromeliads, like the Pitcairnioideae, have dry pods with tiny, tightly packed seed, each with a fixed wing resembling a miniature maple seed. The larger genera, *Neoregelia*, *Billbergia*, and *Aechmea*, belong to the subfamily Bromelioideae. The seeds of these plants are contained in a fleshy capsule or fruit and are surrounded by a sticky jelly.

Tillandsia seed can be sown on a window screen or even a coarse piece of bark, and hung in a place where the air is humid. Frequent mistings are needed both before and after germination, preferably with a dilute fertilizer added to the water. But don't keep the seeds constantly moist or they will not survive. For the other subfamilies, sow the seeds on the surface of milled sphagnum or even pieces of damp newspaper. Keep evenly moist by placing the seed flats in a small plastic bag.

The seeds usually begin to germinate within two weeks. When they develop one or two leaves give them increased air circulation but keep them shaded from direct sun. At six months, the seedlings should be ready for their own individual pots using small plastic pots and a potting mix made of equal amounts of fine fir bark, sand, charcoal, and peat moss. There are commercial mixes available if you don't want to mix your own.

Forcing Tillandsias to Bloom

Many bromeliads when kept as houseplants often refuse to bloom. In nature, they flower in response to a shortening of the photoperiod, the number of hours a day they receive light. When in cultivation, there is often too little light to satisfy the plant's requirements and blooming does not occur. If given enough light, however, most species will bloom on their own. Water has little to do with the bloom cycle, except that insufficient water may cause a general lack of health. One way to speed up blooming is to hang your plants outside when the weather warms up. The combination of nightly dews, changing—but not violently changing—temperatures, and the increase in light usually cues the plant to set flowers.

If you want a really stubborn plant to bloom, there are two ways to get the cycle started. First, check at your local nursery for a product called Florel—it's a chemical formula that forces bloom. Following the directions, spray this on the chosen plant. Or, put your plant in a plastic bag with a piece of ripe apple, tie it tightly, and set it aside for a few days. The apple will produce ethylene gas, a chemical that will force the plant into the blooming cycle. This second trick only works with relatively mature plants and if the growing conditions are more or less ideal.

NIGHT-FRAGRANT TILLANDSIAS

Thanks to Mr. Cathcart, I can offer the following list of night-fragrant tillandsias.

The subgenus *Phytarrhiza* contains all the moth-flower tillandsias. These plants are primarily native to the Andean slopes of Colombia, Ecuador, and Peru. They love the high levels of humidity produced by the *neblina* or cloudlike fogs that frequent the mountain slopes. Here the species *Tillandsia acosta-solisii*, *T. cornuta*, and *T. scaligera* are found.

Other moth-flower plants are found in the jungles and western slopes of the Andes. *Tillandsia narthecioides* grows in dense clumps and in some of the valleys in southern Ecuador, and the conditions are just perfect for *T. dodsonii* which grows in massive clusters that may hang down for three feet or more from the branches above. The three-petaled flowers are white and extremely fragrant and, according to Mr. Cathcart, a colony in bloom resembles a cloud of white butterflies.

"Another night-fragrant moth-flower tillandsia," he said, "is a species which lives in a wide variety of habitats from forest to semiarid scrubland. *Tillandsia triglochinoides* is a clump-forming species with narrow, straplike gray leaves. The inflorescence is very narrow, simple, and green. The flowers are white and smaller than some of the other moth flowers but equally fragrant. This species should be mounted and grown in medium light with plenty of humidity.

"But perhaps the grand champion of fragrant tillandsias is *Tillandsia duratii*. It's native to northern Argentina, Uruguay, Paraguay, Bolivia, and southern Brazil where it grows as an epiphyte in the open forest.

"This plant is a true oddity. It begins its life as a normal tillandsia seedling, firmly rooting to the bark of a host tree. After the first blooming, the plant begins to grow rapidly. As it reaches higher into the canopy of a tree, the leaves grasp any nearby twigs with their curling tips. Soon the plant abandons its roots and continues to climb higher with each successive season. As the new growth climbs to the light above, the lower leaves and stem begin to die, a mature plant being about three feet long upon maturity.

"Grow this plant under bright light, suspended from a string or wire looped loosely under the topmost leaves. As the plant grows it will be necessary to move the hanger forward to keep the plant from becoming top-heavy.

"But the best thing about this plant is its wonderful inflorescence. Depending on the size of the plant, this can be as long as two feet or more, and bear dozens of highly fragrant blue flowers that are especially sweet-smelling in the morning and in the evening. The plants bloom successively over a period of several months. Since it is easily cultivated, *Tillandsia duratii* makes a rewarding greenhouse subject and the flowers will perfume your plant room or your evening garden for many months."

More Fragrant Tillandsias

The following tillandsias are fragrant both day and night.

Tillandsia cyanea is native to the forests of Ecuador at an altitude between 1,000 and 3,500 feet. The plants form beautiful little rosettes of forty to sixty thin, grasslike leaves striped with brown toward the center and reaching a length of eighteen inches. The inflorescence forms a pink paddle-shaped structure remarkably like an ab-

Tillandsia cyanea bears blue flowers.

stract fish and bears brilliantly blue flowers that last up to six months. The flowers have a fragrance not unlike that of cinnamon. These plants have been in cultivation for well over a hundred years and are among the most tolerant of plants, adapting to a number of cultural conditions.

Tillandsia streptocarpa is native to the tropical dry forests of southeastern Brazil, Paraguay, Bolivia, and eastern Peru. The narrow leaves are about a foot long and are heavy with silver trichomes arranged at angles around the short stem, forming a delicate, graceful spiral. When in bloom, the spike grows well above the foliage and branches out, forming clusters of long-lasting, heavily fragrant, deep blue flowers. Mr. Cathcart advises growing this bromeliad on cork or a decorative driftwood piece, and keeping it in a bright, airy place.

Tillandsia straminea comes from the mesquite forests of southern Ecuador and northern Peru. The loose rosette of long, soft, silvery leaves produces an inflorescence that bears beautiful and fragrant white flowers that are edged with lavender. This is a species that comes from arid conditions and prefers to be kept dry and airy.

Tillandsia mallemontii is found in eastern Brazil where it forms ball-like clumps on the branches of trees in Brazil's coastal forests. The plants are very fine and must be grown in clumps. They produce masses of very fragrant purple flowers on tiny narrow stems. They are easily cultivated and grow quickly. Simply hang these plants by a string or wire in a place with bright light and plenty of air movement. Plants should be watered often but allowed to dry quickly.

Tillandsia xiphioides is found in arid portions of southern Brazil, Bolivia, Uruguay, Paraguay, and northern Argentina. A stemless plant, the slate gray, succulent three-inch leaves form an upright rosette. The inflorescence exceeds the length of the leaves and produces snow white flowers over an inch wide, the petals having a ruffled edge and a fragrance described as com-

parable to that of a gardenia. There is a varietal form called *T. xiphioides* var. *taffiensis*, differing in having a fuzzy appearance due to larger trichomes, and on occasion, a purple flower. These species are valuable for any collection and take readily to cultivation. Grow them dry, mounted on bark, and keep the plants in a bright and airy location.

According to Mr. Cathcart, *Tillandsia crocata* is perhaps the best of the fragrant tillandsias for cultivation due to its tiny size and powerfully scented yellow flowers. The plants form small clumps in the dry forests of southern Brazil, Uruguay, Paraguay, and Bolivia and are so tightly layered with trichomes that they almost appear to be white. The flowers of this species are stunning for their beauty and fragrance. Grow this species in bright, dry conditions.

Spanish Moss

Spanish moss is probably the most widely distributed of all the bromeliads, with a range that extends from Virginia and along the East Coast into Florida, west to Texas and then again south to Chile and Argentina from sea level up to eight thousand feet.

The stems of *Tillandsia usneoides* are covered with silvery trichomes and, like the angel hair on a Christmas tree, the individual strands can twist together, often measuring up to a hundred feet in length, draping themselves in graceful curves from tree branches.

When I began looking for information on Spanish moss as a nocturnal plant, I called Jan MacDougal, author of *Charleston in Bloom*, and asked her about this well-known but often maligned plant.

"I'm reminded," she said, "of the delicate essence of early summer breezes, especially when they are heavy with humidity. Most people don't recognize the fragrance since it is often shared with other and showier flowers of the evening

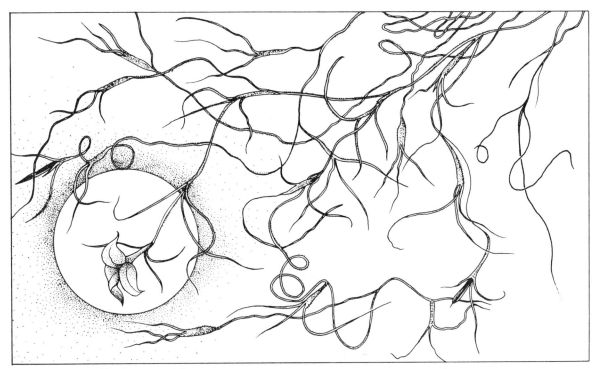

Spanish moss, *Tillandsia usneoides.*

garden. But this elusive perfume comes from an unlikely source: the flowers of the Spanish mosses. The coming of evening triggers the dispersal of scent from the blossoms.

"Most observers are unaware of either the tiny yellow-green, three-petaled flowers, or the fact that they are delightfully fragrant. The tiny green flowers have recurved petals and are no more than one quarter of an inch across. Hidden among the foliage, the tiny blooms can easily go unnoticed. But once discovered, the observer is suddenly aware of many flowers peeking out from their tangled home. After finding these flowers amongst the strands of gray, one is prompted to take a fresh look at this unusual air plant."

Contrary to popular belief, Spanish moss is not a moss nor is it a parasite; it takes no nourishment from the tree branches that act as supports. Rainfall and mist provide all the water and nutrients the plants need.

"In late spring," said Mrs. MacDougal, "the flowers appear and blooming continues for about a month. Pollinated by tiny moths, the flowers are followed by seed capsules, small brown pods that, upon reaching maturity, split open into three parts, and release the seeds to the breeze. One end of the seed has a tuft of white fluff that acts like a parachute and carries the seed into the sky where its inevitable landing is up to the whimsy of the wind.

"When Spanish moss gains a foothold on a tree, a delicate fringe develops. Long, thin, flexible stems grow and sprout narrow, linear leaves. These in turn grow and catch themselves in larger and longer masses of plant and soon they festoon a tree. Hanging from the branches, Spanish moss does not prevent sunlight from reaching the tree's leaves or hinder the tree from manufacturing food."

There are other ways to propagate Spanish

The nettled vriesea, *Vriesea fenestralis*.

moss besides seed. Birds use short lengths to weave into their nests, and can be seen flying with bits of the moss in their beaks; a clump can easily fall from tree branch to tree branch or from a telephone wire to a bush or shrub; and even the wind can tear pieces loose and send them sailing over long distances.

When most people think about Southern nights, they picture the branches of a large oak tree, the Spanish moss silhouetted against the glowing disk of a full moon floating in a starry sky.

"The beauty of this plant," said Mrs. Mac-Dougal, "is best seen with backlighting: moonlight, garden lights, sunset, or sunrise. Add fog or mist and an antedeluvian serenity quietly envelops every evening. A colorful sunset suffuses the moss with a wash of pale color while at sunrise the mossy strands become a luminous silver, radiantly introducing a new day."

Southern gardeners can bring Spanish moss into their evening garden and hang it from the branches of live oaks, dogwoods, and crape myrtles, since these trees will provide especially favorable conditions for the moss. But Northern gardeners need not despair. Just as many orchid growers use Spanish moss in their greenhouses to help with needed humidity, anyone with such facilities can overwinter the plants and, when the spring frosts are over, hang the plants from wire clips and spread them about under the branches of garden trees and bushes.

THE BAT-POLLINATED BROMELIADS

There are other bromeliads that are night-fragrant—and pollinated by bats. Two such genera are *Guzmania* and *Vriesea*, the first being named for Anastasio Guzman, an eighteenth-century Spanish naturalist, and the second for Willem de Vriese, a Dutch botanist. Guzmanias have smooth, glossy leaves that arise from a rosette.

Their natural range is from southern Florida down to western Brazil.

While many members of this genus are found in plant collections, only a few are night-fragrant and, since bats are involved—and their apparent taste for strong, organic odors—one named *Guzmania mucronata* is said to smell like cooked cabbage and another, *G. confusa*, smells of a combination of garlic and burned rubber. Neither of these bromeliads would seem to be naturals for the evening garden.

Vriesea fenestralis is from southern Brazil and a true beauty of the botanical world. The species name comes from the Latin word for window and refers to the rectangular areas of light green on the leaves that look like small windows. The undersides of the leaves are marked with purplish circles and the flowers are reported to have a faint and pungent odor.

Vriesea gladioliflora has flowers that resemble those in the genus *Gladiolus*. This is a vegetable giant with a height of over three feet. According to Mr. Cathcart, the weight of a colony of these plants, each containing a gallon of water, is an enormous burden of the trees that act as hosts. The inflorescence stands well above the foliage and the greenish white flowers are large, tubular, and fleshy, producing an odor described as that of cooked cabbage.

Vriesea bituminosa is named for bitumen, or pitch, referring to the large yellow-green flowers which bear an odor resembling asphalt. Native to wet forests, the species' range includes northern Venezuela and Brazil's Organ Mountains above Rio de Janeiro.

Pitcairinia has over five hundred species with only two reported as being fragrant.

"But few of these make it to civilization," said Mr. Cathcart, "due in part to their size which can range to thirty feet in some vinelike species though some average less than three feet in height. Largely terrestrial, the foliage looks just like grass and the bat-pollinated flowers smell of wet grass.

"Finally *Brocchinia reducta* has the general shape of a pitcher plant and has recently been found to be carnivorous. Enzymes released into the water-filled tank (or trap) of the plant have an odor reported to be very sweet. Found only in the Lost World of southern Venezuela, where it inhabits the boggy summits of the Tepuis or table mountains, this is probably one of the most unusual—and rare—bromeliads—and until it's propagated and becomes known in civilization is not suggested for the evening garden."

The moonflower, *Ipomoea alba*, attracts a hawkmoth on a summer's evening.

CHAPTER FIVE

ANNUALS AND PERENNIALS FOR THE EVENING GARDEN

A black cat among roses,
Phlox, lilac-misted under a first-quarter moon,
The sweet smells of heliotrope and night-scented stock.
The garden is very still,
It is dazed with moonlight,
Contented with perfume,
Dreaming the opium dreams of its folded poppies.

AMY LOWELL, *The Garden by Moonlight*

How Flowers Open

Just as hormones are responsible for controlling many human and animal activities, they also regulate most of the business of cells in the plant world. Auxins, for example, control growth for both stems and roots, including the initiation of lateral bud growth after the gardener has pinched the plant's growing tip. Auxins are also responsible for leaf fall, sex determination, and many other plant processes. Gibberellins appear in cell division, leaf growth, seed dormancy, and flowering. Cytokinins are involved with cell division in leaves, stems, and roots. In addition to these hormones there are other chemicals that are thought to inhibit hormonal activity if such reactions are necessary.

When it comes to flowering, most annuals start the process when they can spare enough food to promote the development of buds and blossoms; they—and many tropical plants—are called day-

neutral since light has little effect on their flowering. But in most biennial and perennial plants, flower production is usually controlled by the length of the day, a process called phototropism. Within that process there are a number of different categories: Some plants are called long-day plants and will not flower unless subjected to a number of days that are about fourteen hours long (examples of such plants are barley, clover, and spinach). Other plants will only flower when days are short, like chrysanthemums. And many plants fall in between in their light requirements.

Or should I say dark requirements. Although the terms long-day and short-day are used, the phototropic response really depends on the length of the night—not the day. A perfect example is the poinsettia. When autumn arrives, poinsettia growers allow their plants to receive no more than twelve hours of daylight as they prepare for Christmas sales. Commercial growers actually cover the plants with black cloths to shut out the light (and a greenhouse full of poinsettias all covered with black shrouds is a strange sight indeed). If someone were to remove the coverings, and the plants were bathed in the light of only a nearby streetlamp, they would not flower and a year's crop would be ruined.

Most botanists suspect there is a yet undiscovered plant hormone—which has been given the name florigen—that initiates blooming. It is probably produced in the leaf and its existence can be deduced from various experiments where a plant that will bloom after twelve hours of illumination is grafted—through a light-tight partition—onto a plant that will usually only bloom after eighteen hours of light and the second plant will shortly flower.

Whatever the hormone, or hormones, that promote flowering, night-blooming plants are simply able to measure day length and light intensity with such precision that a four-o'clock leaf can actually tell when it's late afternoon and produce a measured amount of florigen which will travel throughout the plant's circulation system and up to the blossoms and tell them it's time to bloom.

NIGHT-BLOOMING ANNUALS

It's a pity about annuals. They seem to have lost much of their cachet with the rise of that new generation of consumers who want performance on the line without any sign of failure or hint of death in their future—both at home and in the garden. These folks want perennial flowering to be the result of one mad push of money and energy, all to be followed by an orgy of flowering that will go on and on—at least until the fashion statements of the next decade.

Well, for those gardeners who wish to start an evening garden but bemoan the expenditure of time—and expense—needed to assemble a perennial garden of any note, all is not lost. The following descriptions cover a host of plants that behave in an annual fashion: They will germinate, grow to maturity, flower, and set seed all in one short summer season.

The more unusual annuals (and many tropical perennials grown as annuals in the United States) are not included because, frankly, they are not that easy to come by. Also skipped over are plants like *Hebenstretia comosa*, a South African perennial grown as a half-hardy annual with nocturnal tendencies and mentioned by garden writers for years (especially in England) but never carried by American seed companies or, for that matter, English seed houses. (When I finally found an English source for *H. comosa*, I planted them with anxious anticipation, and on the big night of flowering was disappointed to find the white blossoms were exceedingly small, and they didn't open until the morning.)

The Daturas

The angel's-trumpets are listed in *Hortus Third* as *Datura inoxia* subsp. *inoxia* and subsp. *quinquecuspida*. The first is an annual plant (although under certain conditions, it will behave as a short-lived perennial) and the second is always a perennial, usually grown as an annual.

The subspecies *inoxia* is the sacred datura of the American Indians and while a beautiful flower, is decidedly dangerous. The long trumpet-shaped flowers open in late afternoon and are white and stunning—in more ways than one. At one time they were used in religious ceremonies for their hallucinogenic effects, but please remember that ALL PARTS OF THE PLANT ARE DEADLY, twenty seeds being sufficient to cause poisoning in an adult.

Angel's-trumpets are the second subspecies *quinquecuspida*, called *Datura meteloides* in the *New Britton and Brown Illustrated Flora* and *D. wrightii* in Rickett's *Wild Flowers of the United States* thus guaranteeing confusion all the way around. These plants are not to be confused with *D. metel*, a tropical member from India.

Angel's-trumpets are very common in the

Southwest and appear along roadside in Florida, having arrived from Mexico in the distant past. The trumpetlike flowers are up to eight inches long, white or off-white, and often suffused with purple. They are one of the sources of the drug scopolamine. This plant is decidedly weedy, so would be best in the wild end of the garden.

THE HORN OF PLENTY

These plants are more civilized members of the *Datura* clan. The flowers are seven inches long on plants that reach a height of five feet. The leaves are smooth and the seed capsules covered with stout spines. *Datura metel* 'Aurea' bears beautiful and fragrant yellow blossoms that are often double, 'Florepleno' is a smaller plant that bears twelve-inch double lavender trumpets, and 'Cornucopia' is especially unusual because a second trumpet, or corolla, emerges from the first trumpet. Its colors are white or purple. All are fragrant.

JIMSONWEED

Jimsonweed (*Datura stramonium*) is a North American member of a tropical family that makes its home in barnyards, fields, and other "waste places," but nobody knows how it got to this country in the first place.

This is not exactly the best plant for the evening garden so I advise growing it in a pot. In fact it's listed here as more of a curiosity than anything else. When it blooms, move it into the garden and when it's over, consign it to oblivion. As I write I have a perfect olfactory memory of the odor produced by just brushing against the leaves: it is not horrible or deadly but indeed unpleasant. And for some reason, flea beetles love the leaves so they are usually pockmarked.

Jimsonweed is sometimes grown as a source of alkaloidal drugs including atropine but the plant is violently toxic and many fatalities have been recorded. Jimson is a corruption of James-

Datura metel.

town and refers to first settlers of that town mistaking it for either an edible herb or using the seeds to make a substitute coffee. Either way a lot of people died. In fact, since it is so deadly, it's probably a good idea that gardeners get to know what it's all about. And if you are susceptible to skin irritations, don't touch this plant.

There are two races found: in one the stem is green and the flowers nearly white; in the other the stem is purple and the flowers pale violet. Some references list the second plant as *Datura tatula*.

These annual plants grow up to four feet high but are smaller in poorer soils. The striking flowers are trumpet-shaped, very fragrant, and resemble large morning glories. They are often up to six inches long and open in late afternoon. The eventual seedpods are round, brown, and loaded with prickles.

The Moonflower

A few years ago, some good friends gave me a copy of a garden catalog called *Everything for the Garden* published in 1933 by Peter Henderson & Co. of Manhattan. On page 142, between a top photograph of a pink hydrangea called 'Hortolanus Witte' and one of a giant zinnia, is a black-and-white watercolor of the giant moonflower. A large trellis is cloaked in the vine and, according to my count, there are over three hundred individual flowers, brilliantly white under a half-clouded moon. Just ahead of the trellis, a concrete urn with a giant fern on top casts a long shadow. The copy calls it *Ipomoea maxima* and tells of seven-inch flowers exuding the scent of magnolias, and especially beautiful on moonlit nights.

Moonflowers are perennials in the tropics or a warm greenhouse but are treated as annuals in northern gardens since they bloom the first year from seed. The current botanical name is *Ipomoea alba* but has been called, in addition to Henderson's name, *I. grandiflora*, *I. noctiflora*, *I. bona-nox*, and *Calonyction aculeatum*. Any flower with that many names has to have something going for it.

Moonflowers are vines that can reach a height of ten feet in a good summer season and up to forty feet at the jungle's edge. The flowers are pure white, very showy, and look like large morning glories that have mistaken the hour. They are so attractive and unusual that they can easily become the center of a party as guests gather in the evening hours to watch the buds open.

These blossoms are highlights of the evening garden for they bloom in the early twilight, unfolding their long twisted buds like flowers opening in a nature film taken with time-lapse photography. Within a few minutes sweet-scented, salver-shaped flowers up to six inches wide hover before your eyes and will persist until touched by the first rays of the morning sun, whereupon they quickly close. The leaves are large and heart-shaped, up to six inches long, and the stems have a milky sap.

In subtropic climates the moonflower will often flower within six weeks of sowing but in most parts of the country expect eight weeks to pass. To help break through the hard outer coating of the seed and hasten germination, the seeds should be nicked or soaked in warm water overnight. It is best situated in evenly moist soil in a spot getting full sun or a bit of shade in the South. If insects and moths neglect to pollinate the flowers, use a cotton swab to dust the flower's stigma with a bit of pollen. The developing seedpods are unique and interesting to watch as they mature.

Beverly Nichols, the author of many marvelous English garden books wrote about the moonflower in *Sunlight on the Lawn*. He saw his first moonflowers "in southern India, during the war; they were climbing up the columns of a ruined Hindu temple on the outskirts of Madras. They had a cool, intrinsic innocence against a background which was dark and troubling. In form they resembled the simple wild convolvulus of the hedgerows, but they had a span of three or four inches, and their whiteness was faintly phosphorescent, with a hint of the palest green, such as one glimpses in the fire of a glowworm. Their fragrance could not be caught in words, but to me it suggested a blend of incense and the peel of fresh lemons—I gathered some seeds and eventually took them home. Three weeks later they were blown up by the Luftwaffe, with the rest of my possessions."

I won't suggest that moonflowers will turn your backyard or terrace into another Angkor Wat, but the glow of flickering candles reflected on a trellis of moonflowers and the flower's sweet fragrance mixing perhaps with the sharp and pungent smell of juniper berries in a perfect martini will lead to a memorable evening.

An Annual Gourd

Lagenaria siceraria is a species of gourd with so many variations in the shape of its fruit that it carries such widely diverging common names as bottle gourds, powder horn, the dipper, the club, and the penguin gourd. The musky-scented flowers open at night or on gloomy afternoons. They are large, with the male flowers sometimes up to five inches across and the female flowers easily spotted because of their round ovary—the potential fruit—just below the petals. These petals are white and paper thin, easily torn by a heavy rainfall, and they quickly dissolve under the heat of a summer sun.

The vines can reach a length of twenty-five feet in a good growing season and leaves can measure a foot across. While the flowers are delicately beautiful, the interest of this plant lies with the ghostly shapes of the light green maturing gourds as they hang on thin stems, shrouded by the many leaves. We had a large trellis in our garden in the Catskill Mountains that featured these gourds. At dusk, the pods hung like the shapely sandbags that balance backstage theatrical scenery—with just a hint of the pods from *Invasion of the Body Snatchers*—while the opening blossoms became cellophane stars gleaming against the dark green of the leaves.

Plants are easy to grow, needing only average garden soil, with some compost mixed in, plus full sun, and plenty of water, especially as the gourds develop. They do need a long growing season, so gardeners in the North should start seeds in individual peat pots at least eight weeks before the last frost, transplanting to the garden when all threat of frost is past.

The Evening Stock

Evening stocks, *Matthiola longipetala* subsp. *bicornis*, exude a wonderful scent that is a combination of the heavy scent of jasmine and the light scent of the aromatics. They are hardy an-

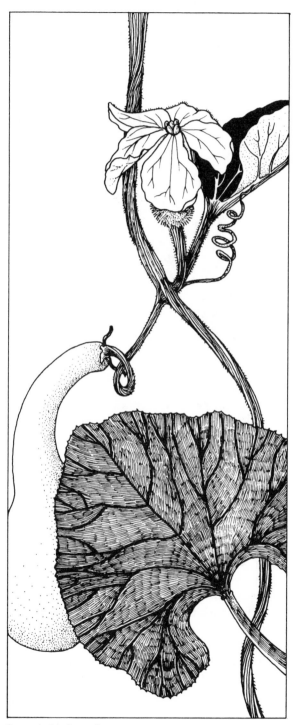

Lagenaria siceraria.

73

The evening stock, *Matthiola longipetala* subsp. *bicornis*.

nuals, about eighteen inches high with thin pale green leaves, best described as straggly. The small pink or purple four-petaled flowers have a small white center and look like bits of windswept, rain-washed tissue paper that some perverse flower arranger has pasted to the stems. By day the best idea is to overlook each and every plant since they have absolutely nothing to recommend them. In fact, all the garden writers over the past two centuries agree that the best place for this plant is at the edge of a shrubbery or between other more florific plants, so that they are effectively hidden by day.

In England, the common name is melancholy gilliflower because of its sad presence during the day but no other nocturnal plant has ever had such outpourings of purple prose dedicated to its presence because by night, according to Louise Beebe Wilder, it becomes: "[A plant] that lifts its head, expands its dim-hued blossoms and looses upon the mild evening air such clouds of sweet-

ness as will cause you literally to take root beside it."

Joseph Jacob, a friend of Wilder's, wrote this about evening stock: "A veritable active volcano of the most delicious perfume," and recommended sowing seeds over the heads of departing bulbs.

Roy Genders wrote: ". . . sow the seed near a window . . . so that the full perfume of these stocks can enter the rooms in early evening."

Alice Morse Earle: "It is the Night-scented Stock, and lavishly through the still night it pours forth its ineffable fragrance. A single plant, thirty feet from an open window, will waft its perfume into the room."

Gertrude Jekyll: ". . . as soon as the light fails the limp plant stiffens, the leaves become firm, the flowers rise up and expand; the whole plant acquires a kind of modest beauty and the bloom pours forth its delicious scent, which is wafted many yards away."

And Vita Sackville-West: "I have just sown half an ounce of [night-scented stock] . . . all along the pathway at the foot of a yew hedge, and now look forward to some warm evening when the pale barn-owl is ranging over the orchard and the strong scent of the little stock surprises me as I go."

Ed Rasmussen of The Fragrant Path reminded me that these plants were once a favorite of German ladies who grew them in pots on apartment window ledges or on balconies where its perfume on summer evenings would penetrate indoors and out into the streets.

With that kind of press, could any gardener overlook this flower? Just to ensure that enough plants survive to scent the entire summer, set out new seed every ten days or so, at least to the middle of July.

The other evening stocks including *Matthiola sinuata*, the great sea stock and *M. odoratissima*, an evergreen stock from Persia, are discussed on pages 34–35.

The Miracle of Peru

The miracle flower of Peru, the four-o'clock, or as the French call it, *belle-de-nuit*, has been in gardens since sometime in the 1540s when seeds were brought to Europe from the Peruvian Andes. *Mirabilis jalapa* caused such a stir in flower and garden circles that the first name for the genus was *Admirabilis*—at least until Linnaeus changed it to *Mirabilis*—from the Latin for wonderful.

The fact that single plants could bear flowers of different colors fired the imagination, especially since the miracle occurred without grafting other strains on the mother root (like the tomato/potato plant of today's supermarket weeklies). And the flowers punctually opened around four o'clock in the afternoon, except for areas with daylight savings time, where five P.M. became the rule. Then there was the perfume, a marvelous scent of sugar and lemony spice that varied from plant to plant.

Gregor Mendel used the plants in genetic experiments to prove that one grain of pollen was sufficient to produce a viable seed. In the early 1900s, four-o'clocks were noticed to have variegated leaves. In one strain, the leaves were mottled dark green and yellowish white, the color being caused by variations in the chlorophyll of individual plant cells; where two zones of color met, there was a band of cells that contained both colors. Experiments showed that seed produced from flowers on green branches produced green plants regardless of the pollen used for fertilization. Flowers from variegated branches produced seedlings that were green, variegated, or white. Thus plastids or cell bodies could be unaffected by chromosomal genes.

The species name of *jalapa* is frankly a mistake. Pharmacists believed that the purgative jalap (named for the Mexican town Jalapa) could be obtained from the tuberous roots of four-o'clocks. But it turned out that that particular

The miracle flower of Peru, *Mirabilis jalapa*.

cathartic was too violent to use and today the only benefit the tubers have is to manufacture a dye that makes Chinese seaweed noodles look more appetizing.

But history aside, four-o'clocks are wonderful plants for the evening garden. They form little bushes often reaching a height of three feet and are covered with flowers. A number of colors are available including red, yellow, white, or rose, and many flowers will be striped or dashed with other colors.

In tropical America, four-o'clocks are perennials and if left alone will soon form tuberous roots that weigh up to forty pounds. In our temperate gardens, the black tubers can reach the size of a baked potato and if dug in the fall, and kept in a warm, dry place over the winter, can be planted out the next spring as soon as the ground warms, just like a favorite bulb. Although self-seedlings from four-o'clocks grow quickly, replanting the tubers will lead to earlier flowers.

The Lure of Nicotine

The generic name of tobacco is *Nicotiana* and was named in honor of Jean Nicot de Villemain, the French consul in Lisbon, Portugal, who in 1560, sent tobacco seeds to France. But the initial discovery of wild tobacco, *N. rustica*, is credited first to some sailors from Columbus's expedition who landed in the Cuba of 1492, and saw natives with smoke pouring from their mouths and noses. Chewing tobacco was discovered by Europeans in the 1560s and cigars—because of their resemblance to the insect they were named from the Spanish word for cicada, *cigaroo*—came along even later.

The plant that produces commercial tobacco, *Nicotania tabacum*, is a stately addition to the back of the larger flower border and where the day-blooming flowers are small but pretty.

But other members of the genus combine nocturnal flowers with especially sweet fragrances, as suggested by Edna St. Vincent Millay in her poem, "There at Dusk I Found You":

> There at dusk I found you, walking and weeping
> Upon the broken flags,
> Where at dusk the dumb white nicotine awakes and utters her fragrance
> In a garden sleeping.

During the day, when many of these flowers are folded up and tragic, they still have an odor. As Alice Morse Earle pointed out in her 1901 *Old-Time Gardens* (The Macmillan Company): "It is a curious fact that some of these night-scented flowers are positively offensive in the daytime; try your *Nicotiana affinis* next midday—it outpours honeyed sweetness at night, but you will be glad it withholds its perfume by day."

Whether annual or perennial, treat the following plants as annuals and start seeds indoors six weeks before your last spring frost. They need good garden soil in full sun or partial shade, and plenty of water especially in dry summers.

Jasmine tobacco, *Nicotiana alata* (synonym, *N. affinis*) is a perennial from tropical South America and, according to Neltje Blanchan, "The tobacco plant that looks rather bedraggled by day, opens its white trumpets at dusk and makes the garden starry at night." Incidentally, Miss Blanchan was the wife of Abner Doubleday and probably the first garden writer to mention gardening for the commuter. In the 1909 *The American Flower Garden* she describes the tobacco plant as looking "like a faded ball-room beauty by day, [that] should be viewed from a little distance; but at evening, when the flowers open and become beautiful and deliciously fragrant, too, one wishes them near the house. They are flowers for the commuter."

While the flowers of the natural species open up about six P.M. (and also in the shade and on cloudy days), hybridizers unfortunately have been busy and the newer cultivars now stay open

Jasmine tobacco, *Nicotiana alata*.

Nicotiana noctiflora, another native of Argentina, has plants that are two to three feet tall and bears tubular flowers that are white within and greenish purple without and very fragrant.

Nicotiana suaveolens, an annual from Australia, grows about eighteen inches high and bears very fragrant two-inch-long pendulous flowers of a pale white within and greenish white without. These plants like a bit of shade, even in the North.

Nicotiana sylvestris, the woodland tobacco, is a perennial native to the Argentine but is usually used as an annual in northern gardens. Reaching a height of four to six feet, the tubular flowers are pure white and have the sweet scent of freesias. Unlike the others, this species will open during the day if the sun is not too strong.

The Nottingham Catchfly and the Campions

The Nottingham catchfly, *Silene nutans*, an English wildflower, is now naturalized in many parts of the United States. The common name refers to the amazing number of these plants described by Ann Pratt, a nineteenth-century writer; Nottingham was the place and catchfly refers to the sticky stems found on some species, thought to catch small insects including ants that might steal pollen without helping in fertilization. Also called the sticky cockle, the plant has sticky, hairy stems up to three feet tall. The five petals are a creamy white, pink at the base, forked at the tip, and very fragrant.

Pratt described hundreds of these plants hanging in masses from the white cliffs of Dover, but nobody else noticed them because all the flowers appeared to be withered. This annual plant is particularly adept at attracting moths and beetles for pollination at night when the blossoms are open. Each flower lasts for three nights, usually opening in the months of high summer. About seven o'clock on the first evening, the flower opens its white petals and sends forth a fragrance

most of the day. These modern creations will, however, still reward you with some fragrance at night. The trumpetlike flowers are about three inches long and an inch across at the lip. Plants can reach a height of five feet but usually stay about three feet tall. 'Grandiflora' is a cultivar with slightly larger flowers, the lip of the trumpet about two inches across. *Nicotiana sylvestris* is a similar plant from Argentina with longer leaves and a spindle-shaped floral tube. They are especially fragrant at night.

Coyote tobacco, *Nicotiana attenuata*, is an annual plant from the West and Southwest. I've never grown this species, but according to Louise Beebe Wilder, the greenish salver-form flowers are nocturnal. But, she warns, the whole plant has a very strong smell.

The Nottingham catchfly, *Silene nutans*.
Flower 1 shows the blossom the first night, flower 2 the second night, and flower 3 the third night.

described as being sweet and reminiscent of hyacinths. Five of its ten stamens mature with great speed, the pollen ripens, and the anthers burst. By three the following morning, the flower stops producing fragrance, the five anthers wither, and the petals close. All the next day, the flowers look as though they're dead but at seven the second evening, the flower opens again and again produces fragrance. The last five stamens now develop and their pollen ripens. Then, in the early morning, the flower closes again. On the third night, the flower opens again around seven in the evening and begins to produce fragrance, only this time the stigma is ready to receive pollen brought by night insects attracted to the flowers during stage one or two. Once the stigma is fertilized, the flower closes again, only this time the act is final.

The night-flowering catchfly, *Silene noctiflora*, has forked petals that are creamy white and pinkish at the base. The flowers are, of course, fragrant. This annual flower was called by John Parkinson "Morpheus's sweet wild Campion" and is often confused with another European import, the white campion, *S. alba*, but the first flower has an attractive calyx that bears a network of green veins; *alba* has a plain calyx. Like the other nocturnal catchflies, this too is a native of Europe.

The white campion is also a nocturnal flower, often reaching a garden height of four feet. In a marvelous merry-go-round of nomenclature, this campion's first name was *Lychnis vespertina*, which became *Melandrium album*, which became *Silene alba* (synonym, *Lychnis alba*). The blossoms usually open at dusk and use both fragrance and the forked white petals to attract moths for pollination. Unlike the Nottingham catchfly, white campions are dioecious plants having male and female flowers on separate plants so they are not forced to follow the catchfly's routine of opening on successive nights to prevent self-pollination.

Depending on growing conditions, the white campion is an annual, biennial, or sometimes a

The night-flowering catchfly, *Silene noctiflora*.

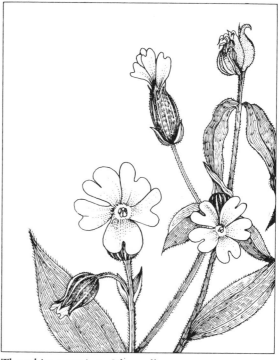

The white campion, *Silene alba*.

short-lived perennial and develops quite a stout root that is easily transplanted. They do best in good, deeply cultivated garden soil with full sun in the North and partial shade in the South.

The red campion, *Silene dioica*, blooms by day and Geoffrey Grigson's *The Englishman's Flora* (Phoenix House Ltd., 1955) calls it a plant of snakes and of death when it's picked, and if picked by day, it could bring death to your father. The white campion, when picked, is said not only to bring death to your mother but you will also probably be struck by lightning. We've used both as cut flowers for years and so far—knock on wood—all is serene and peaceful.

There is a fourth nocturnal annual in the *Silene* genus, called the forked catchfly or *S. gallica*. This is a very pretty plant with small flowers, white and starlike, that form a one-sided row running down an eighteen-inch stem, opening slowly at dusk, just like twinkling stars on the horizon.

All of the catchflies have a place in the evening garden. There along with the starry campion (*Silene stellata*), their clear white petals peek through the overlapping leaves of other plants in a most civilized manner, belying their wild origins. They were once popular garden plants, especially *S. alba*. Unfortunately their use has given way to larger and more blatant blossoms, with either punchier color or stronger fragrances, although in almost every case of bigger is better, fragrances have fallen by the wayside.

The Night Phlox

The night phlox, *Zaluzianskya capensis*, is a half-hardy annual from South Africa named in honor of Adam Zaluziansky von Zaluzian (1558–1613), a physician from Prague and author of *Methodus Hervariae* in 1592. These beautifully fragrant, night-blooming flowers belong in every

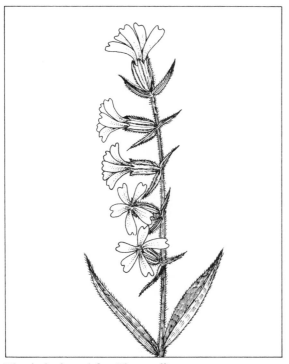

The forked catchfly, *Silene gallica*.

The starry campion, *Silene stellata*.

garden border or planted along the edge of a wall. There the gardener can not only smell the fragrance but will easily see the clusters of pretty but small phloxlike flowers. Each blossom is about a half inch wide and the five white petals are notched at the tip—like the campions and catchflies—and when closed, both the petals and the outside of the floral tube are a satiny maroon with just a hint of white showing where the petals overlap.

I first saw mention of these flowers in the 1936 edition of Norman Taylor's *The Practical Encyclopedia of Gardening*. It was not until 1991 that Thompson & Morgan finally carried the seeds and unlike many pursuits in this world, the flowers were worth the wait.

Either sow the seeds directly in the garden or start them in peat pots as the plants dislike root disturbance. If you do begin indoors, make sure the seedlings get plenty of light or they will be-

come terribly leggy. Give them good garden soil, laced with organic matter and a spot in full sun in the North and partial shade in the South.

NIGHT-BLOOMING PERENNIALS

As noted earlier there are not too many garden perennials that are nocturnal. That plant habit seems to have fallen to the tropicals, the annuals, and many of our so-called wildflowers. The following plants are either perennial herbaceous or bulbous plants and none are native to the United States. The USDA zones are noted with each description.

The Gas Plant

The gas plant, *Dictamnus albus*, should probably not be in a list of night-blooming plants but there is no category in this book for night-burning flow-

The night phlox, *Zaluzianskya capensis.*

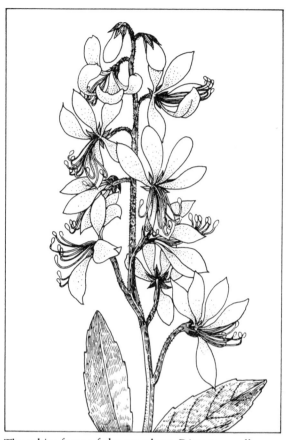

The white form of the gas plant, *Dictamnus albus.*

ers. Because of its odd ability, it is the gardener who must light a match and hope to convince skeptical visitors that a gas plant leaf will produce a tiny gas jet that will ignite and burn. This is the only species in the genus of unusual perennials originally found from southern Europe to northern China. Other common names include dittany and fraxinella. The plant is about three feet tall and produces tall stems topped with unusual-looking, fringed rosy purple flowers with five petals, blooming in late spring to early summer. According to many reports, the crushed leaves smell of a mix of anise, sweet clover, and lavender, but I find the odor to be decidedly citrus in content.

So again, why include it in the evening garden?

Alice Morse Earle tells the tale of an old Swedish lady—she just happened to be the daughter of Linnaeus—who while taking a nocturnal stroll in her garden, saw strange flashes of light sparkling out of the nasturtium flowers one sultry night in 1762 (the great Goethe reported similar flashes of light circling around oriental poppies). Then Linnaeus's daughter did some more checking and finally reported that flames flickered about her fraxinella. These were not the exaggerations of your typical flying saucer believer, but reports from educated people of the day.

There are three sorts of urban myths connected with the gas plant. According to the first, if on a warm summer's night a lighted match is held to a crushed leaf, the volatile oil in the leaf will burn with a blue flame, much like the flame produced by burning brandy. According to the second myth, if a match is applied to the entire plant, it will soon be enveloped in a bluish flame for a second or two, without hurting the plant. The third suggests lighting the flower heads, which will burn with an orange flame and at the same time release the smell of lemon into the night air. Why do I call these myths? Because to my great embarrassment I have tried them all on a number of occasions and none of them have ever worked. But, I must admit, the entertainment value of the entire enactment is worth the effort. And on some warm summer evening, it just might light.

The Iris Family

Surprisingly, a few members of the iris family are vespertine, staying open well into the night. The vesper iris originally came from Mongolia, northern China, and Siberia, found growing in scrublands and grassy places at an altitude of eight thousand feet. Older books call it *Iris dichotoma* but today this iris has a genus all to itself and is called *Pardanthopsis dichotoma*.

My first plant came from Ed Rasmussen at The Fragrant Path and I was amazed to see the wealth of bloom produced over one summer, the flowers opening in late afternoon shortly after the four-o'clocks flowered. The many-branched stems are between two and three feet high, with sword-shaped leaves about a foot long, blooming in August. It's never happened to me but *The Royal Horticultural Society Dictionary of Gardening* warns that plants often flower so freely that they fail to make lateral growth and die.

The sweetly fragrant flowers are a dull greenish white spotted with brownish purple or reddish purple with white splotches, the falls (the flower part that droops) are about three quarters of an inch long. Like many iris blossoms, they become spirally twisted after flowering. According to the description by Brian Mathew in his book *The Iris*, flowers with these characteristics match those of

The vesper iris, *Pardanthopsis dichotoma*.

plants collected at the Ming Tombs in Peking and are probably the typical species. He also describes a variety with deep purple flowers bearing a whitish, purple-spotted splotch in the center of the falls. Mr. Mathews also reports that hover flies are often seen visiting the flowers.

Mr. Rasmussen warned me that these plants are not long-lived; they usually flower from seed by the second year but if plants are started in late winter, they sometimes will bloom the first year. To guarantee a yearly supply of flowers, start new seedlings every year. Give plants a spot in full sun with good garden soil and plenty of moisture. The plants are hardy through USDA Zone 5 but in really cold areas, a layer of mulch is very beneficial.

The Spanish nut, *Gynandriris sisyrinchium*.

A Mr. Samuel N. Norris of Kentucky has hybridized *Pardanthopsis dichotoma* with the blackberry lily (*Belamcanda chinensis*), another member of the iris group, and produced plants that resemble the vesper iris but come in shades of apricot and salmon. They are called × *Pardancanda norrisii*.

Gynandriris sisyrinchium, the Spanish or Barbary nut, so called because the corm is gathered for food and is reputed to taste like a nut, is another member of the iris family that blooms in late afternoon. Although the fragile flowers are short-lived, fading by the following morning, they are so beautiful they're worth the effort. The sweetly fragrant, pale, clear lavender or bright violet-blue flowers are less than two inches wide,

each of the falls marked with a spot of yellow. They are natives of the Mediterranean region from Portugal to Italy, Greece, and on to Pakistan, and south to Turkey and Israel. They are found at an altitude of 6,500 feet and bloom in the spring. And don't be misled by that altitude, figuring that if it grows at that height, it will do well in your backyard. Remember that plants growing in those mountains are covered with snow throughout the winter and that thick blanket of natural insulation prevents the ground itself from ever freezing.

The plants arise from corms and are not hardy if the ground freezes but I got them through one year in USDA Zone 5 by planting them in well-drained soil next to a basement foundation in ground that never froze. Propagate them by taking the little cormlets that form around the mother corm and grow them on for two or three years before flowering. It's also possible to grow new plants from seed. The plants do very well when grown in a greenhouse.

The *Hesperantha* species, or the evening iris, are the last members of the iris family that I know are nocturnal in habit and very night-fragrant. The genus name is from *hesperos*, Greek for the evening star, and *anthos*, for flower. There are about forty species native to South Africa.

All *Hesperantha* species require a frost-free climate or a spot in your garden where the ground doesn't freeze. *Hesperantha baurii* is found in moist grasslands at a height of 6,500 feet and some authorities suggest it is reasonably hardy, but I would take that suggestion with a grain of salt. The plants like full sun and very well-drained soil and can be easily stored over the winter or grown in pots.

For indoor use place six corms an inch apart and an inch deep in a six-inch pot using a planting mix of good potting soil, peat moss, and coarse sand in equal parts. Water once, then keep the pots in a cool, dimly lit place while the roots form and do not water again. When the plants begin to leaf out in early spring, start watering but keep

Hesperantha falcata.

the developing buds out of direct sunlight, especially in the South. After flowering is over, slowly dry the pots, let them rest for a month or two, and start again.

Hesperantha baurii has leaves about a foot long and bears two fifteen-inch flower stems that hold a number of flowers, rose-red on the outside and white within.

Hesperantha falcata is native to the area around Cape Town in South Africa. The flowers are pale white and tinged with green. *Hesperantha inflexa* var. *stanfordiae* closely resembles *H. baurii* but has bright butter yellow flowers.

The Fragrant Hosta

This magnificent plant, *Hosta plantaginea*, originally came from Japan (where it was introduced from China), a country where its nocturnal habits are recognized and valued in the garden. Ah, but that's the country that has soft pine-needle garden pathways so thin slippers will not be torn, path-

ways that are cleared of spiky underbrush, thus guaranteeing the safe passage of silken robes, in addition to stone or iron lanterns to light the garden at night. In America, not one nursery in five tells the buyer about this evening charmer.

The August lily or fragrant hosta (*maruba-tama-no-kanzashi* in Japanese) is especially valuable because the leaves are a genuine garden wonder and the white, waxy, and fragrant flowers are simply beautiful. The leaves are about six inches long and a little over four inches wide on eight- to ten-inch stems, ribbed with eight pairs of impressed veins, plus the midrib, and forming neat clumps. The trumpet-shaped flowers appear on thirty-inch scapes and each is five inches long and three inches wide at the tip. The scent is of pure honey. The plants usually bloom in late August in the North and unfortunately often run afoul of early frosts, so if temperatures are slated to fall below freezing, cover the plants—it's worth the effort.

By day the older flowers look tired, but come dusk they open again, along with newer blossoms farther up the scape. To keep plants neat, worn-out flowers are easily removed. Make no mistake about it, not only are fragrant hostas attractive as specimen plants, they are very fine when planted in groups. They are also valuable for bouquets.

Give these plants some shade, especially in the South, good garden soil, and, in times of drought make sure they get additional water. These hostas are hardy through USDA Zone 5.

Bouncing Bet

Bouncing Bet, or *Saponaria officinalis*, would be a beloved garden plant if her daytime looks matched her nighttime demeanor, for it is in the evening that her tawdry petals perk up and her sweet perfume fills the air. This plant is a stout perennial that spreads by a network of rhizomes and is especially valuable in holding on to the earth in a crumbling slope or bank.

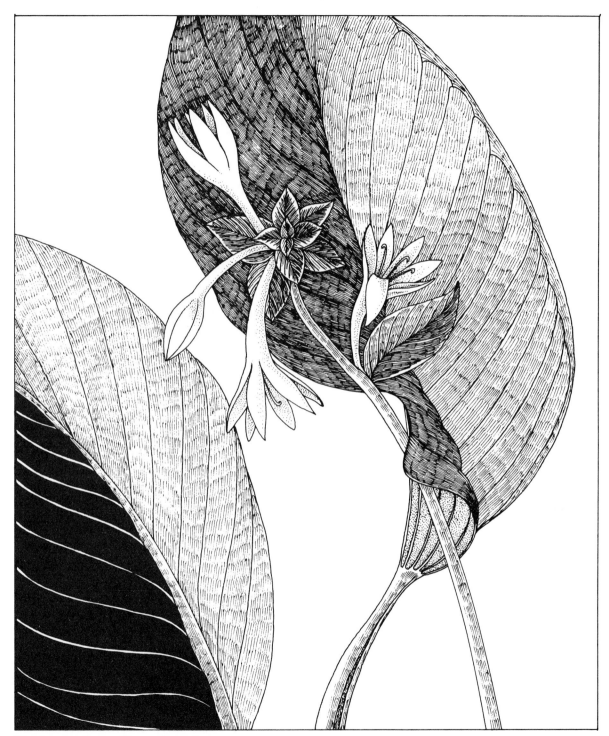

The fragrant hosta, *Hosta plantaginea.*

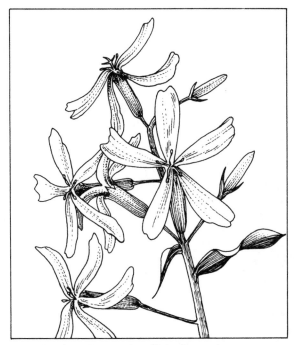

Bouncing bet, *Saponaria officinalis.*

The genus is named from the Latin *sapo*, or soap, referring to the mucilaginous juice in its stems which forms a lather with water. In addition to its use as a detergent, the leaves and roots were used as a remedy for scrofula and skin diseases in general. The chemical concerned is saponin, which easily forms a froth when stirred in water. The lather has been recommended for restoring ancient and delicate fabrics and old tap-estries. Dried plants are placed in muslin bags, then boiled in distilled water, the solution being used cold.

I first realized the evening potential of these plants when I worked at a local newspaper in Callicoon, New York. Across from the offices of the *Sullivan County Democrat* were the raised banks of dirt and cinder that held the railroad tracks and these banks were carpeted with saponaria. During the day everything was dull on the other side of the street, the only color being that of parked cars. But we often worked late hours and many nights we walked out to the bright blossoms and their sweet perfume.

At dusk, these flowers are busy with the whirring wings of the sphinx moth but even during the day various bees including the small halictid bees, come in for nectar. When the blossoms first open, they reveal five outer stamens that shed pollen on moth and bee alike. Next, the five inner stamens do the same. But the female stigma capped by two styles is still protected within the flower's tube, thus preventing self-fertilization. When the stamens wither, the stigma emerges to receive pollen brought from younger flowers.

Give these plants full sun in the North and partial shade in the South but keep them to the edge of the garden, for their afternoon appearance is rather forlorn. They are hardy through USDA Zone 5. 'Rubra Plena' has fragrant double pink flowers on two-foot stems. There is also a white form, 'Alba'.

*N*IGHT-BLOOMING DAYLILIES

I know a little garden close,
Set thick with lily and red rose,
Where I would wander if I might
From dewy morn to dewy night.

WILLIAM MORRIS, *A Garden by the Sea*

hen we moved to our country house back in the late 1960s, the only plants left in the wreckage of a garden ignored for about thirty years were two big clumps of the lemon lily (*Hemerocallis lilioasphodelus*), a lot of the ubiquitous rose, *Rosa multiflora* (sold by the millions in the 1970s as perfect for living hedges and now, in many gardens, a hedge against every other living plant in the neighborhood), and hundreds of the common orange daylily, *Hemerocallis fulva* 'Europa'.

For a number of years gardening took a backseat to work on the house, so we were glad to have the daylilies because they required no work at all, blooming without fail every summer. *Hemerocallis* is Greek for "beauty for a day," so named because each flower opens, matures, and withers in twenty-four hours—at least daylilies seemed to follow that pattern when the genus was named. These plants were first described in John Parkinson's 1629 garden text, *Paradisi in Sole:*

Paradisus Terrestris (A Garden of Pleasant Flowers) after they came to Europe and England over trade routes from China. Culture was simple and the first description claimed them to be at their best when growing in the boggy spots of what was then Germany.

Late in the 1800s, plant breeders saw the potential in the common tawny daylily, *Hemerocallis fulva*, and began to develop new cultivars using the pollen of the lemon lily and three other species from Japan (*H. dumortieri, H. middendorffii,* and *H. minor*). The first hybrid daylily was registered in 1892 by an English schoolteacher, George Yeld. The name was 'Apricot'. When research was slowed in Europe as a result of the two world wars, America took up the daylily banner and from a humble beginning it is estimated that there are well over 32,000 registered cultivars—not all in existence—with a thousand new cultivars introduced every year.

We moved to our country house in July. It

The night-blooming daylily, *Hemerocallis citrina*, pursued by a cecropia moth, *Hyalophora cecropia*.

wasn't until one late afternoon the following May that I saw some dots of pale yellow partially hidden among the grasses in the field just beyond our kitchen door. As dusk advanced, the flowers almost glowed and I have since learned that light yellows are more effective at catching the light than any other color when the last rays of the setting sun fade in the evening sky. Not only were they beautiful, their fragrance was clean and sweet.

The flowers belonged to that marvelously fragrant old-fashioned plant, the lemon lily, *Hemerocallis lilioasphodelus* (synonym, *H. flava*), a plant that older garden books called the custard lily and really old books called Liricon-fancy.

The lemon lily has been grown in gardens since it first arrived from China at least four hundred years ago. There are a number of reasons for its continued popularity: the flowers open early in the season—at least one month before the common tawny daylily, the plants are tough, and the flowers are wonderfully fragrant, with a perfume that is always light and delightful, never heavy or cloying. Many flowers will remain open a second day, and because of the large number of developing buds, two sets will be open at the same time. Because of this habit, lemon lilies are called extended bloomers.

The leaves are a fountain of green and add an attractive accent to the flower border, but for best growth, plants should be divided at least every four years. There are now many cultivars with larger blooms but none of these modern developments can match the perfume of the old-fashioned lemon lily.

As our garden grew, our collection of perennials went beyond those ordinary varieties found at local garden centers, largely as a result of my entering the wonderful world of the mail-order nurseries and by growing a number of plants from seed.

Back in 1977 I first contacted Major Howell's International Seed Collection in Cobham, Surrey, England. Major Howell gathered various seeds from many sources, including a number of botanical gardens from around the world. His collection is said to number six thousand items and the catalogs usually featured two thousand named seeds. Since I keep copies of most of my order blanks—so I have a record of seeds and plants tagged to the right year, in case I forget to label an item or the label just disappears over the years—I easily found out that the most interesting daylily in our garden, *Hemerocallis citrina*, was ordered in 1984.

Now what was so unusual about *Hemerocallis citrina* (synonym, *H. vespertina*), known in the 1930s as the citron daylily? Well, it has long, arching leaves up to forty inches long, leaves that are rippled along the edges and attractive in their own right. Their color is dark green and in autumn the leaves turn to golden yellow, and finally a bright yellow-brown. The base of each leaf as it leaves the ground is white and the part below the soil is stained anywhere from pink to a bright red. But most important, the narrow flowers open in late afternoon and stay open all night, finally starting to decay about noon of the next day (earlier if the day is excessively warm). The three lemon-yellow sepals have streaks of green on their back and the tips are each stained with a blot of purplish brown at the tips, easily noted when the flowers are in bud. The petals are a clear and pale lemon-yellow and the blossoms are sweetly fragrant at night. The plants bloom for a long time. A healthy stem (or, more properly, a scape) will often reach a height of three to four feet, each having up to fifty buds, with two or three opening each evening.

I really get a kick from many early descriptions of this plant's habit. Although they generally admit the citron daylily is attractive, most write it off for having an undesirable night-blooming habit and flowers that are too narrow for true beauty. One team of contemporary writers criticize the foliage for having a tendency to die too early in the fall (undoubtedly a fault if your garden is devoted to only one species of plant, but

I find the fall color very attractive, especially when planted with grasses and other perennials), while another current writer, apparently without his own opinion, just writes it off by repeating the same critique found in A. B. Stout's excellent book *Daylilies* (reprinted in facsimile by Saga-press, 1986), first published in 1934. I have a garden friend who planted a whole row of the citron daylily beneath his bedroom window so that on warm summer nights the light and sweet perfume is wafted upon the evening air.

The citron daylily originally came from north-central China. It was found in the province of Shensi, an area bordered on the east by the Yellow River and covering 72,467 square miles. There in 1890 a Catholic missionary, Guiseppe Giraldi, sent a plant to Antonio Biondi in Italy. Biondi grew the plant and soon one Professor E. Baroni of the Museum of Botany at Florence saw it, describing it for publication in 1897 and giving it the name *Hemerocallis citrina*.

The hybridizing began immediately, with everyone hoping that by mixing the genes of the citron daylily with other species and clones, a flower would eventually be produced that would be open for longer than twenty-four hours. Two Naples nurserymen, Karl Ludwig Sprenger and his nephew Willy Müller, were the first and in 1903 they released 'Baroni', a plant similar to *Hemerocallis citrina* but with fuller flowers.

'Mülleri' was another hybrid released in 1903 by a Mr. Charles Sprenger who turned out to be the same Sprenger with an Anglicized first name and, of course, his nephew Willy. He said it was the best of the hybrids between *Hemerocallis thunbergii* and *H. citrina*. The flowers were described as being very large, with a sweet scent, but unfortunately it opened about four in the afternoon.

'Fulcitrina' resulted from a cross between *Hemerocallis fulva* 'Maculata' and *H. citrina* back in the early 1900s. Once again, the plant was nocturnal with narrow-petaled flowers and was written off as being "dull and worthless."

'Golconda' appeared in 1924, the result of a hybrid between a forgotten clone and *Hemerocallis citrina*. The flowers were described as being large, a light cadmium in color, but because they were night-blooming, this hybrid was abandoned by the Farr Nursery Company.

'Thelma Perry' was listed in 1925 by Mr. Amos Perry as a hybrid between *Hemerocallis thunbergii* and *H. citrina*. This plant was described as having "erect foliage, tall well-branched spikes . . . each with fifteen to twenty flowers, blooming from July to September." Unfortunately, it was nocturnal.

'Citronella' was released in 1926, again the result of hybridizing *citrina* with *Hemerocallis thunbergii*. Although having excellent foliage and pale yellow flowers that were fuller than either parent, they were night-blooming and the plant was discontinued in the trade.

Nineteen twenty-six also saw the introduction of 'Lemon Queen', a nocturnal plant and in 1928 the Bay Street Nurseries distributed 'Lemona', a night-blooming plant reaching a height of five feet and producing numerous pale lemon-yellow flowers almost five inches across that would close by eleven on warm, sunny mornings.

'Golden West', created by a Mr. H. P. Sass, was introduced in 1932, being a hybrid between *Hemerocallis citrina* and *H. aurantiaca*, this last being a plant that appeared in Kew Gardens in 1890, and was assumed to have arrived from Japan at an earlier date. This cultivar appeared in 1951 as one of the plants used to produce 'Ruth Lehman' {('Gypsy' × 'J. S. Gayner') × [('Amaryllis' × 'Golden West') × 'Gypsy']}.

I called a number of people in the American Hemerocallis Society and asked if any of the citron daylily hybrids were still available either from nurseries or perhaps a private collection, but nobody knew of any sources. Obviously the idea of enjoying the evening garden was unpopular over the past eight decades, suffered bad press, or perhaps was simply looked upon as being déclassé.

In the 1930s A. N. Steward introduced a second nocturnal daylily called *Hemerocallis altissima*. The plants were found in the Kiangsu and Anhwei provinces of China. In 1986, Major Howell came to the rescue and I received seeds. Planted out in May, they produced flowering plants in the following year.

Botanical descriptions of *Hemerocallis altissima* call for a plant with leaves to four feet in length and flowers that are nocturnal and fragrant, opening after three P.M., being fully open by nine P.M., and calling it quits around eight o'clock the next morning. The scapes were supposed to be between four and six feet tall, hence the species name.

But my plants had problems. The scapes were over seven feet tall and the orange-brown flowers, while fragrant, opened in the very early morning, stayed open all day, and died at dusk.

Darrel Apps ran the Department of Education at Longwood Gardens for seventeen years and has some forty-two cultivars to his credit and is considered an expert on daylilies. I asked him about my problems with *Hemerocallis altissima*.

"The problem," he answered, "is getting a pure strain of seed. Even though yours came from a botanical garden, in the intervening years some hybridization occurred with the plants that produced your seed. While fragrance is there, along with increased height, the nocturnal habit is gone."

Today, *Hemerocallis altissima* is being used to create a whole new breed of daylilies with added height, suitable for the back of the border and also to impart a new set of night-blooming genes.

Daylily Care

Daylilies are virtually carefree perennials. They require no special attention—although, like most living things, the more care you do provide, the better they will perform. These plants will hold dry, rocky banks together or grow with perfect ease in moist soil by the water's edge. They prefer full sun in the North and partial shade in the

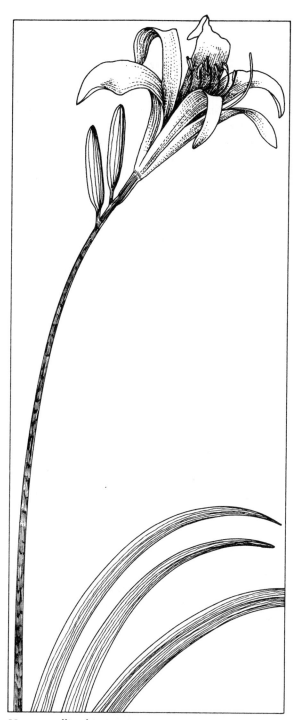

Hemerocallis altissima.

Deep South. Plants may be left in one spot for many years, but once blooming starts to decline, it's time to divide the clumps.

New daylilies can be planted in spring or fall. As a rule I never fertilize garden plants but I give them all a good beginning by mixing new garden soil with plenty of compost and dehydrated cow or sheep manure at the time of planting. Space them about two feet apart, except for the dwarf varieties; here the spacing is a foot apart. Remove the dead flowers every day and the scapes when flowering is over. This last action often helps some plants to remain green, since many have a tendency to turn brown after blooming is over. Most daylilies are hardy in USDA Zone 5. Gardeners in colder zones should check to see that the plants they choose are hardy in these colder climates.

By carefully selecting daylily cultivars, you can have bloom in your garden from spring, through the heat of summer, and on into fall. Today's daylily nurseries list plants according to their blooming time: EE (extra early); E (early); EM (early midseason); M (midseason); LM (late midseason); L (late); and VL (very late). These times must be adjusted to your part of the country, but midseason daylilies come into bloom about May in the South, but as late as July and August in the North.

Hybridizing Your Own Daylilies

Daylilies, with their large flowers, are fine subjects for interbreeding experiments. You can transfer the pollen (the yellow powder that contains the male sex cells) from one blossom to the female stigma (the flattened top of the long rod that stands in the middle of the six anthers), thus starting the plant's process of seed production.

Start when the flowers first open. Using a cotton swab, transfer pollen from another flower of choice, touching it to the tip of the stigma. After this, cover the blossom with a small paper or plastic bag to prevent any other pollen from

The parts of a daylily flower.

reaching the flower. The next day you can remove the bag and within three days, the flower will dry and fall away leaving the ovary that will soon swell and mature. Remember to keep careful records of your crosses.

When fully ripe and ready to split, remove the shiny black seeds. Put them in the refrigerator for four or five weeks, then sow in a sterile mix. Seeds will begin to germinate in about two weeks. In the South where winters are warm, most seedlings will flower the first year but in the colder parts of the country, new plants require two years before blooming.

HUNDREDS OF NOCTURNALS

In 1954 Ben Arthur Davis wrote a book *Daylilies and How to Grow Them*. Mr. Davis, born in Richton, Mississippi, was a southern garden writer and an accredited judge of the American Camellia Society. In a chapter entitled "Daylilies as Cut Flowers," he speaks of the importance of nocturnal daylilies, especially as cut flowers.

"Hemerocallis that hold their blooms open in the evening are not only among the choicest of all material for arrangements displayed at night but are unequalled for planting on certain outdoor situations," writes Mr. Davis. He then goes on to extol the virtues of the evening garden not only for the enjoyment of the family or for entertaining friends, but for evening meetings, especially since the trend is to light gardens at night. Some forty years later, the trend is finally picking up but unfortunately nobody that chairs any committees that I sit on has given much thought to the beauty of meeting outdoors in the evening garden rather than indoors on hot afternoons under fluorescent lights.

Davis also speaks of the nocturnal daylilies as having potential in the creation of tudaylilies (see below) and mentions the search for more of these forty-eight-hour daylilies, flowers that open during the day, remain open all night, all the next day, and all the following night. In 1954, there were four such cultivars: 'Advance', 'Repeater', 'Tuday', and 'Tudor'. (I can find no record of these flowers today.) He follows with a list of over 250 cultivars that are either nocturnal or will stay open until at least ten at night.

The term for tudaylilies in the 1990s is extended bloomers, meaning flowers that are open for sixteen hours or more. Lewis and Nancy Hill in *Daylilies: The Perfect Perennial*, describe a cultivar called 'Pat Mercer' as not having really great flowers but opening in the evening with bright red flowers with a green throat, staying open all the next day, and then a second day, with the flower turning orange and the throat white.

I compared Davis's choices with the over 750 cultivars listed in the Hills' book. Only the following plants appeared in both lists: 'Calypso' (created by Luther Burbank), 'Dauntless', 'Flavina', 'Hesperus', 'Hyperion' (particularly valua-

ble because of its especially pleasant scent both day and night), 'Painted Lady', 'Rajah', 'Salmon Sheen', 'Symphony', 'Talisman', 'Valiant', and 'Wau-Bun'. That's twelve out of hundreds, with the rest in limbo after less than forty years. That's one of the problems with breeding thousands of plants—thousands come and thousands go!

But the daylily breeders continue to work with nocturnal characteristics. Since many of today's gardeners are at work during the day, it has become increasingly important for daylily blossoms to open early in the morning and remain so for at least a few hours after dark. And the search is always on for daylilies that will bloom in the afternoon and remain open all of the following day. Finally, breeders hope to develop a successful tudaylily, or extended bloomer, that will remain open two days or even more—but what a good popular name of such a flower will be has yet to be suggested.

Nocturnal Daylilies Today

There are literally hundreds of nocturnal and extended-bloom daylilies available today. The problem is that most catalogs and nurseries neglect to pass the information along, believing that gardeners are uninterested in the garden after the cocktail hour rolls around. For example, in his book *Hemerocallis, the Daylily* (Timber Press, 1989), author R. W. Munson, Jr., never even mentions the nocturnal aspects of daylilies, except to describe *Hemerocallis citrina* and *H. altissima*.

Enter R. Donald Spencer. Mr. Spencer is responsible for the proposed nocturnal and late-closing rating system for daylilies.

"Daylilies have widely different behavior," says Mr. Spencer, "especially with respect to the time of day their flowers open and how long it takes for their flowers to unfurl after the process has begun. Why, with some cultivars, the petals start to separate a full day before the flower actually opens, although with most cultivars the opening process takes only a few hours. Northern growers, such as a friend of mine in Montana, have to be very choosy about which cultivars they acquire because they get many cool nights in the summer, and after such a night, many diurnal daylilies never fully open. These are the daylilies that in warmer climates would normally start opening around sunrise and be fully open by noon. When nights are cool, only the nocturnal or partially nocturnal daylilies can be relied upon to open fully in the morning.

"When daylily flowers start to die and the petals begin to soften and wilt, the term melting is used. Melting occurs when enzymes in the flower start dissolving the cell walls. If the edges of the petals appear distinctly transparent when one looks through them toward a bright background or the edge of the petal feels or looks limp, the blossoms are melting."

In order to gather as much information as possible about the nocturnal activities of daylilies, Mr. Spencer has a number of garden friends who belong to a round robin and report from around the country about daylily habits as observed in their gardens.

But there is a slight problem: plants do not use timepieces; they function by solar time, not civilized time. In order that observations made about nocturnal daylilies can be useful when recorded in countries as large as the United States and Canada, where eight time zones are in use, solar time must be used.

The simplest definition of solar time is that it's local time reckoned according to the sun. Noon occurs not when the clock proclaims it, but when the sun crosses the observer's meridian, that spot directly overhead when the sun appears to be the highest in the sky. But observers just a few miles to your east or west will have a different meridian than yours, so their local time will be slightly different. Thus standard time is solar time at the center of each time zone. And that is standard time, not summer or daylight savings time.

In the United States, the seventy-fifth meridian

marks Eastern Standard Time, the ninetieth marks Central Standard Time, the 105th for Mountain, and 120th for Pacific. Thus, at the center of any one time zone when the clock reads, for example, nine A.M., solar time will be thirty minutes later at the western border of that zone and thirty minutes earlier at the eastern border. Also remember that solar time is measured on the twenty-four-hour, not the twelve-hour clock, so two P.M. is really fourteen hours and seven P.M. is nineteen hours.

"It really isn't hard to make observations by solar time," says Mr. Spencer, "after you calculate the number of minutes by which it differs from Daylight or Standard Time in the gardener's time zone. And it can be pretty well estimated by looking at a map of your part of the country."

Mr. Spencer's classification system for nocturnal/diurnal daylilies has five categories:

NOC 0: The new flower is at least eighty percent open between twelve and sixteen hours solar time and remains fresh all night.

NOC 1: The new flower is at least eighty percent open between sixteen and twenty-two hours solar time.

NOC 2: The bud is less than eighty percent open at twenty-two hours solar time but at least eighty percent open by six hours.

NOC 3: The bud is more than twenty percent but less than eighty percent open at six hours solar time.

NOC 4: Bud is less than twenty percent open at six hours and the flower does not stay open all night.

The first three categories define nocturnal daylilies, while the plants in the noc 3 and 4 categories are not nocturnal at all, but diurnal, since their flowers do not open until after daybreak.

Nocturnal Daylily Cultivars

The list that follows features a number of daylily cultivars that are nocturnal. The flower color, its fragrance, and, if possible, the noc number is included when available; if not, the notation is "noc." I have included a number of choices since few daylily nurseries or garden centers will have them all. In addition, where possible, the average width of the flower, the height of the plants, and when they bloom are noted.

'After the Fall'; noc.; 2½-inch flowers of a tangerine-and-copper blend with a yellow halo; plants are 20 inches high and bloom very early in the season.

'Agape Love'; noc 2; 7-inch flowers of an ivory tone, washed with pink; plants are 15 inches high and bloom midseason.

'Alice Gibson'; noc 1–2; flowers are light gold with green-gold throat.

'American Bicentennial'; noc.; 6-inch fragrant flowers of dusty rose with green throats; plants bloom midseason on 28-inch scapes.

'Angel Tears'; noc 1–2; flowers are near white with green throats.

'Angel's Voice'; noc 1–2; flowers are near white with green throats.

'Apple Tart'; noc.; dark red flowers with a green throat that bloom early to midseason.

'Best of Friends'; noc 2; 6½-inch deep pink flowers with a green throat; plants bloom early to midseason on 19-inch scapes.

'Betty'; noc 0; rich orange flowers dusted with glitter.

'Bitsy'; noc 1 (except after a very cold night); 2-inch fragrant yellow flowers on 20-inch scapes above 6-inch-high grassy foliage; plants bloom all season.

'Bonnie John Seton'; noc.; 7-inch fragrant pale yellow flowers on 26-inch scapes; plants bloom early to midseason.

'Border Giant'; noc.; 7-inch flowers of a frosty melon-pink with orchid ribs on 16-inch scapes; plants bloom midseason and are reblooming.

'Born Yesterday'; noc 1; cream flowers dusted with rose with a red halo.

'Bridget'; noc 2; dark red flowers with a yellow throat.

'Butter Curls'; noc 1; 4-inch creamy yellow flowers with a green throat and wavy edges.

'Butterpat'; noc 1–2; 2½-inch creamy yellow fragrant blossoms on 26-inch scapes; plants bloom midseason.

'Butterscotch Ruffles'; noc.; 3-inch peach-colored flowers with a green throat on 24-inch scapes.

'Chirper'; noc 1–2; peach-colored flowers on short scapes.

'Coastal Empire'; noc 1–2; 8-inch flowers of melon-yellow with greenish yellow threads.

'Colt'; noc 2 (or 1–2); near white flowers with green throats.

'Cosmic Hummingbird'; noc; 3½-inch peach flowers with a ruby eye on 26-inch scapes; plants bloom very early.

'Cosmic Treasure'; noc.; 5-inch flowers of almond-shell with dark halo and green throat on 22-inch scapes; plants bloom early.

'Country Club'; noc.; 6-inch pink flowers with a green throat, dusted with glitter on 20-inch scapes; plants bloom midseason and will rebloom.

'Crystal Chandelier'; noc. 1; near white flowers with chartreuse throats.

'Cutie Pie'; noc 2 (or 1–2); yellow flowers with good form.

'Dee Dee'; noc 0–1; lovely yellow flowers with deeper yellow veining.

'Dr. Darrow'; noc.; 4-inch fragrant flowers of golden yellow that bloom late in the season.

'Eenie Weenie'; noc.; 1½-inch fragrant blooms of light yellow on 12-inch scapes that last well into the night.

'Erin Hanley'; noc.; 6-inch flowers of shrimp pink veined with rose and a deeper rose halo on 32-inch scapes; plants bloom midseason.

'Erin Prairie'; noc 2; golden yellow flowers with a grass-green throat.

The small but elegant flowers of 'Golden Dewdrop'.

'Evening Bell'; noc 2; 7-inch flowers of light yellow with a green throat on 22-inch scapes; plants bloom early to midseason.

'Everblooming Doll'; noc 2 (even after a cold night); light gold flowers with an excellent habit of reblooming.

'Fairest Love'; noc 2; ruffled purplish pink petals with deeper veins and edging and light apple green in throat.

'Fairy Tale Pink'; noc 2; lovely pink flower with a green throat.

'Gentle Shepherd'; noc 2; near white flowers with a yellow-green throat.

'Gleeman Song'; noc 2; light lemon flowers with ruffled petals.

'Golden Dewdrop'; noc 2; 3½-inch flowers of yellow-gold on 18-inch scapes; almost a continual bloomer down South.

'Green Dragonfly'; noc 1–2; greenish yellow with a deep green throat.

'Green Ice'; noc.; 7-inch fragrant flowers of pale yellow with a green throat on 36-inch scapes; plants bloom middle to late season.

'Guardian Angel'; noc 1–2; 4-inch almost white flowers with a green throat on 26-inch scapes; plants bloom early to midseason.

'Happy Treasure'; noc 1–2; yellow and rose are intermixed with a rose halo and a yellow throat.

'Hazel Monette'; noc 1–2; pink with green throat.

'Ida Miles'; noc.; fragrant pale ivory-yellow blossoms on 30-inch scapes blooming until after midnight; plants bloom midseason.

'Ishmael'; noc 1–2; gold flowers with a bright green throat.

'Iron Gate Iceberg'; noc.; 6-inch fragrant near white flowers with a green throat on 26-inch scapes; plants bloom midseason.

'Java Sea'; noc 2; deep yellow flowers with green throat; a good rebloomer.

'Jewel of Hearts'; noc 2 (3 after a cool night); dark red flowers with a red-black center.

The magnificent yellow flower of 'Ida Miles'.

A rose daylily cultivar, 'Margaret Guillory'.

98

'Joan Senior'; noc 1–2 (or 2); near white flowers with a green throat.

'Jomico'; noc 1–2; light yellow flowers with a green throat and wide ruffled petals and sepals.

'Kazuq'; noc 2; near white with yellow-green throat.

'Lemon Mint'; noc 2; lemon-yellow flowers on a number of scapes.

'Lily Fields'; noc 1 (or 1–2, but doesn't open fully after cold nights); light gold flowers with a green throat, flower turning orange as it ages.

'Lime Painted Lady'; noc 0 (or 1–2); greenish yellow flowers lightly dusted with glitter.

'Little Brandy'; noc.; 5-inch fragrant flowers of pink on 20-inch scapes; plants bloom very early in the season.

'Lolabelle'; noc 1–2; chrome yellow flowers with a chartreuse throat.

'Louise Latham'; noc 2; gold flowers with green throats.

'Lucky Girl'; noc 1–2 (or 2); pink flowers with a green center.

'Lullaby Baby'; noc 2 (3 when nighttime temperature is in the 40s); light pink flowers with green throat.

'Lusty Leland'; noc 6¼-inch fire-engine red flowers with a gold throat on 28-inch scapes; plants bloom midseason and rebloom.

'Margaret Guillory'; noc.; 6-inch fragrant flowers of two-tone rose with a green throat on 21-inch scape; plants bloom early in the season and repeat bloom.

'Mary Sue Mills'; noc 2; deep cream-yellow flowers.

'Master blend'; noc.; huge 7½-inch fragrant flowers of rose-pink with a green throat on 25-inch scapes; plants bloom midseason.

'May May'; noc 2 (even after 45°F night); pale purple-pink flowers on a white base and chartreuse in throat.

'Meadowbrook Green'; noc 2 (3 after 43°F low); greenish gold when opening but turns a deeper gold after 24 hours.

'Mint Condition'; noc 1–2 (or 2); gold flowers with green throats.

'Moon Frolic'; noc 1–2 (or 1); near white flowers to pale yellow.

'Mormon'; noc 2 (3 after a cold night); near white ruffled petals almost three inches long, dusted with glitter.

'Moroni'; noc 1–2; peach-colored flowers with a green throat.

'Mumbo-Jumbo'; noc.; 6-inch fragrant flowers of rose-pink with a green throat on 21-inch scapes; plants bloom early.

'My Belle'; noc 2; flesh pink flowers with a green throat.

'Neon Yellow'; noc.; 5½-inch fragrant lemon-yellow flowers with pink overlay and lemon-yellow throat on 32-inch scapes; plants bloom early.

'Nettie Ergene Conley'; noc 2; nearly white flowers with a green throat.

'Norma Lamb'; noc 1–2; yellow flowers with a golden tinge and apple-green centers.

'Our Love Song'; noc.; light yellow flowers.

'Pardon Me'; noc 2; cranberry-red flowers.

'Pat Mercer'; noc 1–2 (or 1); 7-inch flowers of rose-red with a green throat on 28-inch scapes; plants bloom midseason.

'Paul Bunyon'; noc.; huge 8- to 9-inch flowers of light gold dusted with glitter on 40-inch scapes; plants bloom midseason with a repeat bloom.

'Prairie Charmer'; noc.; 5½-inch melon-pink flowers with dark purple and a green throat on 20-inch scapes; plants bloom early midseason.

'Princeton Point Lace'; noc 2; 6-inch fragrant flowers of deep yellow with laced edges on 33-inch scapes; plants bloom very early, continuing until fall.

'Puddin'; noc.; 2½-inch fragrant lemon-yellow flowers on 20-inch scapes that stay open until midnight; plants bloom midseason.

'Purity'; noc 0; small flowers of pale yellow with a marked fragrance on 5-foot stems; a cultivar with *Hemerocallis altissima* as one parent.

'Radiant Greetings'; noc.; 5½-inch flowers of orange-yellow with ruffled petals on 38-inch scapes; plants bloom midseason.

'Red Bantam'; noc.; 2-inch flowers of bright red with a tangerine throat on 18-inch scapes; plants bloom early midseason.

'Rosella Sheridan'; noc.; 7-inch flowers of a lovely pink on 21-inch scapes; blooms midseason.

'Siloam Powder Pink'; noc.; 3¼-inch pink flowers with a yellow to green throat on 20-inch scapes; plants bloom midseason.

'Siloam Rose Dawn'; noc.; 4-inch rose flowers with varying shades of color and a chartreuse throat on 18-inch scapes that open late in the evening; plants bloom early midseason.

'Silver Circus'; noc.; 7-inch fragrant flowers of bright yellow suffused with pink with ruffled edges and a green throat on 30-inch scapes; plants bloom early midseason.

'Southern Nights'; noc.; 4½-inch fragrant light yellow flowers with glitter on 32-inch scapes; plants bloom midseason.

'Spanish Ruff'; noc 2; light yellow flowers with ruffled petals and sepals.

'Stella D'Oro'; noc 1; 2¾-inch fragrant golden yellow flowers on 12-inch scapes with flowers remaining open until at least eight P.M. in the evening; plants bloom throughout the season; does not do well in the Deep South.

'Toltec Sundial'; noc.; 7-inch fragrant sunshine yellow flowers on 28-inch scapes that open late in the evening; plants bloom early to midseason.

'Tootsie'; noc.; 3½-inch hot pink flowers with a yellow throat on 20-inch scapes; plants bloom early and rebloom.

'Top Honors'; noc 1–2; 7½-inch fragrant lemon-yellow flowers on 24-inch scapes; plants bloom midseason.

'Touched by Midas'; noc.; 6-inch golden flowers on 30-inch scapes; plants bloom midseason.

'Treasured Bouquet'; noc. 5½-inch lavender-rose flowers with a green throat on 28-inch scapes that stay open for 24 hours; plants bloom early midseason with a late summer repeat.

'Weeks Show'; noc.; 7-inch lavender-and-yellow flowers on 26-inch scapes that open late in the evening; plants bloom early to midseason.

'Witches Dance'; noc.; 6½-inch flowers of a dark red with a green throat on 30-inch scapes; plants bloom early midseason.

'Yearning Love'; noc.; 5½-inch ivory flowers overlaid with pink and slightly darker pink veins and rippling edges of ivory on 30-inch scapes that flower late into the evening; plants bloom midseason with some repeat bloom.

'Zarahelma'; noc.; 5-inch fragrant pink-lavender flowers with magenta halo and veining and a green throat on 20-inch scapes, flowering late into the evening; plants bloom midseason.

Daylilies in the Evening Garden

Just about dusk on many summer evenings, I walk into our formal garden where the majority of the night-blooming daylilies are planted. Here they flower against the dark green backdrop of a rhododendron hedge, with ferns and a star magnolia to the right and our viburnum tree to the left. I have set flagstones underneath the magnolia and moth orchids and cymbidiums spend their summers there. All the night-flowering plants from the greenhouse hang on various branches of the viburnum.

The large ivory-yellow blossoms of 'Ida Miles' next to the pinks of 'Erin Hanley' are fronted by a large patch of 'Stella D'Oro', its golden yellow trumpets gleaming in the fading light of day. Mixed with the other fragrances of a host of tropical plants are the fragrances of the daylilies, drifting on a slight breeze coming up from the lake below—light and sweet on the evening air.

CHAPTER SEVEN

EVENING PRIMROSES AND OTHER NOCTURNAL WILDFLOWERS

You know the bloom, unearthly white,
That none has seen by morning light—
   The gentle moon, alone, may bare
   Its beauty to the secret air.
Who ventures past its dark retreat
Must kneel for holy things and sweet.
   That blossom, mystically blown,
   No man may gather for his own
Nor touch it, lest it droop and fall. . . .
Oh, I am not like that at all!

DOROTHY PARKER, *The Evening Primrose*

America builds. The fields and country roads are shoveled up, redug, revamped, and instead of being home to both plants and animals of the field and forest, we get concrete, asphalt, and people.

Few worthwhile things survive the disruption. Occasionally a bindweed blooms or wild roses (unfortunately sometimes even multifloras) spread over gravel and clay. Giant moth mulleins (*Verbascum blattaria*) will dot the landscape like Giacometti sculptures in gray and the ubiquitous daylily (*Hemerocallis fulva*) blooms straight and tall. And here and there the common evening primrose (*Oenothera biennis*) stands, its leaves as pert as if starched, yet its flowers worn and tattered.

Back at the turn of the century, Neltje Blan-chan described these night-bloomers as ballroom beauties (a description she also used to portray the flowering habits of nicotianas), their flowers having a jaded and worn-out look by day—as though the partying of the night before had left them wasted and forlorn. In the evening, new pale yellow petals unfold to expose new blossoms to the night's delight. But from today's viewpoint, I like to think they are worn out from traffic and noise and wait for everyone to go home before they attempt to open.

Living by Dracula's clock, the blossoms both new and old are tightly closed in daylight and look as if they belong along the side of the road. Then once the sun sets, however, fresh buds quickly open to the evening, and again the plant is glowing with a mildly incandescent sulfur yel-

The Missouri evening primrose, *Oenothera macrocarpa*.

low, the combined effect of dozens of fragrant flowers.

The genus name *Oenothera* is from the Greek words *oinos*, "wine," and *thera*, "to hunt." When first named these plants were confused with another genus that had roots bearing the aroma of wine.

There are many evening primroses but the genus is a mixed lot. Like a family of shift-workers who only meet at the breakfast table, some are true night-bloomers, opening only in the late afternoon, while the others, called sun-drops, open their flowers only when the sun is up. Both types have flowers with eight stamens, and all but one species have four narrow stigmas, crosslike, at the tip of the style.

The petals of the flower are held together by tiny hooks at their tips. As the pressure of sap forces the petals to expand, they part at the bottom but remain fixed at the top, until finally the hooks snap apart and the corolla opens up almost instantaneously, then slows as the petals spread out flat. It takes about thirty minutes for each flower to open.

Today many evening primroses are found around the world, having traveled along with other visitors but originally they were all Americans, their range stretching from the deserts of the Southwest to the East Coast. Parkinson noted in 1729 that it was imported to England from Virginia. The common evening primrose (*Oenothera biennis*), a biennial, was introduced into gardens sometime in the eighteenth century as a root vegetable called yellow lamb's lettuce or German rampion. It was also used as an ornamental plant. "[It's] among the handsomest of hardy flowers," wrote William Robinson, England's great gardener. "The yellow species, and varieties allied to the common evening primrose, (*Oenothera biennis*), may be readily naturalized in any soil. These noble and fragrant flowers are easily grown and beautiful. They, however, from their boldness, are suited for shrubberies, copses, and the like, sowing themselves freely."

Plants growing where conditions are favorable often reach a height of five feet, but those along the roadsides are usually shorter. The first-year seedlings form rosettes of leaves that lie flat upon the ground. The second year a tall, branched stem appears and the plant begins to bloom with the heat of summer. Strong stems bear alternate, lance-shaped leaves and clusters of unopened buds, opening flowers, wilted flowers, and near-bursting seedpods all crowded together in a nest of the willowlike leaves.

We have many evening primroses in our garden, both day and night-bloomers, but we've always put aside a spot of good soil in full sun where the garden proper meets the wild garden for a large plant of *Oenothera biennis*. Between the open glow of dusk and the pitch black of impending night, there is a short period of time on summer evenings—ten to fifteen minutes at most—when the atmosphere takes on a luminous quality, magnifying its primrose yellow; that is the time when this plant is at its best.

Louise Beebe Wilder suggested that some writers credited *Oenothera biennis* with the power to give forth a mysterious phosphorescent light, but she (and I) never saw it. What they probably were referring to is the luminous quality of primrose yellow at dusk. One Mrs. Deland in one of her poems described a "silver burst of sound" that often accompanied the opening of this flower; I've never heard that either but it's nice to think that someone once thought they did.

The busiest time for the sphinx moth is after four o'clock in the afternoon. It is then that this insect is up and flying about—often mistaken for a hummingbird. As dusk deepens and the sweet lemony scent of the primrose increases, hawk-moths cease their fluttering and home in on their search for nectar. Since the flower tubes of the primrose are very long, only the tongue of the hawkmoth can reach to the bottom, draining the very last drop.

If a flower escapes pollination by the horde of moths descending, it will remain open for a few

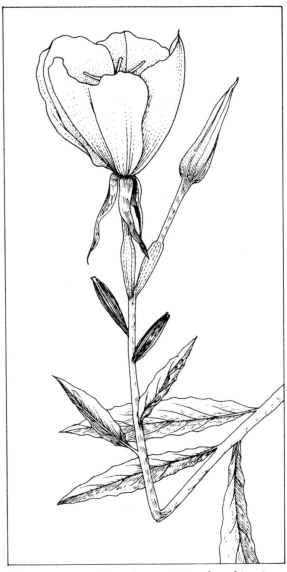

The common evening primrose, *Oenothera biennis*.

hours of morning, hoping to attract a passing bumble bee.

W. J. Holland, one of America's foremost lepidopterists, wrote of evening primroses and moths in *The Moth Book*. He advised the reader to stay by a bed of evening primroses at the hour of dusk. As the blossoms open, the hawkmoths will fly like meteors through the air, rushing from flower to flower faster than the eye can see.

"My friend, Henry Pryer," he wrote, "has a great bed of evening primroses in his compound on the Bluff in Yokohama. Well I remember standing with him before the flowers, and, as the light began to fade upon the distant top of Fuji-no-yama, with net in hand capturing the hawkmoths, which came eagerly trooping to the spot. When it grew quite dark O-Chi-san held a Japanese lantern aloft to help us to see where to make our strokes. A dozen species became our spoil during those pleasant evenings. Ah! those nights in Japan! Can I ever forget them?"

American Indians used a root tea of *Oenothera biennis* to treat obesity, one problem that I, having grown up on movies about the West, did not realize they had problems with. The Indians also used it for bowel pains and the liquid was rubbed on sore muscles to give added strength. Recent medical research indicates that the oil from its seed might be useful in treating metabolic disorders and alcoholism. Since evening primrose oil is a natural source of essential fatty acids like gamma-linolenic acid, various preparations are found in every health food store. I called our local outlet and they told me the oil is used to treat PMS and for reducing inflammations due to arthritis.

There is one last thing to cover regarding the evening primrose and it concerns the Dutch botanist, Hugo de Vries (1848–1935). In 1901 de Vries published his monumental study *Die Mutationstheorie*, in which he formulated the idea that evolution occurs through sudden mutations rather than a series of gradual changes. His results were based on a wide knowledge of plant behavior but most were centered on his backyard garden and a species of evening primrose, *Oenothera lamarckiana* (for many years known as *O. erythrosepala* but now known as *O. glazioviana*). The flower was originally named for Jean Baptiste Lamarck, a French naturalist who lost out to Darwin in the evolutionary sweepstakes. (Although

O. glazioviana is said to be a complex hybrid first found in cultivation, its origins were still American.)

De Vries found his first clump of lamarckiana growing in an abandoned "waste place" at Hilversum in Holland and noticed that in addition to the normal plants, two obvious variations were present. He dug up all three and brought them home to his garden where he studied these and other mutations, noting that they bred true generation after generation. He thought they were new species—although today they would be called cultivars—and, at the same time, rediscovered Mendel's laws of heredity that were based on garden peas (for which de Vries gave Mendel full credit).

OTHER EVENING PRIMROSES

There are at this time 124 species of *Oenothera*. They represent annuals, biennials, and perennials, many of them night-blooming. Add to this dozens of subspecies spread over much of the United States and Mexico and you have a large number of potential plants for the evening garden. If you have exhausted all commercial sources and still hunger for more, check the various wildflower groups and botanical gardens in your area of the country. Meanwhile, here are some that are often found in cultivation. Their Latin names are correct as of 1991.

As to cultivation, evening primroses are exceptionally easy to grow. The desert-dwellers insist on well-drained soil while the otherfs prefer a good well-drained garden soil; the common wildflower, *Oenothera biennis* will even stake a claim in a mix of red shale and clay. The plants should be divided every three years or they slow down in flower production. Give them full sun in the North and partial shade in the South. Most are hardy in USDA Zones 5 to 9.

Oenothera acaulis (synonym, *O. taraxacifolia*) from Chile is known as the dandelion-leaved evening primrose because the leaves are deeply toothed. It's a low, trailing plant bearing large white blossoms up to three and a half inches across, changing to a delicate pink as they age. Robinson thought it one of the finest and suggested using it in the rock garden where its creeping stems can fall over the edge of a wall or block of stone. It is only marginally hardy in USDA Zone 5.

Oenothera argillicola is known as the narrow-leaved evening primrose and is found in the shale barrens of the Appalachian mountains of Virginia and West Virginia. In the wild, these plants grow in clay and shale (which is consolidated clay). They are biennial or perennial depending on their moods but are worth having for the lovely yellow flowers, over three inches wide, that turn a lovely orange-red with age. Plant height is up to four feet.

Oenothera brachycarpa (synonym, *Lavauxia brachycarpa*) is called the largest of the Great Plains species by Claude A. Barr writing in *Jewels of the Plains*. The plants are nearly stemless and the long floral tubes hold the four-inch yellow flower above the long gray, wavy-edged leaves. The fleshy roots can form open colonies of plants. He also says they are unequaled treasures for the night garden. These plants like lime and do well in the rock garden. They are native from western Kansas through central Colorado and south to Mexico.

Oenothera caespitosa, the cowboy primrose, or gumbo lily, gets that last name from growing in the gumbo clay of the great prairies. Those gardeners who complain about average clay soil in their backyards should know about gumbo clay and thank their stars. This material was the result of mud shales laid down over the Great Plains by the late Cretaceous sea that covered that area; when wet it turns into a tenacious mud and when dry has the consistency of steel.

The gumbo lily is a low-growing perennial about two to four inches high with gray-green leaves that lie close to the ground. It bears fragrant white flowers that have four large heart-shaped petals, opening in late afternoon.

The following description of its flowering was quoted by Louise Beebe Wilder in *The Fragrant Garden* and in turn was taken from the August 7, 1927, issue of a once popular magazine called *The Garden*.

> The rough green buds prepare to open an hour or two before sunset when the pleated white petals begin to bulge out between the sepals and if they are plucked and brought into the house at this stage their flowering may be watched during dinner. The sepals under the pressure of the swelling petals suddenly spring apart and bending downwards about as fast as the minute hand of a clock, allow the petals to unfold into a great white chalice, some four inches across, tinted pale green at the throat and enclosing a green style and five delicately designed stamens looped about with ropes of sticky yellow pollen. All through the night the flower pours out the strong sweet scent, rather like that of *Magnolia grandiflora* but a trifle heavier (it has been compared to a combination of Lemon and Tuberose) till about eight o'clock the next morning when the petals begin to flush with rose, which deepens to bright pink as they fade limply an hour or two later.

Oenothera deltoides subsp. *deltoides*, or the birdcage evening primrose, is a creeping annual plant with diamond-shaped leaves up to three inches long and a height that varies between two and twelve inches. The white flowers are three inches wide and open in the evening especially after heavy desert rains. There are areas in the California deserts where hundreds of these flowers open almost at once, carpeting the sands with glowing white lamps. The common name refers to the shape produced by the curving stems of dead plants. They are also found in Arizona and Utah.

The attractive golden yellow flowers of *Oenothera erythrosepala* are often three inches wide

gracing a three-foot biennial plant. In late afternoon, the calyx of a flower ready to bloom exhibits a longitudinal slit like a run in some green material and a bit of yellow will show through. After nightfall, the slit fully expands and the calyx bends back to the stalk releasing four yellow petals. Then the style unfolds its crosslike stigma. It only takes a few minutes from the first split to the final flowering.

Oenothera grandis is known as the yellow evening primrose or sometimes buttercups. These annual plants are erect when young but begin to sprawl with age. The yellow flowers are three inches across and quickly close with the heat of morning. Its pollen often appears to be held together with cobwebby threads. They prefer to grow in sandy soil and can colonize large areas. Ellen D. Schulz in *Texas Wild Flowers* wrote, "Like the mentzelia, [they] are only open in the evening, throughout the night, and on cloudy days. Unbroken prairies are often one gorgeous flower garden."

Oenothera lavandulifolia received its species name in honor of the lavender tint of its small leaves. Long yellow flowers arise from a woody crown, turning red with age. This is another flower for the rock garden. It is found in Texas and Oklahoma and reaches to Kansas.

Our garden also features the more demure and low-growing perennial known as the Missouri evening primrose or the glade lily. The plant was discovered by Thomas Nuttall, English plant explorer who roamed the American continent. In 1812, Nuttall sent seed to Fraser's Nursery in London where it appeared under the name *Oenothera macrocarpa* (the species name referring to the large seedpods) in their catalog entitled, "A Catalogue of New and Interesting Plants, Collected in Upper Louisiana, and Principally on the River Missourie, North America."

In 1913 John Sims, the editor of *Curtis's Botanical Magazine*, described the new plant in his publication. For some reason—probably to make the plant more appealing to the gardening public—he chose to ignore the proper name of *O. macrocarpa* and named the plant *O. missourensis*, and adding insult to injury, he misspelled it, dropping the "i" in Missouri. The second name has stuck through the years but the first is correct.

Sometimes erect but more often creeping, this lovely flower is best planted in well-drained soil with plenty of rocks to tumble over. The buds are spotted with red and the showy yellow flowers—often four inches wide—opening on cloudy afternoons with the slow moves of a desert cactus flower in a Disney nature film. They remain open all night. Eventually large seedpods are formed. There is a new and stunning cultivar called 'Greencourt Lemon' now available that is suited not only for the wild garden but the perennial border as well—and it's open most of the day as well as at night.

Oenothera odorata has gotten press over the years. Not only did William Robinson call it the most interesting flower he had ever seen in a garden at night, but H. E. Bates (1905–1974), author and garden writer (he also wrote *Love for Lydia*, which was made into the PBS hit) praised it to the skies. Bates was especially fond of watching the flowers unfurl petal by petal, "as if excited by some hidden spring, from the slender soft coppery buds." Not only are the flowers extremely fragrant, their lemony scent is magnified by the dark. Treat this plant as a biennial. It will readily reseed itself.

Oenothera pallida subsp. *trichocalyx* is usually marketed as *O. trichocalyx*. Like all but the biennials in the evening primrose clan, plants bloom the first year from seed. The white flowers open first in the evening remaining open throughout the day and turning pink with age but at night they produce a beautiful perfume in addition to their other assets. They are native to western Wyoming, Colorado, and Utah.

Oenothera rhombipetala is a biennial that forms a rosette of basal leaves that produce red stems a little over two feet high bearing many yellow flowers in a terminal spike. It is found in

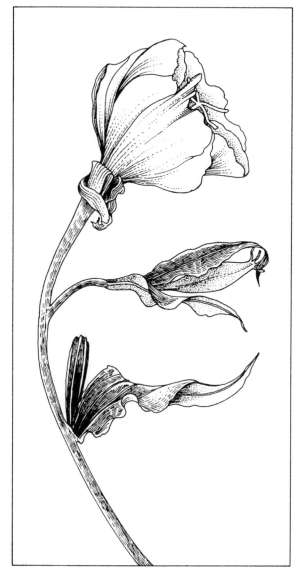

Oenothera odorata.

Texas and southern South Dakota.

Oenothera serrulata is now called *Calylophus serrulata*. Its common name is the tooth-leaved evening primrose because the small, narrow, dark green leaves are edged with tiny teeth. The bright yellow flowers are sometimes flecked with red and bloom on upright stems up to a foot tall and remain open for most of the day. The plants are Texas natives.

Oenothera speciosa (synonym, *Hartmannia speciosa*) has many names, including the white evening primrose, white buttercups, Mexican primrose, and amapola. The large three-inch white flowers are very showy and very fragrant at night. They open in the evening and stay open on cloudy days. The simple leaves are about four inches long and the plant can reach a height of some fourteen inches. *Oenothera berlandieri* is another name for this plant and is now considered to represent a pink or rose-colored form of *O. speciosa*. To add to the confusion over color, many white-flowered forms of this plant will turn pink after pollination. Like most evening primroses, *O. speciosa* will not survive extreme drought and at the same time will rot from excess moisture. It's native from Kansas through Texas.

Oenothera triloba (synonym, *Lavauxia triloba*) is also known as the Mexican primrose or sometimes buttecups. The low-growing plants have wavy, coarsely toothed leaves and bear two- to four-inch flowers of bright yellow with plants that flare from a narrow two-inch-long tube. Ms. Schulz wrote, "The flowers are wrongly called buttercups. The blossoms open in the evening, and remind one of lamps lit at dusk; or open again for a while on a misty morning." This is another Texas flower.

THE YUCCA

A great number of American plants were imported into Europe during the sixteenth century including tobacco, the potato, nasturtiums, sunflowers, and the yucca.

In 1629 John Parkinson (1567–1650), one of England's great botanists and the apothecary to King James I, published his monumental book *A Garden of Pleasant Flowers*. He wrote of the Indian yucca as, "a rare Indian plant [that] hath a great thicke tuberous roote (spreading in time in to many tuberous heads) from the head

whereof shooteth forth many long, hard, and guttered leaves, very sharpe pointed . . . of a grayish greene colour, which doe not fall away, but abide ever green on the plant." Along with this accurate description is a beautiful woodcut showing a branch of flowers engraved by a hand that is very fine indeed.

Following the description is the news that the yucca first came into England from the West Indies by way of a servant who gave it to his master, Thomas Edwards, an apothecary of Exeter, who kept it unto his death.

The word yucca is said to come from *yuca*, Spanish for manioc (*Manihot esculenta*), a major source of the bitter cassava, itself based on a Taino Indian word for this plant. Although used in error, the name stuck. There are about forty species native to the warmer regions of North America many of which have now spread throughout the country. They all belong to the Agavaceae family.

Most people are familiar with these very imposing plants with their sword-shaped leaves—often possessing very sharp points—since the yucca has been used in the landscape for hundreds of years. But few people realize that its tall spires of white, summer-blooming, bell-shaped flowers are pollinated in its native desert home at night by a species of moth. The same agent of pollination—though sometimes of a different species—does the job in many of the new areas where the yucca has settled.

Yuccas are not specifically night-blooming plants since the flowers are open during the daytime hours. But the flowers exhibit nyctinasty, the art of being nyctitropic or, in other words, they move about at night.

During the day, the white, six-petaled blossoms hang down like bells at rest. At dusk, they turn up to the evening sky, open wide, and release a sweet soapy smell to the night air. The reason for this behavior comes in the form of a particular genus of moths, the yucca moths, *Tegeticula yuccasella* (synonym, *Pronuba yuccasella*).

A yucca moth, *Tegeticula yuccasella*, hovers above the blossoms of an Adam's needle, *Yucca filamentosa*.

According to Holland's *The Moth Book*, in 1872 one Professor C. V. Riley discovered the relationship between these moths and the yuccas. He proved that the pollination of the flowers and the development of fruit were not an accidental meeting of insect and pollen but the result of an insect purposely collecting pollen with a mouth modified by nature for the task and the subsequent application of the pollen to the stigma of a yucca flower so that the yucca produce seed and the moth progeny have food upon hatching.

The female moths enter the yucca flowers at night and with a specially modified first joint of their extended jaw or maxillary palp are able to roll the pollen in a tight ball. This is held under the moth's head as it flies to another flower. Here the moth clings to a few stamenal filaments and with her ovipositor neatly lays her four or five eggs in the side of the pistil. She then pushes the pollen ball into the funnel end of the stigma and ensures pollination.

A few days later, the moth eggs hatch and larvae move into the blossom's ovary where they consume eighteen to twenty seeds, gaining enough strength to eat through the ovary's wall to the outside where, using a self-produced thread, they lower themselves to the ground where they burrow into the earth and a juvenile existence is completed and they eventually emerge as full-grown moths. The hundred or so seeds not consumed by the larvae continue to ripen, enough to guarantee the continued existence of the yucca. Since most yucca flowers are incapable of self-pollination as their pollen is so like putty and the anthers and stigma would never touch, without the intervention of this particular moth the plants would have perished eons ago.

Tegeticula yuccasella pollenizes the blossoms of *Yucca filamentosa* in the East and does the same in the West for *Y. angustifolia*, while *Y. brevifolia* (the Joshua tree) is pollinated by *T. synthetica* and *Y. whipplei* by *T. maculata*.

Because of their size, yuccas work well as specimen plants surrounded by lawn, or planted on the edges of slopes and banks. When not in bloom their architectural form is valuable in any traditional garden. But when the spikes of flowers are ready to glow in the moonlight and their perfume scents the air, these are magnificent plants for the evening.

Yuccas like a good garden soil but will cheerfully accept less. Once established, however, its long taproot—which does make the plant very drought-resistant—makes it difficult to move. Give the plants full sun. And watch your eyes and body when working around yuccas—the spines at leaf tips are needle-sharp and can do great damage.

All the plants listed below are hardy to USDA Zone 4. Do omit the Joshua tree from your garden; not only is it too big, but the flowers have a disagreeable odor.

Yucca baccata, the Spanish bayonet or the banana yucca is a clump-forming plant bearing leaves up to twenty-eight inches long. Its flower panicles are over two feet high with creamy white flowers, often tinged with pink. It's native to the Southwest.

Yucca filamentosa, Adam's needle, also grows in a clump. The spine-tipped leaves are gray-green, up to thirty inches long, and are edged with long, curly threads. The flower panicles can reach a height of fifteen feet but are usually much shorter. The blossoms are white but often tinged with reddish brown. It's a Southwest native.

Yucca glauca (synonym, *Y. angustifolia*), the soapweed, is another plant that forms clumps with leaves up to twenty-eight inches long. They are pale green and edged with thin off-white bands and marginal threads. The white flowers are tinged with green and bloom along a three-foot scape. There is a cultivar 'Rosea' with pink-tinged flowers. The plants come from the central United States.

The *Hesperaloe* is a small genus belonging to the Agavaceae family—*hesperos* is Latin for western and *aloe* refers to the family resemblance to the aloes. Of the three species recorded, two are interesting perennials for the American garden. Like the yuccas, they form grasslike clumps of leaves, the margins lined with threads. Like the yuccas, they are pollinated by moths of the deserts.

The first is often called the red yucca (*Hesperaloe parviflora*). The leaves can reach a length of three feet and in midsummer four-foot-tall spikes are lined with nodding, bell-like flowers usually pink but often of darker shades of red. As evening approaches, the flowers slowly turn to the sky but their color is such that except on moonlit nights, they would be better in an alba form—but I've yet to find one.

Hesperaloe nocturna is a ruly nocturnal plant, opening its inch-long flowers as the sun sets and the desert sky turns to flaming purple. These flowers are a greenish purple with a white interior especially suited to guide a moth's tongue deep inside the floral tube. Its soil must be well-drained and full sun is necessary for the best bloom. Unlike the yuccas, both these plants are hardy only to USDA Zone 6.

Another nocturnal American wildflower that closely resembles a yucca, also a member of the agave family, is known either as *Agave virginica* or *Manfreda virginica* and commonly as the false aloe. The dark green leaves form rosettes on an underground rhizome and can grow up to two feet long. The flowers are a greenish white, about two inches long, appearing in terminal racemes and opening their sweet-scented flowers in early evening. Plants are found in dry, well-drained soil in North Carolina, west to Texas, and as far north as Ohio. They are hardy only to USDA Zone 6.

OTHER NIGHT-FLOWERING WILD PLANTS

The following are American wildflowers that bloom in the late afternoon and evening. There are probably many, many more that I've overlooked or that have not come to my attention.

A few have not been included because they are

Hesperaloe parviflora.

plants like the sandbur (*Tribulus terrestris*), a plant with seedpods that can puncture rubber bicycle tires and bare feet, or perhaps the Devil's bouquet (*Nyctaginia capitata*), a strange plant that bears attractive bright scarlet flowers, but whose musky odor and sticky petals are decidedly unattractive—even though they both bloom at night.

Of the flowers included you will note that twelve out of fifteen genera come from the American Great Plains and the Southwest. This could be the result of the greater humidity or more rainfall in the eastern part of America impacting on moth populations or the presence of damp flower petals. I would welcome any other interpretations.

Sand Verbena

Abronia fragrans is the white abronia of the Rocky Mountains, native from Nebraska to Mexico and also known as sand verbena, heart's delight, and Lasater's pride. Stout stems bear ob-

The sand verbena, *Abronia fragrans*.

long leaves that are pubescent, hence the botanical name from the Greek, *abros*, or soft. Numerous white showy flowers, often touched by green, bloom in round-topped umbels that are reminiscent of verbenas—and miniature snowballs. The blossoms open in late afternoon and produce a delicate vanillalike fragrance that is intensified at night. Don't take them indoors as the perfume can be very powerful in a small, closed room. They remain open the following morning. The plants sprawl about and reach a height of about a foot, blooming in summer and early fall. There have been reports over the years of various plants bearing pink and sometimes a light lavender tint. Because the flowers have long tubes and a sweet fragrance, they are probably moth pollinated.

Since the plants like sandy, well-drained soil in full sun and are charming in bloom, the first two common names are readily understandable. The third refers to a Mr. Edward Lasater, who introduced the plant to Falfurias, Texas, in the 1920s. And there is one more important note about names: The genus *Abronia* was the first western plant to receive a scientific name when specimens were sent to the French Academy at Paris.

For years I tried to grow this plant from seed only to find that the outer coat of the seed should be removed before planting—by soaking the seed for a day—and even then germination can take a long time. They are hardy to USDA Zone 5 but need snow cover in areas with long periods of intense cold.

Angel's-Trumpet

Acleisanthes longiflora is a perennial wildflower first reported by botanist Asa Gray and commonly called angel's-trumpet and with good reason: The very long, white fragrant flowers closely resemble the type of instrument that one imagines would be played to announce an important heavenly event. The floral tube can be up to six inches

Angel's-trumpet, *Acleisanthes longifolia*.

or to a place at the back of the border where other more leafy plants can fill in the gaps. The name ringstem refers to a sticky area that surrounds the stem between nodes. The leaves are somewhat heart-shaped and bear small hairs.

Natives of western Texas, parts of Arizona, and Nevada, these plants are found growing in soil with a large gypsum content, so if growing them in the average garden soil, make sure the drainage is perfect and that it tests on the alkaline side. They are hardy to USDA Zone 7.

Like other four o'clocks, ringstem flowers look bedraggled by day but in late afternoon new flowers will open, ready for the night ahead.

long and points toward the heavens above. These flowers are known in Spanish as *yerba-de-la-rabia* or plant-of-the-rabies but I have been unable to find out the connection to this dreaded disease.

After sunrise the previous night's flowers bend over like melted candles while the long buds set to bloom the coming night look like dark greenish brown tubes waiting to open at dusk.

The moth-pollinated blossoms arise from trailing plants with long, vinelike forking stems and simple leaves that are very thick, about two inches long.

Angel's-trumpets need full sun and a perfectly drained alkaline soil laced with sand.

They are native from southeastern California down to Mexico and only hardy in areas where the ground does not freeze.

Southwestern Ringstem

The ringstem, *Anulocaulis leisolenus*, is a member of the four-o'clock family, bearing one-and-a-half-inch long, white or pale pink flowers at the top of rangy plants that can reach four feet. Its ungainly growth limits it either to the wild garden

The ringstem, *Anulocaulis leisolenus*.

The night-nodding bog dandelion, *Chaptalia tomentosa*.

The Night-Nodding Bog Dandelion

For a country supposedly opposed to poets and poetry—except in the guise of Tin Pan Alley—the poetic license that early settlers took with wildflower names is constantly surprising. The night-nodding bog dandelion is such a plant.

I first ran across reference to this flower in a battered copy of *The Natural Gardens of North Carolina* by B. W. Wells. There on page 444, one *Thyrsanthema semiflosculare* was described as a low perennial with three- to seven-inch flower stalks, each bearing a single terminal head that are erect in the sunshine but, like tired heads everywhere, begin to nod on dark days and at night. Since the description included a reference to white ray flowers, I knew it to be a form of daisy.

Ken Moore at the North Carolina Botanical Garden led me to the current name of *Chaptalia tomentosa*, and I found it described in the *Manual of the Vascular Flora of the Carolinas* (The University of North Carolina Press, 1964) as the sunbonnet flower—referring again to the nodding habit—and pictured in Rickett's *Wild Flowers of the United States for the Southeastern States* where it is described as growing in most pinelands on the coastal plain from North Carolina to Florida to Texas. The plant's habit of nodding at night would make it a great conversation piece for the evening garden but its natural range seems to put it out of reach for most evening gardens.

The night-nodding bog dandelion will only grow in bog conditions and is hardy to USDA Zone 7.

Wavy-Leaved Soap Plant

Amole, or the wavy-leaved soap plant (*Chlorogalum pomeridianum*), is a member of the lily family. The long narrow leaves can be two feet long and have wavy margins. They arise from a bulb that like bouncing bet, contains saponin and was used by early settlers as a shampoo. Indians roasted the bulbs to produce a sticky sap used to glue feathers to arrows.

The nocturnal flowers appear in clusters on top of a scape that can vary from two feet up to

The wavy-leaved soap plant, *Chlorogalum pomeridianum*.

Cottonweed, *Froelichia drummondii*.

ten feet high. The blossoms are white, sweet-smelling, and have six narrow petals that are reflexed, or bend backward. They are about one and a half inches wide.

Amole needs full sun to partial shade and well-drained soil. The plants are found from southwestern Oregon down to California. They are hardy only in areas where the ground does not freeze.

Cottonweed

Cottonweed is called snake cotton in some parts of Texas, where it is a native. The botanical name is *Froelichia drummondii*, with the genus named after a German botanist. These are annual plants just like their commercial relatives, globe amaranth and the cockscomb.

Cottonweed is a stiff and upright plant sometimes reaching five feet in height with the stems covered with brownish hairs. The white or pinkish flowers are small, about three sixteenths of an inch long, and are found in dense clusters at the ends of the stems. They are difficult to see

because they are imbedded in the midst of five small sepals, each covered with wooly hairs. The leaves are up to four inches long at the stem bottoms but are smaller and fewer at the stem tips.

The hairs are responsible for the plant's wooly appearance and at night the flowers assume a silvery cast, making them especially attractive when grouped in a wild garden.

They are hardy to USDA Zone 7, prefer full sun, and a well-drained soil.

The Gauras

Elizabeth Clark is a Texas garden writer who first introduced me to the scarlet gaura (*Gaura coccinea*). I had already used white gaura (*G. lindheimeri*) in the moonlight garden because its four-petaled white flowers winding up and down four-foot stems were especially attractive. But I had no idea that the beautiful scarlet gaura and an annual species, the lizard-tail gaura (*G. parviflora*) were night-blooming. Because spent flowers fall cleanly away from the stems, even in bouquets the new flowers continue to bloom. I

The scarlet gaura, *Gaura coccinea*.

had already noticed that rangy plants could easily be cut back to provide new and thicker growth. Knowing that *Gaura* is from the Greek word for superb is no surprise.

Miss Clark pointed out that Texas soil makes great bricks and brought the gauras to her garden because they were "tough as a boot and delicate as a butterfly," so I knew they would be undemanding plants.

Gauras are woody at the base, surrounded by a rosette of narrow simple leaves. The flowers of white gaura are an inch and a quarter wide, and, like many members of the evening primrose family, turn pink with age. Those of the scarlet gaura are smaller, about half an inch across, and begin as white, turn pink, and often become scarlet with age.

In the waning light of day, the scarlet gaura comes into its own. The intensely fragrant white to pink flowers attract a circus of moths and fill the evening garden with their sweet perfume.

In our garden white gaura is planted with boltonia (*Boltonia* 'Snowbank') so that as the flowers of the first begin to fade in late summer, the

white accents are picked up by the stars of the second. Scarlet gaura hovers above an edging of white caladiums. Give plants full sun in any resonably well-drained garden soil and you will find that once established, they are extremely drought-resistant.

Gaura parviflora, the lizard-tail gaura, is a winter annual or biennial and too weedy for all except a wild garden, although the tiny pink to rose flowers that open in the evening are pretty enough when seen close up.

The gauras' native range stretches from South Dakota to Texas, down to Mexico and east to North Carolina. They are hardy to USDA Zone 4.

Sweet-Scented Heliotrope

Sweet-scented heliotrope is an American member of a genus that contains the common heliotrope (*Heliotropium arborescens*), that fragrant summer flower from Peru. The American species name of *convolvulaceum* points to the fact that it looks more like a morning glory than most anything else. The white funnel-shaped flowers are very fragrant, up to an inch wide, and bloom on a sprawling annual plant. The hair stems bear ash gray leaves and never grow more than sixteen inches high. Here is another candidate for a rock garden setting, especially as it wants good drainage and full sun.

The blossoms open late in the afternoon and stay open until the hot sun of the following morning causes them to wilt.

Plants come from the deserts of western Texas and extend to southeastern California.

The Desert Lily

The desert lily, *Hesperocallis undulata*, is a one-species genus from southeastern California and southwestern Arizona and in this case *hesperos* (Greek for the evening star) refers to evening rather than the direction west and *calli* is Greek

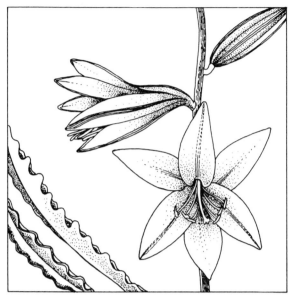

The desert lily, *Hesperocallis undulata*.

Granite snow, *Leptodactylon pungens*.

for beautiful. Strong stems grow to two feet and support two-foot leaves with such strongly waved edges they look like a fluted pie crust. The white funnel-shaped flowers have a greenish band on each petal and closely resemble Easter lilies. Although they are open during the day, the flowers become especially fragrant at dusk. Plants prefer full sun and well-drained soil. They are not hardy where the ground freezes.

Evening Snow and Granite Snow

At one time evening snow and granite snow were both members of the *Gilia* species but botanists have moved them to other genera. But both flower in late afternoon and early evening.

Evening snow (*Linanthus dichotomus*), a native of California, Nevada, and Arizona, is an annual plant that prefers an area with full sun in soil that is basically poor, but laced with sand or gravel so that the roots have perfect drainage. The flowers appear in the spring and have satiny petals of white with a brown or purple throat and are one and a quarter inches long. For three

days they open in the evening, remain open all night, and close by day.

Granite snow (*Leptodactylon pungens*) is a perennial rather like a small shrub reaching a sprawling height of not more than a foot and covered with prickly, needlelike leaves. At dusk honey-fragrant and funnel-shaped flowers about three quarters of an inch long begin to open in colors of off-white or pink. Claude Barr writing in *Jewels of the Plains* suggests that gardeners with a taste for knickknacks might like this flower. It likes the same conditions as evening snow, being native from southern California to the Rocky Mountains and New Mexico. Granite snow is hardy to USDA Zone 4.

Evening Stars

For years I wanted to grow the annual flower *Mentzelia lindleyi* since all the garden books said it was a spectacular night-blooming plant. Finally I received seed and managed to grow three seedlings that were promptly moved, after frost danger was past, to the evening garden. Buds swelled and I waited. Then one morning in July, they bloomed. Note, one morning. Day after day I waited for just one flower to open at dusk, or even in late afternoon. No luck.

But the genus did not let me down—just one species. Other members of the clan do bloom in late afternoon and when dusk comes around. The petals resemble crushed silk and they have a light but sweet fragrance. Mentzelias are perennials especially suited for a rock garden site because they must have full sun and perfect drainage to succeed.

I've found no mention of pollinators in any of my references but assume that desert bugs and beetles do the job, climbing about the pollen-bedecked anthers after the hot sun has set and the evening air has cooled. The plants come from Texas, Colorado, and Nebraska.

Mentzelia nuda is known as star flower, stick-leaf, and good woman, the last two names refer-ring to the small Velcrolike hairs that cover the simple, alternate leaves and stick to one like, ap-parently, a good woman would. The genus is named for Christian Mentzel (1622–1701), a German botanist.

The plants grow from one to three feet high and produce many pale, starry flowers that open in the evening and close the next morning. Flower color is creamy yellow to golden yellow and the two-inch-wide blossoms have many stamens of different lengths.

Mentzelia decapetala, the evening star or stick-leaf, bears large, ten-petaled creamy white star-like blossoms up to four inches wide, and opens at sundown. Like many perennials, they will not bloom until the second year. Plants can reach a height of three feet. All the mentzelias are hardy to USDA Zone 5.

Umbrellaworts, the Prairie Four-O'clocks

There are a number of native Americans that be-long to the four-o'clock family in addition to the

The stickleaf, *Mentzelia decapetala*.

most famous of all, the original marvel of Peru (*Mirabilis jalapa*). The Peruvian member of the clan is covered on page 75 but two important Americans are treated below.

Mirabilis multiflora is a plant in many ways superior to others in the genus. The flowers open in late afternoon and on cloudy days, closing the next morning but the color of the flowers is a brighter purple-rose than that found even in cul-tivars of *M. jalapa*, and they are larger, too. The plant itself is large with branchings capable of making a circular mound four feet wide and up to twenty inches high. Because the flowers open in succession, the plants are often smothered in color, the blooms continuing throughout the summer. And unlike *M. jalapa*, this plant is hardy to USDA Zone 5.

Mirabilis nyctaginea, or in the older books, *Allionia nyctaginea*, has the common name um-brellawort because the developing seedpods re-semble an umbrella with several warty seeds fastened at the center. The plants reach a two-foot height and are not as attractive as *M. mul-tiflora*, but are still worth having around for the

The prairie four-o'clock, *Mirabilis multiflora*.

The multibloom tephrosia, *Tephrosia onobrychoides*.

small clusters of pink or purple flowers that open later in the evening and drop off the plants early the next morning. Hardy to USDA Zone 5, both these mirabilises are found from Montana to Wisconsin and south to Mexico. They will adapt to any well-drained garden soil in full sun.

Multibloom Tephrosia

Multibloom tephrosia or *Tephrosia onobry-choides* is a night-blooming member of the pea family. The snow-white pealike flowers open in late evening and are tightly closed by morning of the next day unless the sun is hidden behind clouds. Shortly before closing, the flowers turn a beautiful shade of rosy pink. Often both colors are found on the same plant.

The botanical name is from the Greek word, *tephros,* or ash-colored, referring to the color of the leaves. Some of the species were used by Caribbean natives to poison fish and a few yield the insecticide rotenone but in very small amounts. Because of the rotenone content some gardeners may be susceptible to contact dermatitis

from touching the leaves or roots so care is advised.

Plants usually grow upright to about two feet but can sprawl. The leaves are a little over two inches long and have thirteen to twenty-five small leaflets.

Tephrosias are perennials but grow readily from seed, preferring well-drained soil in full sun and are found in the wild along fencerows and the edges of woodlots and thickets in Texas. They are hardy to USDA Zone 6.

Plants are found throughout Texas.

Rain Lilies

The rain lilies, field lilies, and prairie lilies belong to the genus *Zephyranthes* and are still called *Cooperia* in older reference books. I must confess I've only seen them grown in pots but even just a few blossoms are exquisite. When you see a photograph of a rain-washed desert plain covered from near to far with thousands of these fragile flowers, you begin to understand how beautiful something can be. The common name rain lily

119

The rain lily, *Zephyranthes pendunculata.*

refs to their blooming within twenty-four hours of a heavy rain.

The plants were first discovered in Texas by a Scottish plant explorer, Thomas Drummond (1780–1835), who is most famous for his discovery of *Phlox drummondii*, the annual phlox that is parent to a vast number of cultivars including the ever-popular star phloxes of summer bedding fame.

In parts of the country where frost can freeze the bulbs, they are best grown in pots, where they will bloom in July. After blooming is finished, let the foliage ripen and die. Keep the bulbs in a warm place and give them six months rest before adding water to start the cycle again. Or they can be planted out in the garden when the danger of frost is past, about three inches deep, in well-drained soil with added compost. The leaves are grasslike with parallel veins and up to a foot long. Make sure you plant them in an accessible spot like the top of a wall or up in the crevices of a large rock so you can get close to the flowers. Again, when foliage as ripened and died, collect the bulbs and keep them in a warm, dry place until next season.

Zephyranthes drummondii and *Z. pedunculata* are the only members of the genus for the evening garden. The first produces solitary, lily-like white flowers on stalks up to a foot high. The flowers open in the cool of the evening and produce a sweet spicy aroma. They begin to turn pink by morning and, except on cloudy days, wither by early afternoon. The second species blooms later in the summer and bears three-inch-long pink flowers on five-inch scapes with the same sweet fragrance.

CHAPTER EIGHT

WATER GARDENS AND WATER LILIES OF THE EVENING

All through the deep blue night
The fountain sang alone;
It sang to the drowsy heart
Of the satyr carved in stone.

The fountain sang and sang
But the satyr never stirred—
Only the great white moon
In the empty heaven heard.

SARA TEASDALE, *The Fountain*

Years ago when we began collecting night-blooming plants, I bought a used fiberglass pool. The design was called Palette, and the shape resembled the outline of an artist's paint tray. The fiberglass was black and it measured about five by three feet and was fifteen inches deep, holding some seventy-five gallons of water.

Digging the hole and working my way through the compacted shale and rock that were first brought to our backyard by a glacier was quite a job. But after the installation was finished, the pool's edge hidden underneath a ring of field-stones and the pool itself filled, the sight of an evening sky reflected in the ripples made all the work worthwhile. We had no limestone or granite satyr and the rippling fountain was a so-called lily bubbler, a lead ornament made in the shape of an open water lily that worked off a very cheap electric pump, but that great white moon above immediately became two, the second sparkling on the water's surface.

Even the soft sounds of water trickling from a hose casually wound among some rocks or the splashing of a small fountain set in the center of a partially buried plastic wash-tub can add a whole new set of wonders to the evening garden.

"Water in a landscape is, as a mirror to a room," wrote Neltje Blanchan in *The American Flower Garden*, "the feature that doubles and enhances all its charms. Whoever may possess a lake, a pond, or a pool to catch the sunbeams, duplicate the trees and flowers on its bank, reflect the moon, and multiply the stars, surely will."

BUILDING A WATER GARDEN

While the evils of plastic in the environment are almost beyond count, there have been a number of enjoyable benefits, too. One of these is the

The giant water lily, *Victoria amazonica*.

development of PVC sheeting or butyl rubber liners for the easy construction of garden pools; a garden can now include a pond of decent size for a very reasonable price without hiring a team of excavators, building complex forms, and supporting a parade of workers to mix and pour concrete. And if the gardener does not have the time to properly install such a pool, he or she need only excavate a small hole and set within it one of the many free-form fiberglass pools like the one we used as our first source of water in the garden.

If you live in a zoned community, remember that it is a good idea to check with local authorities about any regulations concerning pools. Usually no fencing is required for pools twenty-four inches deep or less as they are considered safe for children and animals. But if you plan a pool deeper than thirty inches, fencing might be required for safety.

PVC liners come in many thicknesses but I suggest a minimum of sixteen mil. Most nurseries devoted to water gardens usually sell single ply twenty mil with a guarantee of seven to ten years of use and double ply thirty-two mil with a fifteen- to twenty-year life estimate. Butyl rubber liners are black, have an estimated life span of thirty years, and are more expensive.

The color of both types is usually black or green. Remember to eschew turquoise! It is unsuitable for the daytime since your pool will resemble the facilities at a second-rate motel and be off-putting at night. With black there is no color visible except that of the water.

As to cost, a thirteen by thirteen foot thirty-two mil PVC liner will cost in the neighborhood of $180 and when installed will give you a nine-by-nine-foot pool, eighteen inches deep.

If you happen to inherit an old cracked concrete pond, a new PVC liner can be glued to the old surface and everything will be as new. A stone coping will be needed to cover the liner's flap at the top of the old concrete edge.

For a pool choose a level spot that receives at least a half day of full sun. Shade pools are all right, too, but without at least three hours of direct sun will be unable to support blooming tropical, or for that matter, hardy water lilies.

If possible, locate your pond close enough to an electric outlet to allow for the installation of a pump, not only to filter the water but perhaps to support a small fountain or a set of lights to illuminate the pool at night. Usually local electric codes require a minimum setback of six feet from the outlet to the pool's edge.

A simple rule of thumb for figuring how much liner to buy is to add twice the depth to your maximum width, plus two feet, to allow a one-foot overlap on each side. Do the same for the length.

To make your pool, first dig a hole eighteen inches deep using a garden hose to lay out the shape. Most pond owners sadly report that their first pond was too small. So if in doubt about eventual size, think big. With water gardening, bigger ponds are easier to balance and keep clean than smaller ponds.

Use a line and line-level to make sure your excavation is level; this is the time to be careful. Nothing is more disconcerting than a pond where, when full, the water runs over the edge at one end and exposes two to three inches of liner at the other.

Remove all the rocks, pebbles, or other debris. If you plan on growing some bog plants it's a good idea to excavate a shelf, about eight inches wide and ten inches below the top edge. It need not completely extend around the entire pool.

Make sure all the sides slope toward the center rather than being straight up and down, and slope the bottom slightly to one end to help in future cleanings. One inch for every ten to twelve inches is excellent. Also, make a two- to three-inch depression at the lower end to hold the pump. This allows the pump to remove the maximum amount of water when in operation.

Now, using a sharp shovel cut a shallow twelve- to fifteen-inch trench around the edge to hold the excess liner. Next spread a half-inch layer of sand on the bottom and work the sand up the sides to fill any holes left by removed stones. If you have especially rocky soil, put down a layer of .002-inch commercial building polyethylene, an old carpet, or a layer of geotextile over the sand before you lay the liner.

Drape the liner into the hole, placing bricks or smooth stones on the sides to hold it down. Now start filling it with water. As the pool fills, occasionally remove the stones to allow the liner to fit tightly into the hole. After the pool is full, trim the exposed liner to an eight-inch overhang and cover that with a layer of fieldstone slabs or other stone. If you want a formal look, you could lay stone paving on a bed of mortar, remembering to use metal reinforcement if you garden in a frost belt.

If you plan to add fish—always a good idea—let the water settle for a week before they join in the swim.

Algae in the Water

During the first few weeks of life, the pond looks worse every day since algae will find its way into any new pond or container of water. About sixty percent of the pond's surface should be covered with lily pads by midsummer in order to cut down on the sunlight that prods the algae to growth. Use one bunch of submerged plants for every one to two square feet of surface area to help naturally reduce the algae since these water plants compete with algae for nutrients in the water and usually starve algae out after the sixth week of pond life. Fish will help, too. And they are necessary to eat any mosquito larvae that will soon find the water.

It's important to realize that chlorinated water is bad for plants and fish, although treated drinking water will not bother plants. Regular chlorine will dissipate if the water is left to sit for forty-eight hours or so, depending on the size of the container and the water temperature.

But a new problem is now on the horizon.

Many city water plants are converting to chloramine, a chemical that does not dissipate. This new form of chlorine kills fish slowly over weeks instead of in days or hours. So it's important to check with your public water department to see what they use. If they say chloramine, you can treat your pond water with a chemical called DeChlor, available from most water garden nurseries, before putting in your plants and fish.

If you like your water clear, you can use a biological filter—they use bacteria to clean the water—connected to an electric pump to keep the water sparkling. Mechanical filters rely entirely upon filter wraps to do the job and need a lot of help from submerged plants to keep the water clear. In any event, when fish are added and the plants have a chance to balance themselves, the water will start to clear, usually in four to six weeks.

You can use a siphon to empty the pool at summer's end, but such an installation is usually perfectly all right to leave all year round.

Tips on Planting Aquatic Plants and Pools

When planting any of the following water plants, do not use commercial potting soils or mixes as they often contain various materials such as vermiculite, perlite, and numerous other fillers that immediately float and make the water's surface resemble a liquid landfill. Instead, use good garden topsoil that's on the heavy side.

Instead of tossing soil directly on the pool's bottom, put both water lilies and other water plants into individual pots, either clay, plastic, or one of the new fiberboard pots. Cover any pot drainage holes with a few sheets of newspaper to prevent any soil leaks.

To plant water lilies, fill the container half full with topsoil, carefully set the rootstock on the soil, then add more soil, pushing it around the roots, keeping the crown free of soil. Cover the soil with a half inch of pea gravel or very small stones, still keeping the crown uncovered. This not only keeps fish from stirring up mud but keeps the dirt from riling the water. Next saturate the pot with water. Gently lower the tub into the water.

Today most water garden nurseries grow their lilies at the same depth that gardeners usually do. Set the blooming or budded plants at the prescribed depth, making sure that the stems of the lily pads are long enough so they float on the water's surface. Set the containers on bricks or stone piles if you need to. As the plants grow, you can remove the supports to maintain the correct level.

To plant bog plants, use good garden topsoil with some humus added. Fill the container with soil, then push in the roots of the plant, tamping the soil and covering the surface with one inch of pea gravel or small stones. Saturate the pot with water, then lower it gently into the pool or pond, setting the plant at the correct water depth. Use bricks or fieldstones to adjust the plant to the appropriate level.

A note of caution: It sounds like a good idea to use natural muck from a swamp or bog as a planting mix but that type of dirt contains undecayed matter and while continuing to decompose will produce gases, causing parts of it to float.

Never plant out tropicals until the temperature of the water is 70°F or above. And remember that water lilies will go into a rest period if confronted with a sudden drop in water temperature, so when changing water in an ornamental pool make sure to cut the cold water by mixing it with lukewarm water.

Finally, be sure to remove dead and dying leaves. If you don't, bacteria will soon begin their time-honored job of decay and the rotting vegetation will quickly cloud and foul the water— and such debris is not too aesthetic either. And here's a word to the wise: Don't put this job off for another day. It's probably the only unpleasant activity associated with water gardening.

Fertilizers

Over the years I've often run out of the commercial fertilizing tablets designed for feeding water lilies. My alternative was to take a handful of 5-10-5 granular fertilizer and put it in cheesecloth or a few layers of newspaper, making a little ball that I pushed into the soil of the pots. But the formula of the commercial tablets is 10-14-8, a combination best suited for water lilies, so I always eventually replaced the tablets. The amount of fertilizer needed depends on the size of the containers so just follow directions on the package. Fertilizing is done on a monthly basis during late spring and summer, when the plants are actively growing.

THE TROPICAL WATER LILIES

Water lilies have been in gardens since the time of the ancient Egyptians. Not only were they used for religious ceremonies, the flowers decorated homes and dinner tables. When important guests arrived, they were given an Egyptian lotus, the men to hold and the women to wear in their hair. These were not the familiar lotuses (*Nelumbo* spp.) of Buddhist lore, for they bloom only during the day, but two species of water lilies. One, *Nymphaea lotus*, bears white, night-blooming flowers perfect for evening celebrations, and the other, *N. caerulea*, is a pale blue species that opens in the daytime. The Romans, by-the-by, used the word lotus for both *Nelumbo* and *Nymphaea*.

Today night-blooming Egyptian water lilies are hard to come by, but for the evening garden we now have a large selection of tropical water lilies. These are tender plants and in climate zones colder than USDA Zone 10, they are usually treated as disposable annual flowers. This is unfortunate since the tubers can easily be taken up and stored underwater in a warm greenhouse— or a warm basement—and with the increasing daylight of spring new leaves will appear.

The flowers described below are all night-blooming, opening soon after sunset or at nightfall—the time varies greatly from June 21 to October 21—remaining open until nine A.M. to noon of the following day. If the sky is overcast, they will remain open until early afternoon. The flowers will last three days. The very fragrant blossoms stand above the water's surface and will bloom all summer. Tropicals all make excellent cut flowers. Remember that day-blooming flowers will not complement the evening garden since they open in midmorning and close tightly by late afternoon.

Most plants will produce a large number of leaves—usually up to two feet wide—that lie flat upon the water. These plants need room to spread out but most will adapt to cramped quarters and still bloom.

Those designated full sun will need five to six hours of direct sunlight in order to prosper and bloom. If marked partial sun, they will need at least three hours of direct sun. All require at least six inches of water above the rootstock.

All of the water lilies described below belong to the genus *Nymphaea*. At one time water lily nurseries offered many species; *N.* × *omarana* with magenta blossoms and *N.* × *sturtevantii* bearing bright pink flowers, both come to mind. An old catalog from the early 1900s describes *N.* × *devoniensis* as a single plant that will bear as many as thirty-six flowers and buds at one time. It is a hybrid that first flowered at Chatsworth in 1851 and was named for the Duke of Devonshire. Over the years, however, many such flowers have been replaced by new cultivars.

The following plants bear flowers in various shades of white:

'Juno' has especially beautiful and large, pure white flowers, and needs (at minimum) a bit less than five hours of sun to bloom. The leaves are green. Plants will spread to twelve square feet and grow well in shallower water, with a minimum of ten inches.

'Wood's White Knight' is a hybrid developed from 'Sir Galahad' and 'Missouri' by hybridizer Jack Wood of El Rancho Tropi-Cal and combines the best traits of both parents, resulting in a four-star water lily bearing vanilla-white petals surrounding lemon-tipped stamens. The green leaves have a deckled edge. It can spread well over six square feet and needs a ten-quart or larger tub in full or partial sun.

'Sir Galahad' bears pure white petals surrounding a golden center that are held above parrot green leaves with scalloped edges. Although it will adapt to a small or large container, it's best in a ten-quart or larger tub in full or partial sun.

'Missouri' was originally developed by George H. Pring, an early director of the Missouri Botanical Garden in St. Louis, a horticulturist who was responsible for introducing a number of tropical water lily cultivars to the trade. This particular lily has six- to eight-inch-wide blossoms of creamy white held high on slim stems. The flowers will open late in the evening following sunset, the exact time varying from spring to fall. They last three days and on the last day in the fall or on cool and cloudy days, will be open for twenty-four hours. The rust-colored leaves turn green with age. Unlike most night-blooming water lilies, 'Missouri' will bloom in a winter greenhouse. Use at least a ten-quart tub for planting and if given the room, this plant will spread over twelve square feet. If you keep the leaves down to five or six, it will cover less water. This water lily will adapt to full or partial sun.

'Trudy Slocum' is a many-petaled white with a gold center and very, very fragrant. The flowers may stay open on cool overcast autumn days. The leaves are green. Use a ten-quart or larger container and the plants will spread up to twelve feet. Provide partial sun.

The following water lilies are classified as rose-red:

'Emily Grant Hutchings' has clusters of light rose-red flowers that open late in the evening, following sundown. The blossoms hover like

'Sir Galahad', a white tropical water lily cultivar.

warm, glowing jewels held above foliage that has a decided bronze cast. The plants cover an area of six to twelve feet, depending on the size of the pond and growing conditions, but will adjust to a ten-quart container in full or partial sun. It is the least likely of the water lilies I've described to react adversely to cooler water. It's been gracing water gardens since 1922 and is one of the night-bloomers that will overwinter in a greenhouse and continue to bloom.

'H. C. Haarstick' is an especially fine plant blooming with six- to seven-inch-wide, rose-red flowers with a hint of purple at the base of the petals and surrounding red-gold stamens. The foliage has a bronze cast. This lily will spread over twelve square feet and wants full sun but will flower in the winter if protected from cold, since water temperatures below 70°F will send it into dormancy. A ten-quart container or larger is best.

'Red Flare' bears brilliant vermillion petals surrounding deep maroon stamens, all in contrast to its mahogany-red foliage. This beautiful, cup-shaped flower will continue to bloom in the winter if given greenhouse protection. When well-grown, this plant will spread over twelve square feet. Provide full sun and use at least a ten-quart container.

'Maroon Beauty' matches maroon-red flowers and bronze-red foliage but needs full sun to bloom well. Plant spread is six to twelve square feet. Use an eight-quart container.

'Mrs. John A. Wood' has petals of maroon, almost the same hue as the leaves. Full sun is best and the roots will adapt to most any container but prefer an eight-quart minimum. It's perfect for a small pool.

'Antares' is a cultivar developed by Patrick Nutt at Longwood Gardens. The flower is a cross between 'H. C. Haarstick' and 'Emily Grant Hutchings'. The deep red flowers are seven to eight inches wide. The foliage is green, suffused with purple, and the pads are between fourteen and eighteen inches across. Use a ten-quart container in full sun.

The following water lilies are classified as pink:

'Mrs. George C. Hitchcock' has always been termed a stunning cultivar bearing large pink flowers that open wide and surround orange stamens. The blossoms hover over maroon foliage and bloom late into the season. Full sun is best and use a ten-quart container.

'Texas Shell Pink' remains one of the best night-blooming tropicals with its large shell-pink flowers and orange-yellow stamens. The foliage is green and the plant will spread over six to twelve square feet. Provide full or partial sun and use a ten-quart container.

Nymphaea × sturtevantii is an inhabitant of older water gardens and was described by Peter Bisset in *The Book of Water Gardening* as having eight- to twelve-inch-wide flowers of a beautiful rosy pink, the broad petals giving the flower a fine cup shape. The stamens are orange-brown in color and the large leaves are a fine bronzy green with wavy edges. Mr. Bisset recommended planting these water lilies directly in the bottom of a large pond, spacing the plants about eight feet apart and giving them full sun.

The Amazon water lily, *Nymphaea amazonum*, is more for the collector of oddities than the average evening gardener. In the 1907 *Waterlilies and How to Grow Them*, authors Henry S. Conard and Henri Hus described this flower's beginning as a bud rising above the water's surface on day one. Between three and four A.M. of day two, it opens to a narrow cup shape, and closes before six A.M. On day three, it begins to open about 6:30 P.M., and by eight it has four white petals spread out around a firm white bud. There it remains until 3:30 A.M., when the whole flower bursts into bloom and remains fully open for about fifteen minutes. By six A.M., it is tightly closed and already retreating into the water. They point out that the flower would most likely appeal to a night watchman.

The Largest Water Lily in the World

The blossoms of the giant water lily (*Victoria amazonica*) are somewhat larger than most and its leaves are best described as gigantic. In fact, Richard Spruce (1817–1893), the famous Amazon explorer, said of this, the grandest of the water lilies that ". . . when viewed from the bank above, [it resembles] a number of green tea-trays floating, with here and there a bouquet protruding between them." He went on to write that the six-foot-wide leaves looked like cast-iron constructions just taken from the blast furnace. Besides being called the giant water lily, other popular names include the water-platter and *Mayz de l'Eau*, or water maize or water corn.

Peter Bisset in *The Book of Water Gardening*, wrote that "the flowers, measuring from eight to fifteen inches across, open at dusk and remain open all night, partly closing about 10:30 A.M., and again opening at nightfall. The color of the flower when first expanding is a pure creamy white gradually changing, as the flower grows older, to pink, and then to deep purplish red on the second night." Before blooming, the pear-shaped buds are about eight inches in length, and large flowers can have up to sixty petals.

But its best quality is the nighttime fragrance, a sweet odor of pineapple with a dash of apples and peaches thrown in for good measure. The fragrance drifts across the water's surface and throughout the garden, and at times, like any perfume, can become almost overpowering.

The second evening the flowers open an hour or so earlier than the night before and they lose their scent. By the second morning, nothing is left but a half-wilted pile of petals, and during the day it sinks quietly into the water.

The giant water lily's leaves resemble rimmed platters of a rich green while the lower surface has a decided purplish cast. Kew Gardens has clocked the growth of these leaves at one square inch per minute. A number of prominent, spiny veins divide the leaves into quite regular compartments like the ribs at the bottom of the World Trade Center in Manhattan.

Because these spiny veins are full of air and extend to a raised lip that surrounds the entire leaf margin, each leaf becomes a flat-bottomed raft and will hold a reasonably heavy load if that load is evenly distributed over the surface. Some sources report that *Victoria cruziana* can support up to 150 pounds. But while small children and their pets float with ease, the popular Edwardian pictures of a leaf embellished with a charming girl playing a violin or some adult with a parasol were really faked, the lily pad usually having been supported by an underwater chair.

Today the giant night-blooming water lily flowers in water gardens around the world but at one time it was only found where swirling river waters slowed to just moving currents and in lagoons along the banks of various South American rivers. And judging from the number of plant explorers who literally rowed over this prize, it's amazing that it took so long to reach commerce.

This Brobdingagian's long history began in 1801 when it was initially found by a little-known Bohemian, one Thaddaeus Haenke (1761–1817), a doctor hired by the Spanish government to work in Peru as a mineralogist. Haenke's discovery died with him and the plant was not described again until 1820 when Aimé Bonpland (1773–1858), a French botanist and explorer who was traveling where the Parana and Paraguay rivers converge in Argentina, again found the plant.

Bonpland was involved in investigations concerning the maté tree (*Ilex paraguariensis*), a tree whose leaves were used to make a tea considered valuable to the mine workers of Peru, since its high caffeine content probably allowed them to work long hours underground. The tea monopoly was controlled by the Jesuits, who sold it in powdered form so that nobody could identify the leaves.

Shortly after finding the water lily, Bonpland was taken prisoner for nine years by a consortium out to overthrow the Jesuits. In 1830 he was released, whereupon he married a native woman, and died in 1858 at the age of eighty-five.

Another French explorer/scientist, Alcide Charles Victor Déssalines d'Orbigny, found the plant in 1827 at Corrientes in Argentina and again in 1833 in Bolivia. In 1840 he found the Santa Cruz water lily, *Victoria cruziana*, the only other species ever recorded, also at Corrientes. This is the species that was first introduced to American gardens in 1894. Because it succeeds at lower temperatures than *V. amazonica*, it is usually recommended for outdoor culture in cooler climates. Unfortunately, d'Orbigny waited too long to announce his findings and is overlooked by most reference books.

Next, a German doctor, Eduard Friedrich Poeppig (1798–1868), immediately after receiving his medical degree, sailed for South America where he became the first scientist to report the existence of glaciers in the Andes. In 1832, while canoeing along the Igaripes River—a tributary of the Amazon—he, too, found the giant water lily and, upon his return to Leipzig, named the plant *Euryale amazonica*. He mistakenly thought it to be allied to the *Euryale ferox*, the prickly water lily of Japan and China. While the two plants are very similar, each has a genus of its own.

Enter Sir Robert Hermann Schomburgk (1804–1865). In 1836, while traveling up the Berbice River in British Guyana, he found *Victoria* and immediately sent specimens to Kew Gardens. In 1837 Kew named the flower *Victoria regia* in honor of the Queen. But according to the rules of priority in naming, the first person to name a plant is considered the final authority, so the honor went to Poeppig and the species became

Euryale ferox, the prickly water lily.

amazonica. Sir Robert was the first to note that a certain type of beetle lived within the flowers and this insect is now considered one of the plant's pollinators. These insects are attracted by the blossom's perfume and remain inside when the petals close over during the day. They are released on the second night.

Then Thomas Bridges (1807–1865) came upon the scene. This young man left Norfolk, England, for Valparaiso, Chile, where he began his horticultural career by working as a brewer of beer until collecting enough money to start plant explorations. In 1845 on the Yacuma River in Bolivia, a tributary of the Mamoré, he found and collected seeds of *amazonica* that he returned to London carefully packed in red clay where they were sold to various gardeners for two shillings apiece. Unfortunately only two seeds germinated and those seedlings died before flowering.

Finally, in 1849 two physicians named Rodie and Luckie found *amazonica* growing in the Essequibo River of Guyana and sent seeds back to Kew, this time packed in water. On November 8 of the same year, the first plant bloomed at Chatsworth House under the care of Joseph Paxton (1802–1865), the gardener and architect. It was a horticultural sensation!

Paxton built a special house for the water lily, the design inspired by the rib structure of the leaf. He later designed the famous Crystal Palace for the Great Exhibition of 1851 and here, too, the veining of the leaves "like transverse girders and supports," were used as an inspiration for this, the biggest glasshouse ever built.

The *Illustrated London News* for November 17, 1849, reported that one leaf could hold up Paxton's seven-year-old daughter and that she "was borne up for some time in perfect safety."

One Douglas Jerrold was quoted as saying:

> On unbent leaf in fairy guise,
> Reflected in the water,
> Beloved, admired by hearts and eyes,
> Stands Annie, Paxton's daughter—

From Kew Gardens seed went to Europe and America. The first plant in the United States grew in the garden of Mr. Caleb Cope of Philadelphia and flowered on August 21, 1851.

GROWING THE GIANT WATER LILY

We had a pond that covered over one and a half acres and was ten feet deep at the center when we lived in upstate New York, and for two seasons we grew *Victoria cruziana*. Besides the ability of *V. cruziana* to withstand cooler water, it can be readily distinguished from *V. amazonica* by its floral sepals since these are smooth, not spiny as in *amazonica*. There is also a pronounced difference in the color of the leaves: when young, *cruziana*'s are green with a purplish tinge, in addition to having a more robust appearance.

I wondered why the plant never bloomed; then I realized that the pond was partially fed by a very cold spring and never got warm enough for flowers to appear before the plant was cut back by the first frosts of September.

There is a hybrid between *Victoria cruziana*

and *V. amazonica*, developed by Patrick Nutt of the famous Longwood Gardens in Pennsylvania. It tolerates cooler water temperatures than *V. amazonica* and has a red tinge to the outside rim of the leaves. In addition, the sepals have spines at the tips.

Not all the suppliers of aquatic plants carry the various giant water lilies, and some have years when they do and years when they don't. As a result, you might have to search around a bit. Most botanical gardens have giant water lilies on summer display, so perhaps the resident horticulturist might be willing to let a gardener have a few seeds.

Don't attempt growing this plant unless you have a pond at least two feet deep and no less than fifteen or twenty feet across. There is room for experimentation, however, since blooming plants have been reported with only eight inches of water above their soil. And the water temperature must be above 70°F.

STARTING FROM SEED

Both species of *Victoria* produce fruit described as being about the size of a man's head and containing many pea-size, brownish seeds which native South Americans use to make pastries. Authors Conard and Hus wrote that seeds at that time retailed for twenty-five cents apiece and could be found at any good seed house where they were shipped to customers in small glass tubes filled with water.

They also advised the grower to keep the water at no less than 60°F and never to let the temperature go higher than 70°F. A small heater from a tropical fish store will keep the water at the right temperature.

Nick the seeds with a file just as you would with morning glory or canna seeds. Sow the seeds in small clay or plastic pots, pushing them into—but not covering them with—heavy garden loam. The pot should then be submerged in a water-filled container—an old glass fish aquarium works best—until the top of it is under two or three inches of water. Seed should be sown four months before the lilies are to be planted out.

Keep the tank in a bright spot and germination will usually begin within a week to ten days but most of the seeds will take a month before the first root breaks out of the seed coat and the first threadlike seed leaf appears.

When the second arrow-shaped leaf appears, transplant the seedlings to three-inch pots, using a mix of heavy garden loam, and continue to keep the pots underwater. Repot when the first floating leaf appears and continue to repot as the plants become larger, eventually using fifteen-inch pots.

Take the plants out to the pond when the water warms to 75°F, about May 20 in St. Louis, early June in Philadelphia, and toward the end of June farther north.

PLANTING OUT

Now comes the hard part. Using wooden two-by-fours and planking (if you wish to continue growing these plants over a number of summers, invest in cypress), make a tub about two feet square and at least twelve to eighteen inches deep to hold the roots. Fill with heavy garden loam. If you haven't the time or patience to build a container, buy a thirty-quart plastic tub from a water garden supply house. If using a wooden tub, start this a few weeks before planting out the water lily roots so the wood has a chance to soak up enough water so it won't float. Place the tub in the pond keeping the top of it just above the water's surface. This can be done by placing the four box corners on a stack of fieldstones or bricks.

After carefully planting the plant's roots up to the neck, cover the dirt with a layer of crushed gravel to keep the fish from riling up the soil. Remove a brick or stone every three days or so until the top of the container is eighteen inches below the surface of the water. A bathing suit or fly-fishing waders are convenient for this task. Following this treatment, the water lily will bloom the first year.

Over the summer, fertilize two or three times a month using commercial tablets available from water lily nurseries or your own mix as described on page 125.

This seems like a lot of trouble for just a flower—but what a flower! When you plan a garden party using *Victoria* as a centerpiece, your friends will talk about it for years.

OTHER PLANTS FOR THE EVENING WATER GARDEN

There are a number of white flowers that are perfect for the evening water garden. *Chelone*

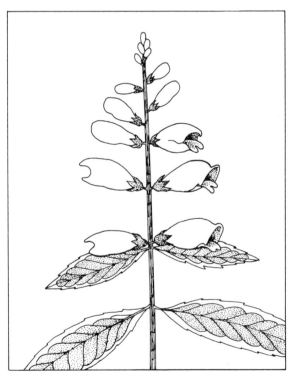

The turtlehead flower, *Chelone glabra.*

glabra, or the turtlehead flower, grows to a height of four feet with narrow, oval leaves up to six inches long. Clusters of white (or sometimes pink) flowers, resembling those of snapdragons appear in late summer or early fall. These perennial plants need full sun to light shade in moist, humusy soil and are best along the water's edge. They are hardy to USDA Zone 5.

Crinum americanum, also known as spider lily or the southern swamp crinum, is a truly exotic plant that bears very showy and evening-fragrant white flowers often reaching a length of five inches. The strap-shaped leaves are shiny green. They adapt to either full sun or partial shade and reach a height of two feet. Water depth can be up to six inches but these plants will adapt to higher, drier ground. They are not hardy north of USDA Zone 8 but do well in pots and can be overwintered in a greenhouse or warm basement.

Dichromena latifolia, the white-bracted sedge, bears white bracts just below its insignificant flowers that seem to glow in the evening garden. More like tiny fairy lamps than plants, they grow one to two feet tall, bloom through September, and while adapting to moist soil, prefer up to six inches of water in full sun or partial shade. They are not hardy north of USDA Zone 7.

There is a South African species of the white-bracted sedge found in the mountains around Capetown called *Ficinia radiata*. Here the ornamental bracts are a bright yellow rather than white.

The true spider lily, *Hymenocallis* spp., is best described as son of crinum. The fragrant white to greenish white flowers resemble a flock of narrow-winged white moths. There are a number of gardenworthy species native to the American Southeast and the West Indies. As I write this book, I have a blooming *H. macrostephana* (*H. narcissiflora* × *H. speciosa*) in a large, self-watering pot. The first flower opened late Friday afternoon and now, on Monday evening, the sepals have spread to a diameter of seven inches surrounding a seven-inch tube, and the scalloped

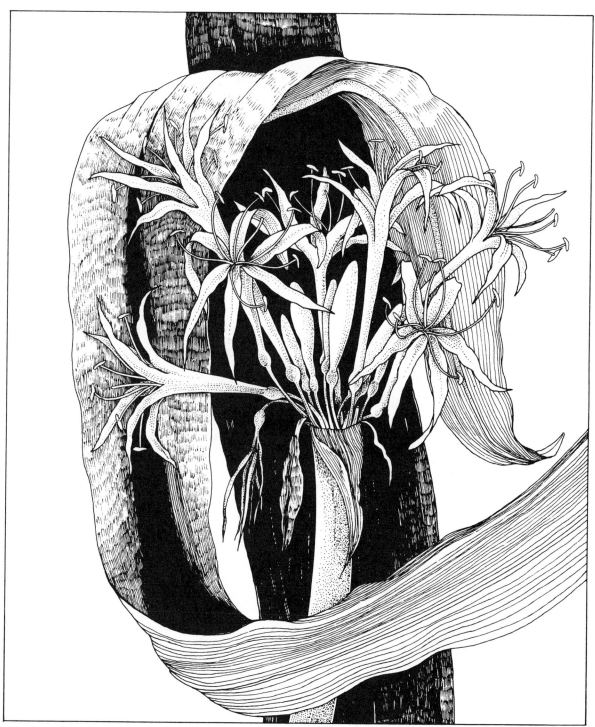

The Australian crinum, *Crinum pedunculatum*.

The white-bracted sedge, *Dichromena latifolia.*

corolla is three inches across. Soon four more buds will open. Like crinums, the strap-shaped leaves are a shiny green but these plants can reach a height of four feet. Keep water depth at six inches or less and provide full sun in the North and partial shade in the South. These bulbs are also not hardy north of USDA Zone 8 but can be collected in the fall, overwintered in a warm spot, and planted out again the next spring.

Iris sibirica, or Siberian iris, is a June-flowering perennial that reaches a height of three feet. Clumps of sword-shaped leaves surround flowers of many colors but for a beautiful white, look for the cultivar 'White Swirl'. They need full sun but adapt to partial shade, using any good garden soil. They also adjust easily to moist, boggy con-

ditions, tolerating a water depth of four inches and are hardy to USDA Zone 5.

Iris ensata, Japanese iris, is a perennial bearing huge handkerchieflike flowers that look more like large butterflies or orchids than the typical iris. They bloom for several weeks after the Siberians are finished. While not surviving in water, they need continually moist soil to grow and bloom. Choose either 'Moonlight Waves' or 'Frosted Fountain' since both have lovely white petals. They are hardy to USDA Zone 4.

Miscanthus sinensis 'Gracillimus', known as variegated maiden grass, is a perennial that will grow to seven feet. Its thin, arching blades with narrow white centers are very effective at night. In early fall, plumelike flowers with a metallic cast open, becoming buff-colored with age. They like full sun but will adapt to partial shade in moist, fertile soil and are best planted at the water's edge. Maiden grass is hardy to USDA Zone 5.

Scirpus tabernaemontani 'Zebrinus', the variegated bulrush, is a perennial cultivar reaching a height of two feet. Its round stems with sharp points resembling porcupine needles are banded with white, an effect that sparkles under moonlight (the leaves are brown sheaths at the base of the stem). They need full sun or partial shade in boggy soil or shallow water. This is a striking plant for the water garden. Not hardy north of USDA Zone 6.

Typha latifolia 'Variegata', the variegated cattail, is not the intruder that its plain green brother is but it's still best to grow this plant in a pot. Reaching a height of five feet, it has slender grassy leaves edged with white. Give it full sun to partial shade in boggy soil or up to ten inches of water. It's hardy to USDA Zone 5.

Zantedeschia aethiopica, the white calla lily, originally came from the Transvaal. Today they are found in gardens of USDA Zone 8 and warmer (though they will overwinter in Zone 7 if mulched enough to keep the earth from freezing). Unlike

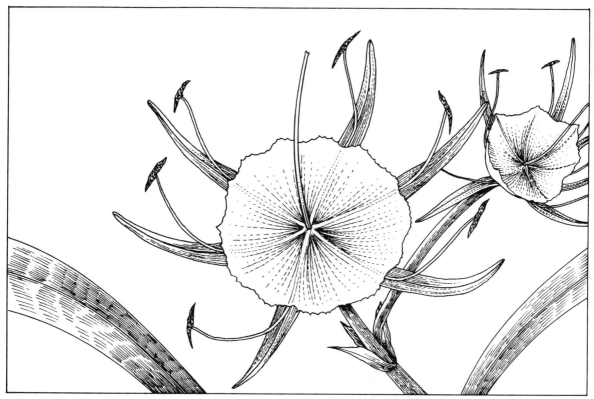

A spider lily hybrid, *Hymenocallis macrostephana*.

many flowers, they are not dependent on day
length or temperature to initiate flower production. Dormancy is brought about by a lack of
water, so if kept wet—in up to four inches of
water—they will bloom for a long time. Any
good soil mix is adequate but I use a mix of equal
parts good potting soil, sharp sand, and composted manure. Use at least a six-inch pot. Provide full sun or in the South, partial shade. Calla
lilies can overwinter in a greenhouse or heated
garage or basement.

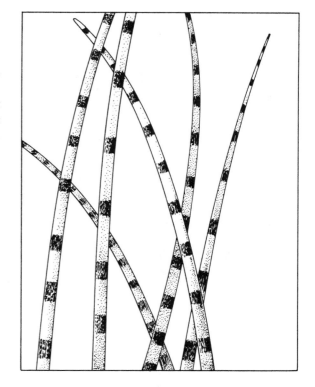

The variegated bulrush, *Scirpus tabernaemontani*
'Zebrinus'.

An eight-spotted Forester moth, *Alypia octomaculata,* heads for the blossom of a night-blooming cereus, *Seleni-cereus coniflorus.*

CHAPTER NINE

𝒩IGHT-BLOOMING CACTUSES

The flowers of the majority of the species of Cactuses are unsurpassed, as regards form and size, and brilliancy and variety of color, by any other family of plants, not even excluding orchids.

WILLIAM WATSON, Royal Botanical Gardens of Kew

No doubt it is an acquired taste alone that leads one to admire greasewood and Cactus.

JOHN C. VAN DYKE, *The Desert*

𝒞actuses are mostly plants of the New World. Their natural range extends from southern Canada down to almost the tip of South America, including Cuba and the West Indies. In fact, these spiny plants are native to every state in the United States with the exception of Maine, New Hampshire, and Vermont.

As with everything else in this world there are a few exceptions to the New World rule and they revolve around the genus *Rhipsalis*. For years botanists thought the rhipsalises found in Ceylon and southern Africa were originally brought over from America but it's possible that they are native populations and so the argument goes on today.

It is also interesting to note that the term cactus originally meant a prickly plant found in Sicily called the cardoon (*Cynara cardunculus*) and Linnaeus incorrectly applied the word to cactuses in general. As for the correct plural form of the word

cactus, in English it is cactuses, although many people use the term cacti, the plural form of the Greek or Latin *kaktos*. Both are acceptable.

Cactuses are members of a plant group called succulents, and are characterized by fleshy leaves and stems that are often swollen with a watery sap. Most succulents are native to areas of the country that are arid (or semiarid) for at least part of the year, and, as a result, have become masters at the art of storing water.

When asked about cactuses that bloom at night, most people mention the night-blooming cereus and also remark that an aged aunt, somewhere, grew one to perfection; they also promptly assume there are no others. In reality there are over 450 members of the cactus family that flower in the evening. To describe them all would require an entire book on this subject alone, so I've limited my choices to the following plants based on their beauty and market availability.

The night-blooming cereus, *Selenicereus grandiflorus*.

THE NIGHT-BLOOMING CEREUS

People have always loved and been fascinated by the most famous of all nocturnal plants, the night-blooming cereus. According to French gossips of the time, Marie Antoinette had little interest in the art of painting and whenever she passed through the Louvre, she quickened her step. But she loved flowers and she once asked the great botanical artist Pierre-Joseph Redouté (1759–1840), who had been appointed Designer to the Queen's Chambers, to paint this flower in full view of the assembled court. She was, at the time, a prisoner of the Revolution and six weeks after the painting was finished, the Republic was proclaimed.

The next great floral representation of the night-blooming cereus was a portrait of *Selenicereus grandiflorus*, done as plate thirty-one from C. J. Trew's *Plantae Selectae*, and while beautifully executed by Georg Dionysius Ehret (1708–1770), it doesn't hold a candle to the third great representation.

This last was not only one of the best but one of the most fantastic plates in Dr. Thornton's 1799 *Temple of Flora*. Here the flower fills half the picture, its many sepals of bronze-yellow surrounding the thirty-odd chaste white petals like a medieval halo. A full moon plays on dimpled waters while a clock in a partly ruined turret points to three minutes after XII; the face of an owl can just be seen to the left of the dial. The whole picture is especially wonderful because the plant is set within the lush and green landscape of an English summer and the landscape has no bearing on the true home of the plant.*

*The original painting of Thornton's cereus was painted by Phillip Reinagle (1749–1833) but the moonlight was painted by Abraham Pether (1756–1812). In addition to being a fine artist, Pether was a musical prodigy, philosopher, mathematician, and inventor of mechanical gadgets. Because of his passion for painting nocturnal scenes, he was dubbed "Moonlight Pether," and his astronomical accuracy was above criticism. Unfortunately he died in poverty, leaving a wife and nine children.

The lure of the night-blooming cereus is profound. The blooming of this evening flower has assumed the stature of a family ritual in homes throughout the world, neighbor calling neighbor to report the expected opening.

People love to write about them, too. Every book I've found devoted to cactuses mentions the famous hedge comprised of night-blooming cereus that covers a stone wall on the campus of Punahou College in Honolulu. Seven feet high, the hedge has been described as being a half-mile long, and on a single night five thousand blossoms have opened sending sweetly fragrant fumes out to a tropical night. The massive hedge was started in the late 1840s by Mrs. Hiram Bingham, the wife of a missionary assigned to Honolulu. During Queen Liliuokalani's reign, there were elaborate ceremonies to Pau when the night-blooming cereus bloomed.

In fact, in many old Spanish-American homes there was a fiesta the night that the cereus bloomed. Their *reina-de-la-noche* lit up the night. And I've read in the *Journals of John Cheever*, where the Cheever family went up the hill to a neighbor's to see the night-blooming cereus perform at nine P.M.

I have seen the spent blossoms at Logee's greenhouses in Connecticut, the result of blooming on an evening in late July. According to Logee's horticulturist, Tovah Martin, friends and neighbors are called to attend one of nature's best spectaculars. The plant at Logee's is one of a number of night-blooming cereuses, in this case *Hylocereus undatus*. "It takes many years for a hylocereus to reach blooming size," she said, "but when it does bloom, it's a conversation piece. Unfortunately, the thick, three-edged rambling stems are a little too large for the average home."

I have seen it bloom in September at Mohonk Manor, New York's famous resort hotel on the Hudson River. The plant sat in a pot, propped up against a brick wall, the ritual beginning in late afternoon when a desk lamp was fixed precariously over the burgeoning bud since the waning light of an early fall afternoon was not enough to force flowering.

In Virginia, where it was called Christ-in-the-manger, I have seen a forty-year-old plant bloom in late September and produce seventeen flowers the first night, five the second, and three the third.

Two summers ago, late in August, we took care of my aunt's garden in Asheville while the family was away for a week. She told me that the night-blooming cereus was setting buds and could possibly bloom while they were gone.

Over the period of a week, we watched the buds get plumper and the sepals that tightly wrap the flower began to change to a light brown color. On a Thursday afternoon I knew the first flower would bloom that night, but as the plant is over six feet high and sits in a large earthenware pot that is very heavy, moving the plant to our house was out of the question.

At 4:30 I took a sharp scissors and cut the bud from the point where it joined the leaf, plunging it immediately into water. The sepals at the base of the bud and a few surrounding the white-tipped blossom had already started to unfurl and the texture of their surface had the glisten of baked meringue. We quickly drove home.

As darkness fell in our kitchen, the petals began to separate and by nine P.M. the flower was almost wide open and giving off a sweet, spicy scent that swept through the house like fog sweeping a London street. By midnight it was perfect. Hundreds of threadlike stamens, each topped by a dot of golden pollen, surrounded a long, thin pistil with a graceful, many-fingered tip. The flower measured nine inches across and the blossom was six inches long.

By morning the perfume in the kitchen was gone and all the beautiful petals and sepals had collapsed while hundreds of stamens were already beginning to melt together. The baked meringue texture had turned to a lifeless brown. The flower hung lifelessly over the edge of the vase. My wife said it was so beautiful that it deserved a burial.

The Various Night-Blooming Cereuses

The name cereus is from the Greek and refers to the candelabrumlike branching of the first species to be described. But Phillip Miller in his famous eighteenth-century *Gardener's Dictionary* reports that Spanish servants burned them as torches or tapers after the branches were cut down, dried, and dipped in oil. It is probably the oldest common name given to any cactus and it's mentioned in sixteenth-century literature after its discovery by the first explorers to the Americas. The earliest illustration is believed to be in Oviedo's *La Historia General de las Indias*, published in 1535.

Well over thirty genera of the cactus family have nocturnal flowers and at one time over one thousand names were listed as species belonging to the genus *Cereus*. But today, all night-blooming cereuses belong to the following four genera: *Hylocereus, Nyctocereus, Peniocereus,* and *Selenicereus*, while another cactus that shares that common name (but differing in botanical structure) is found in the genus *Epiphyllum*.

THE GENUS *HYLOCEREUS*

The forest cereuses include the best known of all the true night-blooming cereus. *Hylocereus undatus*, the Honolulu queen. The three-angled, undulating stems have tiny groups of spines arising from small spots called areoles at the crest of the wave and the stems also give rise to aerial roots that help the stems cling to walls, tree trunks, and artificial supports. These are the plants that form the famous Hawaiian hedge and ramble throughout Logee's greenhouse, the rambling being important since it flowers on older wood.

The blooming season begins in July and continues until the end of October. The flowers are up to one foot long and shaped like a funnel. Each of the pure white petals is up to five inches long and is surrounded by a collar of yellowish green sepals. As many as eight hundred stamens

The night-blooming cereus, *Hylocereus stenopterus*.

have been counted in a single flower. The long stigma ends in a series of fingers that can total up to twenty-seven. Because these flowers are pollinated by bats, they do not have the sweet and spicy fragrance associated with the moth-pollinated orchids. If the morning following blooming is cool and cloudy, the flowers will remain open until just before noon. Fertilized flowers will produce a dull red, smooth fruit about four inches in diameter and containing edible white pulp studded with black seeds.

Amazingly enough, the exact origin of *Hylocereus undatus* is not known. The species had been long known in cultivation and called *Cereus triangularis*. But the plant that Linnaeus described came from Jamaica and doesn't quite match the plant that is grown all over the world, which is half wild in all tropical countries and first came from China where it was grown for centuries.

Hylocereus costaricens is a native of Costa Rica, described as a vigorous vine and often used for grafting purposes. The three-angled stems start out green and purplish but with age turn white, then to a greenish gray. The young flower buds are globular, and tinted a dull crimson or purple. They open to a width of nine inches and are very fragrant. There are dozens of stamens, each about three and a half inches long, with creamy white filaments and yellow anthers. The style is ivory white and over nine inches long, ending in twenty-four to twenty-seven lobes. Because the flowers stay open long after dawn, they are among the few in the group that can be photographed in daylight.

Other species of *Hylocereus* often found in commerce include *H. stenopterus*, unusual because the nocturnal flowers are carmine red and over seven inches in diameter, and *H. lemairei*, considered by many to be the most beautiful of all in this genus. Although the flowers are only ten inches long, the scales on the tube of the flower are tipped with purple, while the outermost sepals are a greenish yellow with red-purple

margins. The sepals proper are a waxy yellow while the petals are tinged with pink at their lower edge and tipped with white, with a slightly yellow cast.

Cultural requirements for these epiphytic cactuses are simple. They prefer a soil rich in humus, kept moist while the plants are in active growth, and partial sun. Temperatures should be kept about 60°F. They can easily spend summers out of doors, in the shade of a tree or shrub.

THE GENUS *PENIOCEREUS*

In the United States there is only one native night-blooming cereus, known as *reina-de-la-noche* (queen of the night), the thread cactus, the deer-horn cactus, or the sweet potato cactus. The scientific name is *Peniocereus greggii*, and it's a native of Arizona, southern New Mexico, and western Texas. The plants are usually found growing in valleys and on mesas but they are very easy to miss since they look like nothing except some dead sticks poking out of the ground. In fact, for years collectors found the plants only when they were in bloom, guided by their spicy fragrance. In nature they usually flower in mid-June and appear on the same night throughout the desert.

Dr. Lyman Benson writing in *The Cacti of Arizona* describes their blooming as occurring

on one or two nights in May or in June. However, a few flowers may appear earlier or later, and the total flowering period occupies nearly one month. Flowers open just after dusk when the petals and other floral structures begin a series of spasmodic jerks. The perfume of the blossom is liberated in profusion, and a single flower may scent the air for 100 feet. Normally the blooming period is over by about seven o'clock the following morning or later if the weather is cool, but the flower may be removed from the plant and kept open for some time if it is placed in the dark.

The flowers are seven to ten inches long and six inches across, with forty or more petals of pale lavender shading into a soft, waxy white. An unusually large plant in Tucson was reported to have produced forty-four flowers in 1939 and thirty-one in 1940. The flowers can often be preserved by keeping them refrigerated and in water.

The common name of sweet potato cactus refers to the plant's large tuber, which is shaped like a turnip. Weights vary between two and forty pounds. American Indians and Mexicans are reported to slice the tubers and fry them in deep fat. Because this root acts like a reservoir for both water and food, these plants bloom every year, rain or no rain. A sweet, red, egg-shaped fruit ripens in September and is a popular food of birds and has also been used for jam and jelly.

The only way to start this plant for the evening garden is from seed. Use a sandy loam in partial shade and take care when transplanting so the fleshy root is not damaged. The root should be planted at least two feet deep in a loamy soil with good drainage and given some protection from hot summer sun. Water well during the growing season and in dry weather but do not cultivate around the plant. When grown outdoors, the thread cactus will endure a temperature of 5°F and much colder if carefully mulched or protected by a mantle of early snow. If you live in a colder climate, grow this cactus in a large pot and winter it in a sunny window or a greenhouse, remembering to withhold water until growth resumes in the spring.

THE GENUS *NYCTOCEREUS*

If you could enter a time machine and travel back to the 1920s and 1930s, especially the sunrooms or conservatories of many comfortable homes, in one corner you would probably find another night-blooming cereus known as the serpent or snake cactus and botanically called *Nyctocereus serpentinus*. Although these plants were originally found growing wild in Mexico, a note pub-

The Arizona queen of the night, *Peniocereus greggii*.

lished at the Missouri Botanical Garden in 1905 mentions that no wild specimens had been collected in recent years. By that time, *Junco espinoso*, as the Mexicans call it, was widely cultivated in that country, or grew half wild as it poked through hedges and around and over walls.

The tangled and spiny stems of this cactus are about an inch in diameter and can easily reach a length of eight to fifteen feet. They stand erect for the first eight feet or so, then the next few feet begin to bend and twist about, looking for a foothold. If you cut a stem in half you would count about twelve ridges, each lined with half-inch spines of translucent white.

The truly magnificent flowers begin to open soon after sundown, having begun the process the day before. They are eight to nine inches long and when fully open, about seven inches across. Petals are creamy white and the pink-and-tan sepals are touched with green. As the flower matures, both petals and sepals reflex, or bend backward, and the blossoms give off the scent of a spicy tuberose and the perfume from a single flower will fill a large room or backyard. Each plant blooms only one night a year, usually between April and June. If the next day is cloudy, the flowers will remain open until late afternoon.

"... the soft cream-white of the petals, then the corona of stamens, [become] a symphony of pale yellow and white ... and the whole forms a lovely picture against the background of old adobe buildings, evanescent and brilliant in the white rays of the southern moon," is the description in a delightful 1932 Macmillan book by Thornber and Bonker called *The Fantastic Clan*.

All members of the *Nyctocereus* genus prefer warm growing conditions, generally above 60°F., and need as much light as possible. Keep plants on the dry side, allowing the soil to dry well between waterings. If grown outdoors, they will endure temperatures in the twenties but if your winters are colder, move them into the greenhouse or a bright corner in the living room.

THE GENUS *SELENICEREUS*

The moon cereuses belong to the genus *Selenicereus*. In their native lands, they either climb trees and hang with aerial roots, or where vertical supports are absent, merely trail over the ground, rambling up and over rocks and cliffs. Popular names include goddess of the night and princess of the night. For years alkaloids have been extracted from these plants and used as a homeopathic heart tonic.

Although the flowers are not quite as succulent as those in the genus *Hylocereus*, they are just as beautiful to see. Usually very fragrant, and often up to fourteen inches across with pure white petals, they open at dusk and close before dawn. The flower tubes have either long, silky hairs or bristles instead of scales.

Margaret Mee (1908–1988) was one of the finest botanical illustrators of the twentieth century and searched for years to find a blooming specimen of a rare moonflower, in this case *Selenicereus wittii* (synonym, *Strophocactus wittii*).

Back in 1901, Karl Schumann wrote in the *Gardener's Chronical*:

Among the numerous novelties which the last decade of the past century brought to Europe, the [*Strophocactus wittii*] is surely one of the most interesting for both the amateur and the professional cultivator. I received the curious plant through the kindness of Mr. N. H. Witt, of Manaos, Erlado do Amazonas, Brazil. He told me long before he was able to send specimens that a climbing species of a genus he was not able to determine, grew in the swampy forest, or Igape, on the Amazon river. Closely appressed to the stems of the trees, and fixed to them by numerous roots, in the region of the early inundation, there creeps a cactus with the habit of a Phyllocactus, but armed with very sharp spines. It is so closely connected with the plant on which it grows that one must look carefully to distinguish it.

Mr. Schumann continued his article, pointing out that this species was the missing link between the genera *Phyllocactus* and *Cereus*. He also noted that the older joints of this cactus turn from green to a beautiful wine-red or purple color, a peculiarity which he had also seen on the plants cultivated in the Royal Botanic Garden of Berlin.

For years Miss Mee tried in vain to be in the right place at the right time, for the plant does not flower every year and, of course, when it does it's for only one night. In May of 1988, she reached the port of Igarapé São Raimundo. Traveling up the Negro River in a boat with a fifty-year-old diesel motor, at dusk they finally reached the Parana Anavilhanas, where the huge trees were draped with bromeliads and philodendrons and wild orchids dotted the emerald green curtains with brilliant color. The next morning they began their search in an area of the river where huge trees stood in the river water like gigantic temple columns, and there on a large tree surrounded by thorny bushes, they found *Selenicereus wittii* with three buds.

The next night the vigil began. As the light began to dim and the forest sounds faded for the night, one of the buds began to open, first one petal moving, then another. Under the light of a full moon and a very dim battery-powered fluorescent light, the flower opened wide, at the same time giving off an extraordinary sweet perfume.

Miss Mee's painting shows four blossoms, each about ten inches long and five inches wide, with a fifth beginning to fade. There are twelve pure white petals and over fifty white sepals, the sepals backed with a hint of pure maroon. The golden-tipped anthers are spread apart instead of being in the usual cluster and the stigma has a number of lobes. There is also a photograph of the open flower, lit in the same manner as a Georges de La Tour painting. Its strange beauty would have made Doctors Glendon and Yorgami white with envy.

Selenicereus grandiflorus is the best known of

The moon cereus, *Selenicereus wittii*.

the genus, first described by Linnaeus in 1753. Discovered in Jamaica and Cuba, it has since been widely planted and has escaped from cultivation in much of tropical America. In the West Indies this flower is called the king of the night and of all the nocturnal flowers I've seen, this is one of the most dramatic, especially since it possesses a powerful fragrance touched with vanilla. The floral cup is over ten inches wide with petals and sepals of pure white inside and tinges of salmon without. The stems are an inch thick and a light gray-green to purple in color.

Selenicereus pteranthus (synonym, *Cereus nycticalus*) is known as princess of the night. The snakelike stems are bluish green and again tinged with purple. The fragrant flowers first appear in June and complete blooming by the end of the month. Each blossom is eleven inches long and fully one foot in diameter, yellow with reddish highlights. The outermost petals are a dull bronze—often purplish brown—and surround an inner core of pure white petals. There are many stamens of light green to a cream while the style is off-white with a touch of green at the base.

Selenicereus macdonaldiae hails from Uruguay and Argentina and is called the queen of the night because the flower is about thirteen inches in diameter with pure white petals surrounded by dozens of thin, golden sepals.

Other species usually available from specialty nurseries include *Selenicereus coniflorus*, bearing large fragrant flowers with white inner petals and reddish or yellowish sepals; *S. inermis* with medium-size white blossoms with a reddish throat and yellow-green sepals; and *S. innessii*, having the smallest flowers of the genus, measuring one and a half inches in diameter, the innermost petals cream-colored and tinged with magenta.

Unlike the other nocturnal cactuses, the selenicereuses prefer a good soil laced with compost that is kept evenly moist with plenty of water when they are in bud. In the summer, plants prefer higher humidity and temperatures should be above 60°F—although cooler indoor temperatures will be tolerated in the wintertime. These plants grow easily in tubs and can be trained to wind about a trellis with ease. In the winter, hold back on the water and either keep them in a greenhouse or in a sunny window. Plants are easily grown from seed. If grown outdoors, this cactus will endure winter temperatures of 7°F to 10°F.

THE GENUS *EPIPHYLLUM*

Epiphyllum represents a fifth genus not allied to the other four but most home-blooming cactuses called night-blooming cereuses belong to this genus, specifically the species *oxypetalum* (or *Phyllocactus latifrons* in old catalogs). They are nocturnal members of the beautiful orchid cactus clan. Plants have broad, leaflike stems and are epiphytic in nature, growing in trees.

When many of these night-blooming plants were first discovered in the jungles of Mexico and Central and South America, they were hybridized with distant relatives and the resulting hybrids became the popular orchid cactuses, those lovely flowers that are not only available in a fantastic range of colors, but, like all these epiphytes, easy to grow as houseplants.

Epiphyllum oxypetalum is the plant that blooms in my aunt's garden. The cool days of spring initiate the formation of buds that develop throughout the summer months. With the cooler temperatures of late summer and early fall, the buds begin to mature and flower about a month later. Thanks to a cutting we now have our own specimen. From November to February it lives in the greenhouse where it's contained in a fourteen-inch hanging pot made of wide-spaced enameled wire. The pot is lined with sheets of sphagnum moss and contains a soil mix of one part each potting soil and sharp sand. If the stems show signs of shriveling, I water. Winter temperatures should be kept above 60°F. Once frost danger is

The night-blooming cereus, *Epiphyllum oxypetalum*.

past, the pot and plant go out to the garden, hopefully to brighten up the nights of August or September.

Other night-blooming members of the *Epiphyllum* genus that are not called cereuses but still possess magnificent flowers include the following four:

Epiphyllum anguliger was first distributed by the Horticultural Society of London after they received plants in 1846 from a collector, T. Hartweg, who found them growing on oak trees in southern Mexico. The branches have such deeply rounded lobes that they are attractive when not in flower and are called rick-rack cactuses. The very fragrant white flowers are over five inches long.

Epiphyllum chrysocardium has foot-long flowers, eight inches across, sometimes called golden heart because of the brilliant yellow stamens surrounded by the pure white petals. The plant was originally discovered in the rain forests of northern Chiapas in Mexico. The lobes on the stems of this plant are so long and narrow, they look like a fern. Stems can reach a length of five feet or more and can be a foot wide, so only those gardens with plenty of room should try this plant.

Epiphyllum guatemalense is described by growers as being a stout plant growing over three feet long and bearing numerous foot-long flowers with white, spidery petals surrounding a bright orange pistil.

Epiphyllum strictum has glorious flowers that consist of over twenty-eight slim white sepals and petals surrounding a vivid crimson pistil. The plant was first described in 1854 and again in 1902, the second time a specimen found growing in the wild state and collected in Honduras. Flowers are up to ten inches long and seven inches wide. This is an especially beautiful orchid cactus for the evening garden.

Epiphyllum thomasianum is probably another bat-pollinated flower since it emits a strong musty or acrid fragrance when opening. The flowers are bell-shaped and white with red sepals.

Provide these last five cactuses with the same growing conditions as *Epiphyllum oxypetalum*.

OTHER NIGHT-BLOOMING CACTUSES

The Giant Saguaro

There is only one species in the genus *Carnegiea* and that is *gigantea*, the giant saguaro (pronounced sah-WAH-roe) cactus of the southern part of Arizona. This cactus is so typical of the Arizona landscape that its nocturnal blossoms are the state flower. While not the largest cactus in the world (that honor belongs to the Pringle cereus, *Pachycereus pringlei*), when entering a forest of these strange plants, there is an immediate feeling of dignity and age, and tourists often lower their voices. After all, an adult plant can tip the scales at fifteen tons and was probably a seedling when the American Constitution was signed.

Unfortunately the adult plants are too large for the average evening garden, but I've included their description for desert gardeners who wish to start plants from seed and to caution those who care that people continue to steal them from the desert and pay large amounts simply to watch them slowly die in their backyards. Unless moved when relatively young and continually cared for while they adapt to their new homes, the breaking up of their gigantic root system, as much as seventy feet in diameter and very close to the surface of the desert floor, eventually does them in. This root system is so efficient that even after years of drought, the trunk holds enough water to allow the production of flowers.

The night-blooming flowers are about five inches long and up to four inches in diameter, with heavy, waxy white petals. They appear in May and June, opening in late evening and closing by midmorning of the next day unless the sky is overcast and the weather is cool. Although bees and other insects visit the flowers, the major pollinators are bats, including Sanborn's long-nosed

The giant saguaro, *Carnegiea gigantea*.

bat (*Leptonycteris sanborni*). This acrobatic flyer approaches the flowers from above, then using its wings like parachutes, hovers over the blossoms for just a second, takes a quick sip, and flies off to try again. Meanwhile, its fur is completely dusted with yellow pollen.

Saguaros grow easily from seed in well-drained, sandy soil. Transplant when they are a half-inch tall. Soil should be moist but never wet. Transplant young plants up to six feet high in spring to a gravelly clay soil, taking two feet of the roots and being careful not to injure them. Water once a month during dry seasons. These cactuses will endure an occasional winter temperature of 12°F without harm but longer cold spells can spell death.

The Barbed-Wire Vine

Acanthocereus pentagonus was first described by Linnaeus in 1753 and are native to the coast of Texas and the Florida Keys. The erect stems are about three inches thick but soon begin to bend under their own weight, making a series of McDonald's arches of green rather than gold. When grown outdoors, the arches soon form an interlinked colony and hence earn it the common name of barbed-wire cactus. The fragrant flowers are about seven inches long with light green sepals and narrow white petals. Many, many stamens with white filaments and pale yellow anthers crowd the center of the blossom. If grown indoors, provide full sun, keep temperatures above 60°F, keep the well-drained, sandy soil on the dry side, and give the plants a winter rest by withholding water.

Anthony's Rick-Rack Cactus

Anthony's rick-rack cactus gets its popular name from the form of the stems, since they look exactly like the zigzag braid used for trimming and decoration. *Cryptocereus anthonyanus* is a climber but will also do well in a hanging pot.

Anthony's rick-rack cactus, *Cryptocereus anthonyanus.*

The pinwheel-shaped blossoms are four inches wide and have alternate petals of yellow and maroon. They are extremely fragrant with a sweet and spicy odor and last but a single night. Grow in an evenly moist soil heavily laced with humus and give partial shade in the summertime—it's perfect to hang underneath a tree. Winter temperatures should be kept above 60°F.

The Tortoise Cactus

Deamia testudo represents one species of epiphytic cactus that is native to Central America. The usually three-winged stems clamber over and cling to the bark of living trees. The common name comes from the look of its ribs. It was first described in 1837 and for years collectors called it *Cereus pterogonus*. It's amazing how such a strange-looking cactus can produce such large and beautiful flowers. They are over eleven inches long and yellowish white. Plants like warmth and full sun. Let the sandy, well-drained soil dry out between waterings. Temperatures are best kept above 60°F. These strange cactuses are best grown in pots, though the creeping stems will easily cling to a section of log like those used to grow philodendrons.

The Eriocereus *and* Harrisia

The two genera of *Eriocereus* and *Harrisia* are very much alike, the distinguishing characteristics being found in the fruits. The first are usually vinelike with red fruits that split apart and the latter semierect with fruits that do not split.

Eriocereus martinii comes from Argentina where it clambers over rocks and trees, reaching a length of many feet. The stems are covered with stout black-tipped spines. The flowers are about nine inches long and very fragrant. Light green sepals, often flushed with red or pink at the tips, enclose white petals with a greenish base. Many stamens surround a seven-inch style of light green, tipped with twelve lobes. The seeds of this species germinate with ease and seedlings will produce flowering plants within five to seven years.

The red-tipped dogtail, or *Harrisia tortuosa*, also comes from Argentina. The stems are less than two inches thick, very stout, and covered with spines. The flowers are up to eight inches long and have a tendency to remain open on cool and cloudy days. The floral sepals are grass green at the base, lighter to off-white through the center, and pinkish along the margins. The stamens stand in two ranks with a single row clearly attached to the mouth of the throat and the rest going down into the floral tube. The style is chartreuse with fourteen lobes.

Give these plants winter warmth of 60°F, full sun, and let the well-drained, sandy soil dry between waterings.

The Peruvian Haageocereus

The *Haageocereus* cactuses are native to the Pacific slopes of the Peruvian Andes, where they are found at low altitudes. They are more in scale for pot cultivation than most of the plants in this chapter. The cylindrical plants usually creep over the edges of rocks and are covered with dense but attractively colored spines, ranging from golden brown to brown. The flowers are funnel-shaped, usually under three inches in length, and come in shades of white or red. Give plants full sun, warmth in winter—again 60°F or above—and let the well-drained, sandy soil dry between waterings. Withhold water during the winter.

The Lovely Monvillea

Monvillea cavendishii is a prolific bloomer beginning to produce flowers in April and continuing into September. The stems are slender, pale green in color, and bear fine, short spines. The fast-growing stems can reach a height of more than fifteen feet as they ramble on the ground or work their way through tree branches. The flowers are funnel-shaped, white, over five inches long, and borne toward the top of the previous year's growth. The sepals have a greenish or reddish hue, while the petals are pure white. The fruit is a spineless red apple about two inches long that contains edible white pulp embellished with many shiny black seeds, which will readily germinate.

Monvilleas need a good, rich soil with plenty of humus but one that is well-drained. Provide plenty of water when they are growing but allow a rest and withdraw water during the winter, keep temperatures above 60°F, and give this cactus full sun. Provide partial shade in the summer.

The Beautiful Setiechinopsis

There is only one species in the genus *Setiechinopsis*, known as *mirabilis*, and it is simply beautiful! The cactus body itself is small, up to eight inches in height, and cylindrical, resembling those found in the genus *Echinopsis*. The spines are straight and bristly. This is a perfect nocturnal cactus for the gardener with limited space.

In midsummer at dusk, the stylish, fragrant flowers appear. They are about five inches wide when fully open and made up of dozens of thin white sepals and petals.

This cactus is very easy to grow, providing it gets full sun both summer and winter, ample water during the growing season, and a winter rest when the well-drained, sandy soil is kept dry. Winter temperatures should be above 50°F.

The Torch Cactuses

Over twenty-five species are found in the genus *Trichocereus*. Because of their usual upright growth habit and thick branching, they are also called columnar cactuses. Most come from Argentina, Bolivia, Peru, and Chile. The flowers are often over ten inches in length, shaped like a funnel, and range in colors from white to pink, and deeper red. Many are fragrant and most of them

Monvillea cavendishii.

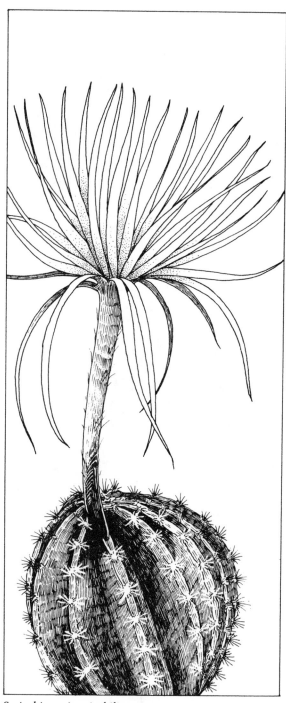

Setiechinopsis mirabilis.

flower in the summer, clustering at the top of the cactus, like the flame on a torch.

The larger torch cactuses are very suitable for gardens if temperatures stay above 40°F. They also do well in tubs—if you have the strength to move them inside when frosts threaten. They like to be kept warm (above 60°F), given full sun in both summer and winter, and let the well-drained, sandy soil dry out between waterings.

Trichocereus bridgesii has blue-green stems to fifteen feet, branching at the base. The funnel-shaped flowers are white, over seven inches long, and are scented with jasmine. They bloom in summer. In La Paz, Bolivia, these plants are often grown as a hedge plant or set on the tops of walls for protection to gardens.

Trichocereus candicans forms a clump rather than a column, the ultimate height being three feet. The funnel-shaped white flowers are very fragrant, over six inches long.

Trichocereus schickendantzii is not fragrant but is probably the most beautiful of the genus. The cup-shaped white flowers are about eight inches long and cluster on top of the plant, as many as ten blooming at one time.

A white-lined sphinx moth, *Celerio lineata*, heads for the blossoms of a ylang-ylang tree, *Cananga odorata*.

CHAPTER TEN

𝒩IGHT-BLOOMING TROPICAL VINES AND TREES

Moonlight walks under the giant bamboos . . . the smell of durian in the Kampong. The soft notes of the bamboo flute player drifting up in the early evenings from Batoe Tulis.

DAVID FAIRCHILD, *Garden Islands of the Great East*

There are literally hundreds of botanically different but nocturnally blooming plants that grow throughout the tropics (with thousands more waiting to be discovered). These flowers run the gamut from bulbous perennials to attractive shrubs to vines that stretch like Tarzan's lianas from the highest tree.

Crinum ornatum, for example, is a bulbous plant found in West Africa, where its three-inchwide bulb produces three-foot stalks topped with eight to ten pendulous flowers striped with pink that open to the jungle's evening air. *Nyctocalos thomsonii*, one of three species of climbing shrubs native to Malaya, bears nocturnal white flowers that somewhat resemble those of a gloxinia, flaring out like the lip of a tuba at the end of a seven-inch tube.

And there are many night-blooming trees. The Indian rosewood tree, *Dalbergia latifolia*, belongs to a genus containing some one hundred species of evergreen trees and climbing shrubs (even though it is deciduous). Found in the jungles of India, the wood is extremely hard and fragrant, and is used for furniture and gun stocks. The white flowers are very fragrant and fill the air at dusk with their sweet odor.

The tree of sadness, *Nyctanthes arbor-tristis*, bears extremely fragrant white flowers with an orange tube, opening at night and falling at dawn, their spent flowers circling the trunks until they are gathered for use in perfumes and as vegetable dyes.

Most of the species of the genus *Posoqueria* bear clusters of tubelike flowers and *P. fragrantissima* from Brazil is especially fragrant at night where the white flowers are pollinated by jungle moths.

The beautiful sorrowless tree, *Saraca indica*, originally found in India and the Malay Peninsula, bears night-fragrant flowers that are often used in temple offerings. A specimen continues to exist in Florida at The Kampong, the famous garden and home of botanist and explorer David Fairchild, but it is extremely sensitive to cold.

Unfortunately many of these plants are difficult to find, usually residing either in their native lands or in large glasshouses around the world. But the following night-blooming vines and trees are quite common in the tropical gardens of the United States, especially in Florida.

TWO TROPICAL VINES

A *lang* is a covered but open-sided walkway in a Chinese garden, usually with a tiled roof held aloft by columns. Between the columns, the weary walker will find benches that offer a shady retreat and a chance to sit down for a moment. Trunks of woody lianas often twine around the *lang*s and become so twisted and gnarled with age, that for a moment in a flight of fancy, a visitor can imagine that he or she is in a far-off land, standing before ancient temples lost in steamy jungles where secret doorways, surrounded with these vines, open into shadowed and strange interiors.

There are two tropical vines perfect for such a setting. The first is called Christmas vine, horsetail or snow creeper, *Porana paniculata*, with flowers open both day and night. It's an evergreen plant grown in Zanzibar, upper Burma, northern India, and parts of Florida, where its many tiny white flowers bloom at Christmastime. Most of the year the six-inch-long, heart-shaped leaves are inconspicuous in the landscape, climbing over trees and fences to a length of thirty feet or more. Toward the end of November, however, and sometimes beginning in mid-December, the flowers appear and parts of the garden look as though they are buried knee-deep in snow.

The individual flowering stems can grow to a foot long and four inches across, but they are often grouped in clusters up to four feet long. The bell-shaped flowers are pure white, five sixteenths of an inch across, and sweetly scented, with the fragrance increasing at night. Strangely enough, all the flowers seem to bloom at once, carpeting everything in a blanket of white, an effect not only spectacular in the daylight but stunning by the light of the moon. The only drawback to these flowers is their short ten- to fourteen-day period of blooming.

Flowers of the Rangoon creeper, *Quisqualis indica.*

These vines are also effective in a greenhouse setting and can be trained to run along the rafters. A mix of potting soil laced with humus and sand is best and temperatures should be kept above 50°F. But growers should be warned, that once comfortable in their environment, Christmas vines can become far too prolific for their own good.

An annual member of the species, *Porana racemosa*, or the snow creeper, is known but is rarely found on the commercial market. If you do find seeds, sow them in early spring using a heating cable to provide needed warmth. When seedlings produce their first true leaves they can be grown in pots or planted directly out into the garden—as long as frost dangers are past.

The second vine is the Rangoon creeper, *Quisqualis indica*, sounding like a character from an old Sherlock Holmes movie. When Dr. Edwin A.

Menniger wrote his classic book *Flowering Vines of the World*, he and fifty collaborators made a list of the fifty most beautiful vines and the Rangoon creeper made the list. Originally from southeast Asia, this is a very large deciduous climbing shrub. Because of its disconcerting growth habit, the Latin name of *Quisqualis* literally means "who? what?" A young plant was first described as a three-foot upright shrub with a few irregular branches and scattered leaves. In six months the shrub sent out a runner from the roots which soon climbed some neighboring trees. It threw out branches in all directions but they did not twist about their support. Then the original shrub ceased to grow and perished—and the result was a climber. Clusters of three-inch tubes are topped with five petals, their outer surface flushed with pink, the inside a pure white. They resemble stars falling from a Fourth of July rocket. Opening at night, the white turns pink at daybreak, then finally a rich red. Since flowers open in succession, there is a simultaneous mix of red, white, and pink—and every evening, a rich and heady perfume. They should be cut back after flowering.

In order to grow and flower, the Rangoon creeper needs temperatures above 60°F and full sun at all times of the year. The plants prefer a soil mix of peat moss and potting soil laced with humus. The soil should be kept evenly moist except during the winter months when it can be allowed to dry out between waterings. These shrubs can be kept to bush size by judicious pruning but they should have a conservatory or greenhouse if grown indoors.

SOME TROPICAL TREES

I talked to Larry M. Schokman about night-blooming tropical trees. Mr. Schokman was a former tea planter in Sri Lanka and today is the assistant director of The Kampong and president of a relatively new society, The Tropical Flowering Tree Society.

"Most of these night-blooming trees are usually pollinated by flower-feeding bats. The flowers are usually large and often have an unpleasant odor. Of course there are exceptions to this rule. For example, flowers of the ylang-ylang tree produce an extract used in Chanel No. 5 perfume."

Among the Bignoniaceae family are the night-blooming sausage trees, chiefly *Kigelia africana*, specifically pollinated by bats. A black-and-white photo in David Fairchild's book, *The World Was My Garden*, shows the curious-looking sausage-like fruits produced by this tree. Each fruit is the size of an uncut delicatessen bologna—and sometimes weighs as much as twenty pounds—and hangs at the end of a long, straight stem, like a puppet on a string. The tree grew beside a gas station in Coconut Grove, Florida, grown from a seed that Fairchild brought back from Egypt. The maroon flowers, which resemble very large squash blossoms, have rounded petals and the texture of crushed silk.

Approaching the midnight horror tree (*Oroxylum indicum*) in twilight could be startling—its four-foot-long seedpods curved downward appear to be the wings of a resting vulture or, perhaps, the sharp blades of a hundred swords of Damocles. This small night-blooming tree from India bears large white or purple bell-shaped flowers, each about two and a half inches long and over three inches wide. In nature the tree reaches a height of forty feet but in gardens, it is somewhat shorter. Rich soil, plenty of water during the summer, and full sun are needed for the development of the pods. *Oroxylum* is hardy in the Gulf states and throughout USDA Zone 8.

"*Crescentia cujete*, the calabash tree," said Mr. Schokman, "is one species with two-inch flowers of yellow lined with red or purple veins, that eventually produce gourds that can be carved with intricate designs. When filled with pebbles or lead shot, they are used as maracas.

"In the Bombacaceae family, there are a number of nocturnal trees, including *Pseudobombax ellipticum*, the shaving-brush tree, where the pods

One of the bombax trees, *Bombax insigne*.

The baobab tree, *Adansonia digitata*.

pop open at dusk. Reaching a height of thirty feet, the trunks have a smooth, green bark and the compound leaves, each with five leaflets, are deciduous and shed in winter. The *Bombax ceiba*, the red silk cotton tree, can reach thirty feet in less than five years and will eventually be 125 feet tall. Large cuttings will root with ease and produce flowers in one year.

"The baobab, or upside-down tree, *Adansonia digitata*, resembles an upside-down carrot, its trunk diameter often being thirty feet while the height is only forty feet. Here, too, the strange pendulous flowers have five white reflexed petals that hover over a round ball of stamens.

"The durian tree, *Durio zibethinus*, is an evergreen that is widely planted in Malaya and the East Indies. The trees begin to flower about seven years after germination and soon produce ten-inch-long fruits that ripen over three months.

This fruit is an immensely popular food item—also considered an aphrodisiac—known chiefly for its delicate flavor combination of vanilla, caramel, and bananas with a touch of onion. But the flavors are coupled with a smell that is by some termed offensive and by others unbearable."

The Ylang-Ylang Tree

I love the Ilang fragrance
at twilight floating down,
the call of bird,
the plodding herd,
Along these ways to town.

—Hugh Curran, *Road to Manilla*

The common name of the perfume tree in the Philippines is ylang-ylang while the Spanish call it ilang-ilang. In Samoa it's mosu-oe and in Sri

Lanka, the name is vana-sapu. The scientific name is *Cananga odorata*. It's a fast-growing and aromatic evergreen tree that's a member of the Annona or custard apple family. These tropical trees and shrubs number about one hundred species. They are all native to tropical Asia and the Philippine Islands and are especially noted for producing flavorful fruits that are eaten raw or used to flavor sherbets and refreshing drinks.

In its native haunts, ylang-ylang will reach a height of eighty feet but when grown in the tropical gardens of southern Florida, the trees stop growth at about thirty-five feet.

"Ylang-ylang has long and slender, partly drooping branches," said Mr. Schokman, "and the foliage is inclined to be sparse unless the tree is trimmed to about fifteen feet every few years. The secret is to pinch the top of the tree after it is ten to twelve feet in height in order to develop a more compact frame. Otherwise it will continue to grow tall and slender, and in our South Florida environment, branches tend to snap off in strong winds."

The leaves of this tree are simple in shape, up to ten inches long and three inches wide. The flowers have three three-inch petals and three three-inch sepals, opening as greenish yellow but ageing to chartreuse. Like the magnolias, ylang-ylangs are pollinated by beetles.

But it's the fragrance that is the hallmark of this tree. Located at the base of the three petals are nectaries that resemble small pinkish red blotches which produce the essential oils. The flowers are best picked at dawn before the aroma dissipates into the tropical heat and a ten-year-old tree will produce about twenty-three pounds of flowers a year. Only two percent of that weight is oil; about two hundred pounds of the flowers are needed to produce one pound of essence, which is used as the base for Chanel No. 5 and other perfumes. Much of today's oil production takes place on Réunion Island where geranium oil is also produced.

Ripe seed germinates with ease, and seedlings are fast growers with flowers appearing two years after planting. Although references suggest that flowering occurs in November, in Florida, ylang-ylangs will flower throughout the year. They need full sun and plenty of water. In the event of a severe freeze, leaves will fall and there will be some dead branches, but the trees themselves will survive.

"In the Philippines," said Mr. Schokman, "the Samoan Islands, and parts of Indonesia, people soak these flowers in warm coconut oil which absorbs the perfume and rub the fragrant lotion on their bodies. Despite the increasing use of synthetic chemicals in modern perfumes, there is still a demand for a number of naturally produced essential oils for use in perfumes, cosmetics, polishes, and detergents. During the nineteenth century, the aroma of Macassar oil for men's hair came from ylang-ylang. The oils are extracted from flowers by steam distillation.

"There is a fifteen-year-old specimen at The Kampong, planted just east of the swimming pool. The scent of the flowers in the early morning and in the evening is subtle and alluring and not as overpowering as the orange jasmine."

The Kapok Trees

Just as the silky fibers that enable milkweed seeds to fly across the sky were once used to fill Mae West life preservers, the fluff of kapok seeds has similar applications. Being resistant to both decay and water, this lustrous yellowish floss has great commercial value as a stuffing for life preservers, bedding, and upholstery, and in addition an insulation against sound and heat.

Fred Berry of the Tropical Flowering Tree Society has been studying night-flowering tropical trees for years and is an expert on the kapok tree.

"There are some fourteen or fifteen species of *Ceiba*," said Mr. Berry, "with five species growing in Dade County, Florida. I've watched closely

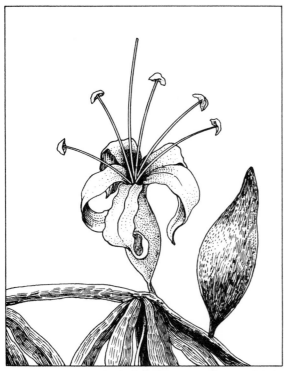

The flower and pod of a kapok tree, *Ceiba aesculifolia*.

the flowering of three of these, including the great kapok, *C. pentendra*, whose many small flowers bloom in clusters, tending to open late at night and in the early morning hours while the sky is still dark.

"While in the Yucatan, I collected seed from the pochote kapok, *Ceiba aesculifolia*, in 1975. In a pot, the seed germinated in six days. After being planted in my front yard, the little tree started blooming in two years and continues to bloom from early March through September, even after heavy pruning. The seedpods are plentiful, so there is plenty of insect pollination. The pods are packed with kapok, each puff loosely attached to one seed. There used to be plenty of opening pods full of kapok but there are so many wild parrots and parakeets around South Florida picking open the pods to get the green seeds that most of the fluff is ruined."

The great kapok tree can reach heights of one hundred feet in nature but is much smaller when grown in home landscapes, parks, and gardens. The pochote is much smaller and its trunk is armed with dense spines for the first twelve years; later the spines are only found on the upper branches.

"When flowering," said Mr. Berry, "the buds start cracking open from noon to late afternoon and the bronze color on the outer part of the petals will begin to show through. The next day the petals form a tube about the diameter of a finger, about an inch long. The following day the bud will reach the size of three and a half inches. The flower is now ready to open between eight thirty and nine fifteen (Daylight Savings Time). The five petals will separate and curve down, this action taking between thirty seconds up to five minutes. Sometimes two or more petals will stick together and the process will be delayed for a few minutes. Every three-inch flower on the tree will open within that time frame.

"Amazingly enough, if you pick a bud on its stem (or pedicle), a few hours before it would normally open and put it in a glass of water, the bud will open on cue. If you pick a bud four to five hours before normal opening, it will slowly open finishing about three o'clock the next morning. If picked much before then, it won't open at all."

The Pitch Apple

The pitch apple, *Clusia rosea*, was described to me by Julia F. Morton, Director of the Morton Collectanea at the University of Miami.

"The pitch apple reaches a height of fifty to sixty feet," she said, "in its natural habitats of the Bahamas, the Greater Antilles, and the Virgin Islands, but stays at about thirty feet in Florida. It is often free-standing, but in the rain forests of Puerto Rico and other moist areas, is usually seen as an epiphyte, starting as a seedling in a crotch or on a branch of another tree, some of its descending aerial roots, to twenty feet long, gradually strangling its host while others anchor themselves in the ground to form a pseudotrunk. The strangling habit is the reason for the nickname, Scotch attorney."

The thick, leathery and smooth leaves are evergreen, up to nine inches in length and over five inches wide. The tree blooms all year around in the tropics but only during the summer in Florida and then only a few flowers at a time over several weeks. The beautiful flowers, borne singly or in twos or threes, open at night and sometimes on overcast days remain open all the next morning. The flowers are circular, three to four inches across, white with a wide pink band across the center of each petal, or sometimes entirely pink.

Dr. Morton is concerned about the use of the tree in the Florida landscape.

"It's usually placed as though it were a shrub in foundation planters, in pots on terraces, or, if in the ground, on small patios and very close to houses or other buildings, and sometimes espaliered against a wall. But the aerial roots and the ultimate size are not taken into consideration and the result is, in time, damage to structures and increasing ugliness as it struggles for space, and finally removal."

The Evening Magnolias

Magnolia spp. have been beloved by gardeners for centuries and a number of magnolia species and cultivars are fragrant not only by day but in the evening, too—and many open their blossoms in the evening. "It always seemed to me," said Phelan A. Bright, Secretary-Treasurer of The Magnolia Society, "as a child growing up in Tennessee, that the scent of magnolias was most heady at dusk, an attribute, real or imagined, which is significantly responsible for my addiction to these plants."

Magnolias are among the most primitive flowers on earth today. They have been found in fossil beds from over fifty million years ago. The trees were named in honor of Pierre Magnol (1638–1751), a botanist and physician who lived in

The pitch apple, *Clusia rosea*.

southern France and was director of the Montpellier Botanic Gardens.

Since magnolias show no differentiation between petals and sepals, the term used for both is tepal. Before the flowers open, they are protected by perules, tough furry covers that resemble pussy willows. The male part of the flower is called the androecium and consists of stamens that are spirally arranged around the base of the female organ, the gynoecium.

As you would expect from an ancient flower like the magnolia, pollination is not achieved by anything as average as a bee or butterfly. Here the agents of pollination are beetles that belong to the Nitidulidae family. These beetles feed on the sap of freshly cut trees, decaying melons or fruit, and, as in the case of the magnolia, floral pollen and nectar. After visiting an open flower, these beetles are covered with pollen. Then, before the next flower opens, they crawl between the overlapping tepals for the nectar and in such close quarters, leave pollen on the gynoecium. After fertilization, the fruit cone turns red or pink, the carpels holding the ripening seeds split, and the individual seeds hang by threads until blown away.

One magnolia, *Magnolia coco*, an evergreen shrub native to China, has nodding, rounded, creamy white flowers that are entirely nocturnal in habit, the flowers opening at dusk or shortly after. They are extremely fragrant, especially at night. Plant height is between two and four feet bearing thick oval leaves of glossy green. They are only reliably hardy in USDA Zone 9 since freezing will kill the roots but make an excellent greenhouse or houseplant, blooming on and off throughout the year.

Known as the Mexican cow-cumber (I do not know the story behind the name), *Magnolia delavayi* is an evergreen, evening-flowering magnolia originally from southwest China. This large shrub or small tree can reach a height of thirty feet in nature and has a compact conelike form and large oval leaves up to fifteen inches long. The flowers are ivory white, about seven inches across, and sweetly fragrant at night. Although it's only hardy in USDA Zones 8 through 10 (some gardeners report that it is much hardier but up-to-date information is lacking), *M. delavayi* makes a wonderful indoor-blooming houseplant, albeit needing plenty of room.

The Yulan or lily tree, *Magnolia denudata* (synonym, *M. heptapeta*), comes from central China, and Buddhist records tell of its cultivation going back to the Tang Dynasty (A.D. 618–906). It's a small, slow-growing tree reaching a height of thirty feet in about a hundred years, so people with small gardens need not worry too much about overcrowding. Its oval leaves are about six inches long and the flowers grow to four inches long, each with nine white tepals. They are particularly beautiful at sunset when the lemon fragrance becomes especially pronounced, carrying over well into the evening.

Magnolia globosa, introduced from China in 1919, is a shrub or small tree with oval leaves about ten inches long and five inches wide. The three-inch-wide, creamy white flowers are produced in June, the tepals surrounding a ring of rose-red stamens, and are very fragrant, especially at night. This tree is hardy in USDA Zone 7 and south.

The ear-leaved umbrella tree, *Magnolia fraseri*, is an American native that matures to a beautiful multistemmed shrub but if kept to a single stem, eventually becomes a fifty-foot tree. The leaves are about ten inches long and up to six inches wide and the wonderfully evening-fragrant creamy white flowers are up to eight inches across. The large crimson seed cones are produced in late summer and quite attractive in their own right.

Magnolia fraseri var. *pyramidata*, a smaller form of the umbrella tree, becomes either a large multistemmed shrub or a single-stemmed tree growing to thirty feet. The leaves are only eight inches long and the showy night-fragrant flowers are about five inches across, varying in shade from pure white to a creamy white. Like the parent magnolia, this variety has attractive rose-crimson seed cones and is especially suited for the small garden. Both these native magnolias are hardy in USDA Zone 6 and south.

Magnolia sieboldii (synonum, *M. parviflora*) remains a large bushy shrub or small tree reaching a height of twenty feet, with oval leaves about six inches long and a little over three inches wide. Beginning in June and on and off throughout the summer, the trees bear four-inch-wide nodding flowers of pure white. The nine tepals surround a ring of deep red to rich crimson stamens. They are very fragrant, especially at dusk. This magnolia is hardy in USDA Zone 6 and south and it has been reported to withstand temperatures of below 0°F for at least a week without showing damage.

Magnolia virginiana, the sweet bay tree, has a bushy growth habit doing well in poor as well as

The flowers of *Magnolia sieboldii* are especially fragrant at night.

moist soils. The lovely three- to six-inch white flowers appear in the spring and sometimes during the summer, opening in late afternoon and becoming intensely fragrant during the evening, and are described as being cool, fruity, and sweet. The pretty oblong leaves are about five inches long and glaucous-gray beneath, giving a silvery effect when the wind blows, especially at night. There are a number of garden cultivars including 'Dwarf', which is especially suited for the small garden since its ultimate height is about fifteen feet. This beautiful tree is surprisingly hardy from USDA Zone 5 and south.

Another thing about the sweet bay tree is that it needs the hot summers of the eastern United States in order to grow successfully. Well-grown trees can reach a height of sixty feet but in England the tallest on record is about thirty feet high.

Talauma hodgsonii is a close magnolia relative, blooming at night with seven-inch ivory white flowers that are especially fragrant at night. It's a wonderful tree, with very large and attractive foliage, each leaf two feet long and over nine inches wide. The flowers open at dusk, usually about eight P.M. The talauma cannot withstand long bouts of temperatures below 20°F.

The Lacy Tree Philodendron

The lacy tree philodendron, *Philodendron selloum*, has a long history as a houseplant and has often been mistaken for a close relative, the Swiss-cheese plant, *Monstera deliciosa*. Both plants are similar in looks and growth habit and both were among the most popular decorator plants of the 1950s. Any house or apartment that did not have the obligatory orange or red, round-bottomed fiberglass tub on shiny brass legs containing one of these plants was decidedly *déclassé*.

This philodendron is a self-heading plant—it has only one main stem—that at first forms a large rosette of elegant foliage. After many years,

a stout stem develops that will grow up to the light, carrying the beautiful leaves and a host of aerial roots along. The lush green leaves are often three feet across, deeply lobed and cut, and as long as the plants are kept at temperatures above 60°F, in evenly moist soil, and are given plenty of light, they will thrive.

But in addition to being an elegant houseplant, *Philodendron selloum* is a night-blooming plant and when the plant is about sixteen years old and conditions are to its liking—including lots of light—once a year the flower will appear, its greenish white hooded leaf or spath surrounding a foot-long spadix, opening after dark, closing the next morning, and opening once more for a final night.

But this plant is unusual for more than its time of flowering, as it's one of the few plants known to generate heat—up to 114°F—burning fat in special cells that turn it into heat instead of carbohydrates and attracting the scarab beetles native to Brazil that it depends on for pollination. For some unknown reason some jungle beetles—possibly because they enjoy saunas—come for the heat and, while either eating or copulating, will wander up and down the spadix, carrying pollen from the male flowers at the top, past the center where the heat is produced, to the female flowers at the bottom.

Gardeners who live in the warmer parts of America have a better chance to see the flowers in bloom but it also blooms up North, especially if the plants can spend summers out in the garden, shaded from the midday sun, getting lots of humidity—and lots of light.

The Swiss-cheese Plant

Monstera deliciosa is usually called the Swiss-cheese plant but its common names also include breadfruit vine, hurricane plant, Mexican breadfruit, fruit-salad plant, window plant, and split-leaf philodendron. It belongs to the Araceae

The flower of the Swiss-cheese plant, *Monstera deliciosa.*

family, as does the lacy tree philodendron, its genus containing some twenty-five species of epiphytic climbers native to tropical America.

The term *Monstera* is Latin for strange or monstrous and points to some of the oddities associated with this plant, including long and twisting aerial roots that usually never touch ground, large glossy leaves full of holes and deeply lobed cutouts (hence some of the common names), and nocturnal flowers that ultimately produce edible fruits that resemble white pine cones and taste of pineapple. No one has ever proved why the leaves are full of holes, but it has been suggested that it would allow heavy tropical rains to drip right through or hurricane winds to whistle through the holes and not cause structural damage to the plant.

The waxy white floral spathe opens on mid- to late winter evenings, revealing a foot-long greenish yellow spadix with faint honeycomblike markings. It exudes an odor straight from grandmother's kitchen or the local bakery: the yeasty smell of fresh-baked bread—hence yet another one of the common names, breadfruit vine.

The spadix turns into a large fruit, resembling an ear of corn but often much larger. From flowering until the fruit ripens is fourteen months or more. Then the fruit turns yellow and the scales that cover the surface eventually fall off. It ripens from the bottom up and should be kept in the refrigerator to prevent spoiling. The odor is a combination of banana and pineapple and the taste is sweet—but rather boring if you hold your nose when eating.

Following the instructions for *Philodendron selloum* for growing this plant.

$\mathcal{P}$LANTS THAT LOOK LIKE THEY SHOULD BLOOM AT NIGHT

———

Nothing great is achieved without chimeras.

ERNEST RENAN, *L'Avenir de la Science*

$\mathcal{J}$ have spent a number of years in the evening garden and over those years several plants have come to my attention that are not strictly nocturnal in habit. But although they open their flowers during the day, because of their general construction they look as though they were meant only to open after dark—and luckily they remain open all through the night. Some like the stapeliads, have beautiful but strange blossoms; some like the mouse plant are cute but strange; others like the tropical members of the Dutchman's-pipe vine are just strange; and one, the jack o'lantern mushroom, is really a fungus and doesn't flower at all.

In our evening garden when one of these marvelous plants comes into bloom, it's usually set within a grouping of potted plants in front of a low wall under our viburnum tree. There low-voltage lights gently bathe the unusual flowers in soft light. Others have been placed where they are bound to catch a visitor's eye while walking the darkened pathways.

If one of these plants should open during the winter months, I have lights in my greenhouse and at night the flowers are visible through the glass to anyone coming up to the front door.

The Devil's Tongue

I first read about the genus of plants known as devil's tongue (*Amorphophallus* spp.) in a used copy of *Plants with Personality* by Patrick M. Synge (Lindsay Drummond Ltd., n.d.). After mentioning stapeliads in the chapter entitled "Fly-Pollinated Plants," Synge speaks of one of the largest flowering plants in the known world, *A. titanum*, a

> . . . gigantic and monstrous aroid [that] grows at an incredible rate, sometimes six inches a day until it opens at a height of eight and a half feet. The mature inflorescence is said to give off an offensive scent, resembling the smell of decayed fish. The inflorescence consists of a

The infamous devil's tongue, *Amorphophallus rivieri.*

gigantic fleshy spike pale-green in colour, with touches of white. This spike emerges from the centre of a spathe, a sheath, which at first surrounds it and then opens like a rococo seashell with a fringed edge, displaying a rich maroon or liver coloured inside. . . .

Need I say more? This is a flower meant for the more bizarre parts of the evening garden. Unfortunately, up until the 1980s there were few practical sources for obtaining these plants. Then a smaller species called *Amorphophallus rivieri* hit the bulb market.

Upon arrival in the fall I planted the bulb in a ten-inch Rivera self-watering pot (the first scientific name of this plant was *Hydrosme*, referring to its love of water) with a mix of composted manure, potting soil, and sand and left it in the greenhouse. Two weeks later a sheathed and speckled shaft burst through the dirt and continued to grow inches a day until about a week later a twenty-inch spathe began to open with a taller spadix, all standing on a three-foot stem. Unfortunately the blossom is surrounded by flies during the day, so it's not a good idea to flower this plant indoors.

After the flower begins to shrivel, then slowly dissolve, the plant disappears for about a month, then the attractive, fernlike leaves appear, some being three feet across. If kept in an attractive pot, either the flower or the foliage is welcome in the evening garden. When the leaves start to yellow and dry, the bulb goes into a period of rest so withhold water for six months before using water to start a new cycle of growth. Winter temperatures of above 50°F are fine.

The Mouse Plant

Shades of the three blind mice! *Arisarum proboscideum* has arrow-shaped leaves growing about four inches high and in late winter and early spring produces hooded flowers with a dark brown top and a whitish bottom and, at the end of each hood, a long tail that winds about. Together these flowers look like a group of mice at a cheese convention. These plants need partial shade and a soil rich in humus. The tuberous roots form clumps which produce many offsets so once this plant is in your garden, there will be plenty to go around.

They are especially eye-catching when planted at the edge of a wall but be sure to have a small light placed in the middle of the group. They are hardy in USDA Zones 5 to 7.

The Calico Flowers

The calico flowers or birthworts are members of the *Aristolochia* genus. The name is derived from the Greek *aristos*, or best, and *lochia*, meaning childbirth, references to the use of this plant as a medicine. Most of these plants are tropical or greenhouse plants and indoor vines, but one called the Dutchman's-pipe, *A. durior*, is a popular vine used to ramble about summer porches or screen rubbish piles and old tree trunks.

The most bizarre is the pelican flower, *Aristolochia gigantea*, which first arrived in England from Guatemala in 1841. This is a high-reaching vine that can grow up to ten feet, and bears flat, smooth, heart-shaped leaves that have a slightly rank odor when crushed. The six-inch flowers are off-white, veined with purple, and sit on top of a U-shaped tube of a greenish color and with an unattractive odor. But as a flower for the evening garden, this is a showstopper.

The vines do best in pots that hang on wires, allowing plenty of room for growth. They can also be carefully unwound from one wire and rewound on another but remember to maintain the counterclockwise turns.

The calico flower, *Aristolochia elegans*, is peculiar and somewhat smaller. This plant first came from Brazil and entered Europe in 1883. It's a free-flowering vine reaching a length of eight feet once it's settled in. The flowers are one and a half inches long and three inches wide and con-

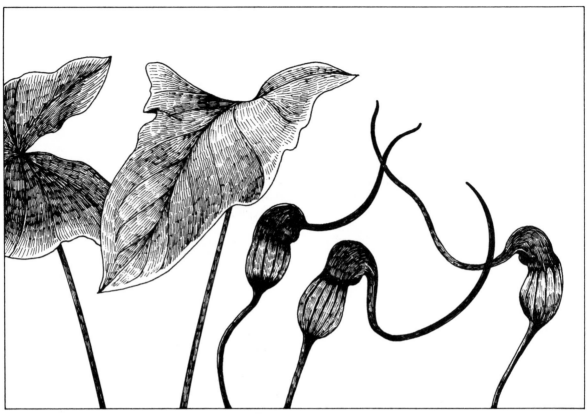

The tails of the mouse plant, *Arisarum proboscideum*.

sist of purple flaps etched with white, sitting on top of a yellow tube.

Both of these plants want warm surroundings with temperatures always above 60°F. A good soil mix is one quarter each potting soil, peat moss, composted manure, and sand. Keep the soil evenly moist but never soggy and keep the vines in partial shade, as hot summer sun can burn the leaves. Once indoors for the winter, you can cut the vines back; new leaves will appear in the early spring.

The Cobra Lily

Cobra lilies were discovered in 1841 in a marsh off a small tributary of the upper Sacramento River, a few miles south of Mt. Shasta. These pitcher plants were immediately seen to be so distinctive as to warrant their own genus, *Darlingtonia californica*. The plant was dedicated and named after Dr. William Darlington of West Chester, Pennsylvania. It's found only in Oregon and northern California in the typical damp and boggy conditions enjoyed by most of the insectivores. Dr. Darlington was a respected botanist in his day and upon his death, left his herbarium of over eight thousand species of plants to Chester County, Pennsylvania.

The dome-topped chimneys of darlingtonias are really modified leaves. The dome itself is unusually firm and dotted with translucent windows, looking very much like a piece of Tiffany glass. A feature peculiar to *Darlingtonia* is the twisting of the tube either to the right or left so

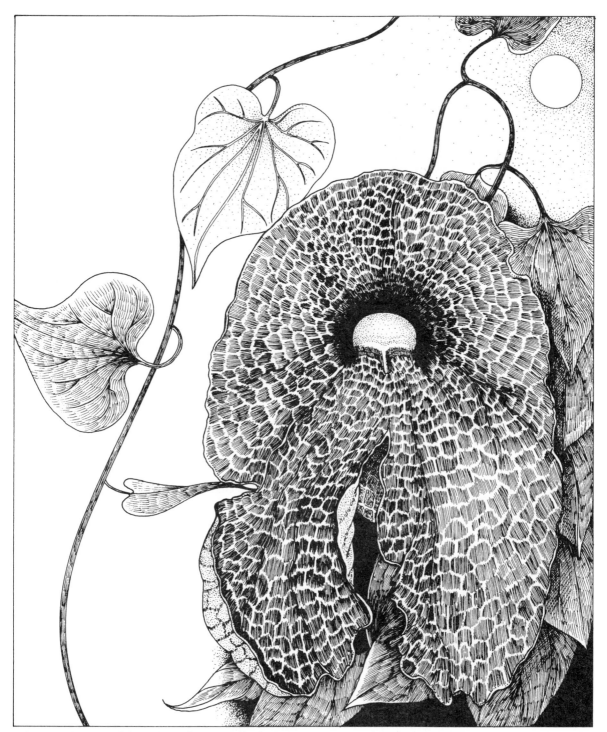

A bizarre blossom of the pelican flower, *Aristolochia gigantea*.

The cobra lily, *Darlingtonia californica*.

that the helmet-shaped dome is turned about 180 degrees from the axis of the plant. The beard in front of the tube's opening secretes nectar to draw unwary visitors. Cobra lilies bear strange nodding flowers composed of yellow-green sepals and dark purple petals early in the spring.

The pitchers are lined with stiff hairs that point toward the well of water below and these, in combination with additional nectar glands, lead unsuspecting insects along the path to oblivion. Once in the water, there is no escape and the insect is drowned and digested by bacterial action. These plants are unique among the pitcher plants because they harbor active bacteria in their wells that do the job of digestive fluids. Other members of the family actually produce their own digestive enzymes.

If you live in an area of the country where temperatures stay above 20°F, cobra lilies can be grown outdoors in a bog garden. Since our garden is too cold, the plants are kept in clay pots set in saucers full of water, spending the winter in the greenhouse. The soil mix is half potting soil and half sphagnum moss mixed well. They want as much winter sun as possible and will do well in temperatures of 40°F or above. Never let the soil dry out.

These plants are spectacular both day and night but are especially fascinating in the evening garden not only because of their shape but because of the way light from decorative lamps shines through the translucent windows found on the hollow stems.

An Orchid Named Dracula

There are a few orchids that, because of their general appearance, were considered too monsterlike for the genus *Masdevallia* and, thanks to some taxonomists with a sense of humor, were moved to a new genus called *Dracula*. It was a wise move since its lip forms a fleshy cup that moves and the sepals constrict to form tails covered with hairs giving the flowers a furry appearance. Frankly, they do have that certain look of the kind of monster often found in Roger Corman movies of the 1950s. (There is an orchid called *Dracuvallia* that is a cross between the two genera, but I've never seen the result of this flight into the unknown.)

The leader of the pack is *Dracula chimaera*. This is the flower that led to the name change. Each blossom has three triangular sepals, about three inches wide at the base, that surround a pink center cup—which is movable. Including the sepals' tails, the flower is fifteen inches long. The background color of the sepals is a creamy tan but they are covered with maroon splotches and the accompanying fur is gray. My description is based on a painting of this floral beauty by Florence Helen Woolward (1854–1936) who was hired to paint all the orchids in the collection of the Ninth Marquis of Lothian, Schomberg Henry Kerr (1833–1900). The Marquis was exceptionally fond of the masdevallias and his specimen of *D. chimaera* was the first to flower in England.

You would expect that these orchids would delight in heat, the hotter the better. But most of the species come from the mountain jungles of Colombia, Ecuador, and Peru, where nights are cool and days only moderately warm. *Dracula chimaera*, for example, prefers evening temperatures between 50°F and 55°F and daytime highs in the seventies, although in the summer draculas will adapt to higher temperatures if the humidity stays above sixty percent. In fact, the blossoms quickly react to a lack of water by wilting and must be continually sprayed to keep them in the pink of health. In areas where temperatures stay above 35°F, these orchids can be set out in the garden. Provide draculas with filtered sunlight and pot them in a mix of chopped osmunda and sphagnum moss, tree fern mixed with perlite, or plain unmilled sphagnum.

There are a number of other species and cultivars including *Dracula bella*, an orchid that is found at an elevation of eight thousand feet.

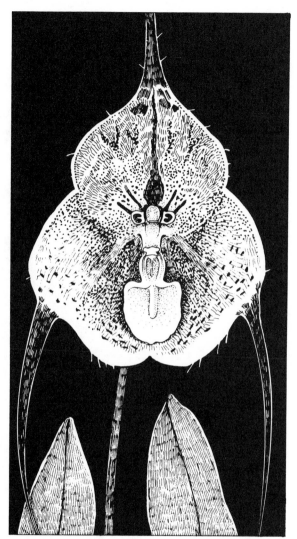

One of the Dracula orchids, *Dracula erythrochaete*.

Tufted nine-inch leaves give rise to slender stalks that bear fragrant flowers of pale yellow spotted with brownish crimson that end in four-inch tails. The lip is described as being white and oscillating.

Dracula tarantula is a species that bears flowers described as being "heavily hirsute," with yellowish sepals overlaid with irregular purple dashes, then rimmed with solid purple that ex-

The dragon lily, *Dracunculus vulgaris*, from Dr. Thornton's illustration first published in 1801.

tends to the ends of the tails. And *D. vampira* has white sepals laced with heavy blackish brown lines.

Draculas should be grown in open baskets since the floral stalks often grow down through the rooting medium. The flowers bend down like a pendant. The flowers open one at a time from a single spike, blooming from winter into spring but, if content with their surroundings, will flower on and off throughout the year.

The Dragon Lily

I mentioned Dr. Thornton's great florilegia the *Temple of Flora* for its amazing portrayal of the night-blooming cereus. But Dr. Thornton did it again with the plate that details the dragon lily, *Dracunculus vulgaris*. Here the tip of the flamboyant flower blooms in the upper left corner of the picture, its livid purple spathe superimposed on a violent orange sky while to the right, the clouds have turned a dark Payne's gray, laced with lightning, and on the horizon an active volcano spews fire to the heavens. At the picture's lower right corner, a dark river laced with white reflections runs on to nowhere, all signs proclaiming that wild is the night.*

These plants are close relatives of the devil's tongue and produce a foot-high stalk that is topped with an eighteen-inch spathe that is greenish without and purple-black within, its edges crisped as though they were made of crepe paper. The spadix is purple. The leaves have whitish stems spotted with purple and, like others in the clan, the flowers have un unkind odor since they are pollinated by flies, but the blossoms are so strangely beautiful, they should be admired both day and night.

*The plate I described above was first painted by Peter Henderson. Dr. Thornton's studio then produced a print using mezzotint, aquatint, and stipple engraving, with hand coloring added. It was first published in 1801, but the plate wore out and subsequent editions show a dull gray sky with the orange highlights, the volcano, and the lightning completely erased.

Unfortunately these are not hardy where the ground will freeze but if you can offer protection, plant them out about nine inches apart, providing good garden soil in full sun. If grown in pots, water well but let the soil dry between waterings and let the corms go dormant during the winter months.

The Serpent Gourds

The following two plants are vines that belong to the Cucurbitaceae, or the gourd family. Of the two, *Hodgsonia heteroclita* is the most difficult to find. The plants come from East Bengal, Burma, and Java. The fruits and flowers appear on fantastic vines often reaching a length of one hundred feet, winding their way through the tree canopy above the jungle floor. The white flowers open in late afternoon and are wasted by the following morning. These blossoms are decidedly strange in appearance being over five inches wide with each of the five petals ending in six five-inch-long threads that curl and twirl about. After fertilization, a fruit is formed that resembles a small pumpkin about six inches across. It's full of a green viscid pulp that is inedible but there are a number of seeds called *kai hior pot*, and the seed centers are used for food.

There is a smaller serpent gourd known as *Trichosanthes anguina*, the genus name meaning hair flower because of the hairlike division on the lobes of the five petals. The flowers are smaller than those of *Hodgsonia heteroclita*, being a little over an inch wide but they are incredibly fringed and like their giant cousin, the flowers are fragile and never last more than a day.

The fruit grows like a snake, long and coiled, and the warmer the climate, the longer the serpent. In our northern garden in upstate New York in USDA Zone 5, the fruits never grew longer than two feet.

H. F. Macmillan writing in the *Handbook of Tropical Gardening* (published in Ceylon), said this is

A serpent gourd, *Hodgsonia heteroclita*.

A quick-growing gourd, bearing long cylindrical, green (sometimes greenish-white) fruits, which not unfrequently reach the length of five to six feet. In an unripe state these podlike fruits are sliced and cooked in the manner of French beans being also rarely used as a curry vegetable in the low-country. Seeds are sown in the monsoons [and] it is customary to suspend a small stone at the end of each fruit whilst growing, so as to weight it down and induce it to grow straighter, and perhaps longer, than it would otherwise do.

In an 1804 issue of *Botanical Magazine* published in London, the following description appeared:

. . . [It] was introduced into Europe about the year 1720, and seems at first to have attracted considerable attention from the singularity of its fringed flowers and snake-shaped fruit, which last is also curious from the rapidity of its growth. The plant was cultivated by Miller in Chelsea Garden, the year 1755, who published a figure of it . . . [and] like many other annuals which excite but a short-lived curiosity, this plant soon disappeared, and perhaps there are few persons now that have ever seen it in this country, though it will produce ripe seeds with us if sown on a hotbed early in the spring and treated in the same manner as cucumbers and melons.

We grew it in well-fertilized garden soil in full sun and provided plenty of water all summer long. The vines grew along a trellis some five feet off the ground and were used as a backdrop for other evening flowers. The ripening gourds are especially fantastic when viewed by torchlight.

The Indian Pipe

Last summer while on a walk in the woods, I spied a very large clump of Indian pipes, or *Monotropa uniflora*, growing underneath the

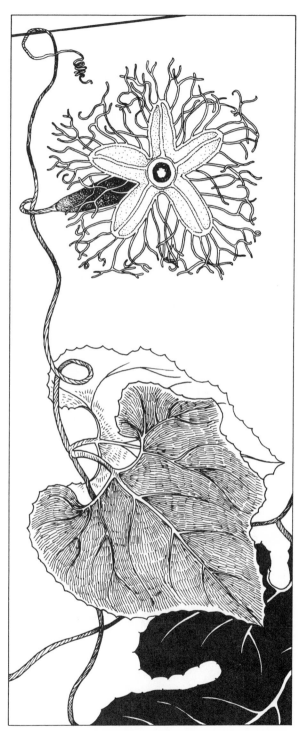

The snake gourd, *Trichosanthes anguina*.

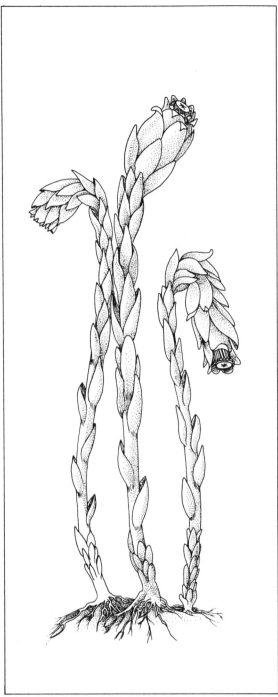

The Indian pipe, *Monotropa uniflora*.

branches of a gray birch. The other common names of ice-plant, ghost-flower, and corpse-plant point to its reputation in the world of wild-flowers. I was struck by the strange beauty of this plant—its soft white pallor seems to shine against the litter of leaves from which it emerges. Although the blossoms usually nod toward the ground, they raise their heads when the waxy petals are ready to open. This particular specimen had changed its floral pitch and was ready to expel a burst of tiny seed.

Neltje Blanchan in *Nature's Garden* gives the following description: "Colorless in every part, waxy, cold, and clammy, Indian pipes rise like a company of wraiths in the dim forest that suits them well. Ghoulish parasites, uncanny sapro-phytes, for their matted roots prey either on the juices of living plants or on the decaying matter of dead ones, how weirdly beautiful and deco-rative they are!"

Mrs. Blanchan was a master of colorful prose and her description is certainly apt, but somehow in the generation that has produced *Night of the Living Dead*, the plant does not seem as funereal as it might have when first she saw it.

In this case the juice of the living is not blood but the sap of a lowly fungus. The two- to twelve-inch pipes do not themselves live on dead or dying matter but, like many orchids, depend on another agent for survival. Their true root system is but a few short, white cords that lie in close arrange-ment with a fungus which in turn spreads its threadlike but false roots, or mycelium, in all directions through the leaf mold.

Mycelium resembles nothing more than a net-work of tiny, white, branching filaments—much like a piece of cheesecloth—which actively search for and digest bits of organic matter and humus. Then the roots of *Monotropa* steal these predi-gested foods.

Hortus Third lists *Monotropa* as a perennial, which was a surprise to me. I thought because of its method of survival it would be an annual en-tirely at the mercy of finding a store of food. But

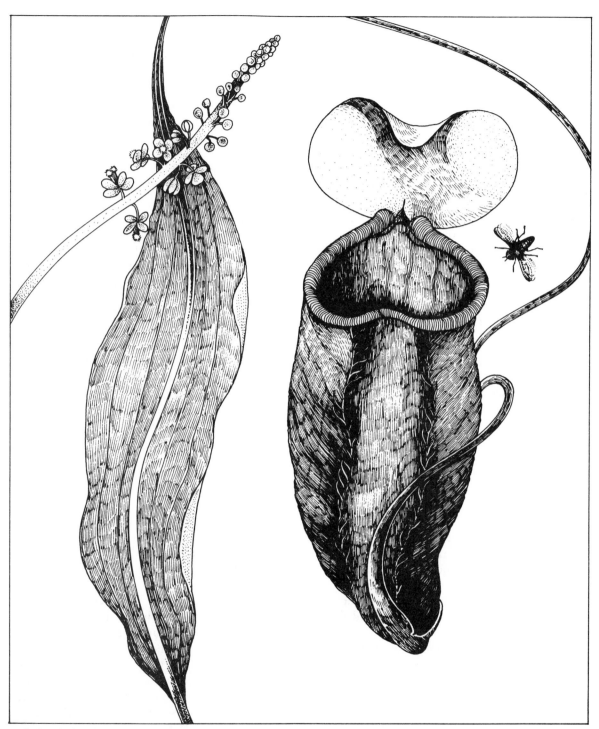

A fly heads for the pitcher of a tropical pitcher plant, *Nepenthes maxima*.

apparently once a plant finds a fungus to live with, a long partnership ensues. Although it's possible to transplant if a good deal of surrounding earth and leaf litter is moved with the plant, it's not a wise thing to do—unless you find plants in the path of developers, then move whatever you can. The easiest thing to do for the evening garden is cast seeds in a specially prepared section of soil where there is plenty of good deep black earth loaded with organic matter. The best place is a spot at the edge of the evening garden where the leaf mold is thick or funguslike coral root abound. As with many other flowers in the eastern woods, close relatives are also found growing in Japan.

The Pitcher Plants

I have in my hand the dried pitcher of a tropical pitcher plant known as *Nepenthes maxima* or sometimes *N. curtisii*. The pitcher itself is over three inches high and about an inch and a half in circumference. The lip is tough and resembles a horse collar in shape. Unfortunately the lid shrank to almost nothing in the process of drying but the whole affair gives one a good idea of what these insect traps looked like in the full flush of life. This particular species is small—many others bear pitchers over a foot in length.

There are about seventy species in this genus of plants and they are native from the Philippine Islands to northern Australia, the Malay Peninsula, and Sri Lanka. The pitchers are usually green, often splotched with crimson and appear at the ends of long tendrils that begin at the ends of a leaf, and are extensions of the midribs. A well-grown plant makes a rosette of these leaves and the pitchers bob up and down like strange puppets on green strings.

Until the pitcher reaches maturity, the lid is held to the pitcher's mouth and whatever minute openings exist are sealed with a dense growth of branching hairs. In some species the lids will keep out heavy rains, while in others, like the plant we grow, the top is useless. The fluid within is sterile and completely free of bacteria but infused with digestive fluids. The interior walls are coated with a waxy substance. Insects are attracted to the pitchers by a honeylike nectar secreted by cells under the collar. Many slip over the edge and once inside are unable to get a grip on the wax and eventually plunge to the liquid below where they become a protein soup.

Our plant summers under the viburnum tree where a shaft of low-voltage lighting illuminates the pitchers with high drama. Winters are spent in the greenhouse. While some pitcher plants need specialized care and enormous applications of heat, *Nepenthes maxima* will tolerate occasional plunges into the fifties although it likes the range between 60°F and 75°F the best. Give the plants partial shade in the summer but full sun during the winter months. The soil should be kept evenly moist at all times. A mix of one part each potting soil, sphagnum moss, and sand does very well. The green flowers are small and not particularly attractive and best glossed over for the pitchers.

The Triffid Orchid

The Day of the Triffids was a popular science-fiction film of 1963. The movie deals with the potential end of the world brought about by the eating habits of giant plants called Triffids, flowers from another star, flowers that walk and devour anything that moves—including the human race.

A number of orchids are spectacular in their beauty, many more are interesting and amusing, but to my mind, there are a few that so resemble nighttime creatures that their beauty could best be termed lurid for they look as though they should be shunned by the light of day. The *Dracula* species immediately come to mind but there are also the members of the *Paphiopedilum* genus that fit this bill. When the special effects crews hunted about for a proper florific horror, someone found these so-called slipper orchids and knew that if the blossoms were enlarged and set upon six feet of tentacles and shaggy bark, they would have a Triffid. The fact that these orchids are terrestrial in habit rather than epiphytic only adds to the illusion.

The long-lasting flowers are thick with substance and look like they have been sculpted from wax. Most have a large pouch veined with opposing colors, a dorsal sepal (or cover to the pouch) that is usually striped, and two petals, one on each side of the pouch, that are dotted with color, bear small warts, and are lined with hairs along the edges.

One of my favorites is *Paphiopedilum callosum*, originally from Thailand and South Vietnam. The bluish green leaves are marbled and the four-inch flowers sit on top of foot-high stalks, the dorsal sepal striped with green and crimson, the eyelashed petals are green, and the pelican pouch a deep purplish brown shade of mahogany. This species flowers in the spring.

Another best bet for the evening garden is *Paphiopedilum lawrenceanum*, a species with a dorsal sepal of white, tiger-striped with deep purple, the side petals green with purple tips with both margins lined with small warts, and the lip of the brownish green pouch of a dull purple. The flowers appear from spring well into summer, with individual blossoms lasting a month or more.

Like the draculas, slipper orchids are not hothouse flowers but prefer temperatures between 50°F and 55°F and daytime temperatures in the mid-seventies. If temperatures reach the mid-eighties, the plants should summer under shade trees, but set the pots on gravel or cinder beds to prevent slugs from attacking. If you live in an area where summers are very hot for long periods of time, look for another flower-of-the-night.

Pot slipper orchids in fern bark as the roots should never be kept in a soggy condition, though they should also never be allowed to dry out.

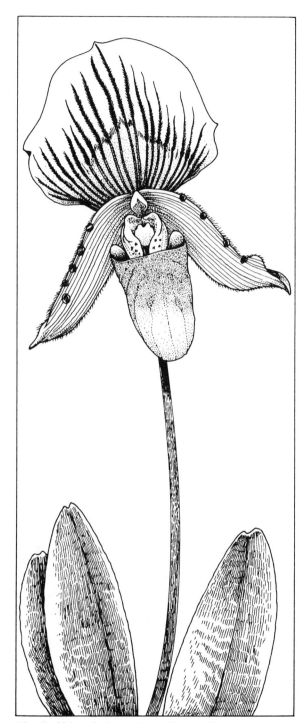

The Triffid orchid, *Paphiopedilum callosum*.

A North American pitcher plant, *Sarracenia purpurea*.

Keep the plants out of the direct sun; they are creatures of the jungles, protected by a high canopy of trees and protected from too much ultraviolet.

The Other Pitcher Plants

There are a number of insectivorous plants that, if they were larger, would provide a shudder or two. The Venus flytrap, the sundew, and the butterwort are all too small to make much of a statement in any but a specialist's collection, but the hardy pitcher plants would make a valuable addition to any evening garden.

The first insectivores to be carefully examined were the pitcher plants, chiefly *Sarracenia purpurea*, found and described in North America by an unknown artist circa 1550. The plant itself was finally traced to Virginia and brought to England, alive, in 1640. Its intriguing shape and its method of obtaining insect food caused quite a sensation in the scientific community of the time.

Nectar-producing glands on the outside of the pitchers send scent signals to passing insects. When the potential victim reaches one of the pitchers—really a modified stem—it follows a honey trail leading to the open mouth. There it either slips or falls over the edge, and being unable to crawl back out due to stout glassy hairs that line the inside walls pointing to the bottom, it winds up in a liquid grave at the foot of the stem.

The trumpet pitcher plant, *Sarracenia flava*, flowers from March to midsummer with yellow blossoms that resemble inverted umbrellas. The trumpet pitchers vary in color from light green to yellow and are hardy from USDA Zone 7 and south.

But the northern pitcher plant, *Sarracenia purpurea*, is hardy all the way north to USDA Zone 3. The pitchers are often lopsided and the lower curve of the stem rests on the ground. The leaves are in varying shades of green and purple and have pronounced veining. The flowers are typical of the genus and are maroon in color.

Grow both these plants either in large containers or in a bog garden where the soil is always wet or evenly moist. They want full sun to produce the best coloration in the leaves.

The Voodoo Lily

Sauromatum guttatum is the voodoo lily, though it's also referred to as the red calla or the monarch-of-the-east. This plant belongs to the same group as the devil's tongue but is less malodorous.

This plant is rarely pictured in plant catalogs, and when it does appear, the likeness is usually presented in a little watercolor or a hurried drawing, never by a photograph.

Because this plant is not hardy north of USDA Zone 7, it's best grown in a clay pot. In the spring shortly after you water the pot that contains the wrinkled, oval-shaped tuber, a pale green tip will push up through the dirt. Day by day it will lengthen, until finally the spathe opens to reveal an inner lining of purple spots on a greenish buff background. Also disclosed will be the lizard's tail, a dark purple bending wand, its bottom hidden within a part of the spathe that doesn't open and itself sitting on a very short, tiny stem, so that the blossom is almost level with the soil. The blossom lasts only a day or two before it deflates and slowly dries up but for those few days it will be the talk of the evening garden.

Soon green tips appear and after that very large and attractive, tropical-looking leaves are borne on spotted stems and will persist until fall. The leaves often reach a height of two feet. The foliage is attractive enough to be grown without the added attraction of the bizarre flowers.

During the days of Queen Victoria, these were popular flowers for the houseplant window and corms were imported to be grown indoors in a bowl, for they will bloom without water or soil. After blooming the corm must be planted so that it gains strength to flower again the next year. Grow this tuber like the devil's tongue (see page 167).

The voodoo lily, *Sauromatum guttatum*, is less malodorous than others of the clan.

The strange color and strong smell of a *Stapelia nobilis* blossom attract a fly.

The Stapelias

Most of the stapelias are native to the tropics, the deserts, and the mountains of South Africa. Their common names include the starfish flower, starfish plant, and the carrion flower. Although the succulent stems are not unattractive, they would not be grown if it wasn't for the strange flowers. Bizarre, unique, and sometimes indelicate, they always elicit response when set out to summer in the evening garden. The genus is named after one Johannes Bodaeus van Stapel, an Amsterdam physician who died in 1631.

The following three species are fairly easy to find and represent just a few of the dozens of species in cultivation. They are all unique additions to the evening garden.

Stapelia pasadenensis bears a five-inch-wide wine-red flower, the flower's corolla forming a huge leathery star, the sections covered with many hairs. If ever a flower looked like a perfect foil for the night, this is it. Strangely enough, the flowers really open during the day so that the odor they produce—of spoiled fruit or a piece of meat just past its prime—can attract the flies that pollinate the blossoms.

Stapelia gigantea, or the Zulu-giant, can produce a flower up to sixteen inches across, a huge star of a bright ochre yellow, with crimson ridges, and fine purple hairs. The plant itself is only five to eight inches high, so a flower of this size is very impressive. *S. nobilis* is a few inches smaller in width and is covered with finer purple hairs.

Stapelias are succulents, so the primary rule of care is to provide adequate drainage. I use a potting mix of equal parts standard potting soil, composted manure, and sharp sand. The plants are fertilized only during the hot days of summer.

While most of these plants will endure a temperature of 40°F, they do not respond with favor to such a chilly atmosphere. If allowed to sit in damp soil when the temperature falls that low, they will usually begin to rot. I withhold water from November to March and give them as much sun as possible during the winter months.

The Bat Plant

Some weeks ago my bat plant bloomed. The botanical genus is *Tacca*, derived from the Malayan name for this plant. The bright green puckered leaves of the plant circled a stout stem ending in a tangle of black blossoms. The blossoms in turn are surrounded by a forest of black whiskers, each between six and eight inches long.

"That's a bat flower," I said to my wife.

"That's the most sinister flower I've ever seen," she said.

This is indeed a strange flower. Among the common names are devil's flower, magician's flower, devil's tongue, cat's whiskers, but I like bat flower the best.

The plants grow in the densely shaded parts of forests in Burma and Bangladesh plus many of the Pacific islands. The nodding bell-shaped flowers are satiny black, lightly brushed with maroon, but the most unusual feature is the long whiskers that fly about in all directions. They begin to bloom in early summer and continue until well into September or October and are naturals for the evening garden.

Tacca integrifolia is the botanical name of the bat plant in my collection. Temperatures should always be above 60°F when the plant is active but I've noticed that winters in the greenhouse can go as low as 50°F without harming the plants. As to other requirements, follow those of the devil's tongue (see page 167).

The Jack O'Lantern Mushroom and Foxfire

It was a dark and stormy night on the tenth of July when I wandered through the oak trees that line the trail down to the lake and the dock. Two weeks of hot, humid weather were about to bite

A flower of the bat plant, *Tacca intergrifolia*, sends whiskers in all directions.

The glowing fruits of *Omphalotus illudens*, the jack o'lantern mushroom.

the dust and lightning forked across the type of sky often seen in Steven Spielberg productions.

I was out looking for our black cat, Maude, and as I passed the oak closest to the house my eye was stopped in its track by a misty glow close to the ground. I turned on my flashlight and in its bright beam saw a group of orange-red, almost pumpkin-colored mushrooms, clustered between two large oak roots. When I turned off the light, they began to glow again.

Later that night, after the storm had passed (and the cat was found), I went out and picked a fairly fresh specimen. Back at the house I took it into the front hall closet and closed the door, prompting my wife to ask: "Why are you walking into the closet with a mushroom?"

Once the door was closed, it wasn't long before the underside of the mushroom began to faintly glow with enough light to remind me of the cereal premiums of the forties—specifically the Lone Ranger's ring powered by atomic energy or the one from Buck Rogers that would stop glowing when placed on the finger of an alien. I was soon able to sort out the coats that hung in front of me and reflect a pale ghostly light upon my hand.

The mushroom that I found is called the jack o'lantern (*Omphalotus illudens*). It's a lightly toxic affair that contains a goodly amount of muscarine, a chemical that is fatal in large doses. Not only does the victim suffer from visual episodes of a frightening sort, there is salivation, difficulty in breathing, decreased blood pressure, plus vomiting and diarrhea, with most victims recovering in twenty-four hours.

The common name refers to the glow of the mushroom's flesh, a glow that in fresh specimens can be bright enough to read a large-print newspaper by. The gills are bioluminescent, giving off a cold light much like that produced by fireflies and foxfire.

Most woods-walkers are familiar with foxfire, the eerie glow caused by the rambling, white, rootlike mycelium of the honey mushroom (*Armillariella mellea*) that travel great distances by running through the soil and feeding on other plant tissues, glowing as they go—although the cap, gills, and stalk of this mushroom do not glow. Legend has it that Indians and settlers marked their trails through the woods with bits of decaying wood that contained these mycelia.

And night-walkers who stroll seaside beaches have seen glowing waves, a phenomenon produced by millions of microscopic one-celled dinoflagellates, which when disturbed by the action of the water, begin to glow.

There has been much discussion about this illumination, but most botanists today believe that as far as mushrooms and fungus go, it is the byproduct of the plant's metabolism and has no specific function. With fireflies it's a matter of species survival, and with dinoflagellates, it's anybody's guess.

Omphalotus illudens is the species found in the East and the South, while *O. olivascens* is restricted to the West Coast. Care must be taken because the *Omphalotus* clan bear a close resemblance to the chanterelles, mushrooms belonging to the *Cantharellus* genes and considered some of the best mushroom eating in the world.

Other luminescent mushrooms include the American form of *Panellus stipticus* where the cap, the gills, and the mycelium glow. And, appropriately enough, two species of the deadman's finger genus, *Xylaria*, are reported as being luminous. In the Far East *Pleurotus japonicus* and *P. lunaillustris* both glow.

Obviously the jack o'lantern mushroom and its cohorts are unsuitable for the garden—even the garden at night—since propagation is chancy at best and the mushrooms only last a few weeks before beginning to decay into a black, slimy mass. But oh, if I could find a variety with a bit more staying power, what a garden sight it could be as we watched the more common flowers of the night unfold their petals in the dim iridescence of Jack and his glowing flesh. The Spider Woman would have been proud of me!

The reflection of the moon in a gazing globe attracts *Actias luna*, the luna moth. The flower is one of the night-flowering gourds.

$\mathcal{T}$HE MOONLIGHT GARDEN

Enchanted ports we, too, shall touch,
Cadiz or Cameroon;
Nor other pilot need beside
A magic wisp of moon.

WILLIAM ALEXANDER PERCY, *March Magic*

In the middle of our walled garden there is a simple concrete stand exactly twenty-one inches high that holds a silver gazing globe. The globe is fourteen inches in diameter and made from handblown glass.

Way back in the 1600s, any fashionable Dutch garden had a gazing globe. In *The Story of Gardening* Richardson Wright wrote: "[Around] 1694 small Dutch gardens began sprouting queer-shaped trees and from then went on to making those toy gardens, some of which exist even today—gardens with miniature bridges and canals and gazing globes and fantastic topiary work and tiny painted garden figures."

Although that description sounds like a miniature golf course, the gazing globe has much more cachet. It's a piece of garden nostalgia that has a special place in the evening garden—and is especially wonderful when used to view the garden under moonlight.

I grew up with a love of the moon. The affection was partly scientific since I've always had a telescope of one sort or another and, as a result, have looked at the moon's craters, when young in hope of finding a rocket ship (not from earth), and when older for the sheer beauty of the lunar landscape. And that affection for the moon (and its effect on the imagination) has also been rooted in my aforementioned love of old black-and-white horror films. This too is wedded to my youth since moonlight never looks authentic; the typical color films of today's Hollywood make the moon a sickly yellow and the night sky is never really black. If you don't believe me, rent the video for *I Walked with a Zombie*, and watch the real power of the moon. There, on a remote island in the Caribbean, a zombie follows two women across the canebrakes of a sugar plantation. Moonlight makes the shadows seem to be a mile long and wisps of clouds slowly pass over that silver orb above.

Thoreau loved the moon. "Now we are getting moonlight," he wrote in volume two of his journals, "we see it reflected from particular stumps in the depths of the darkest woods . . . as if it selected what to shine on,—a silvery light. It is a light, of course, which we have had all day, but which we have not appreciated, and proves how remarkable a lesser light can be when a greater has departed. How simply and naturally the moon presides!"

Thoreau often complained to himself that he had not put duskiness enough into his words when he described his evening walks by the light of the moon. He actually wanted to so develop his style that readers would know that the scene was laid at night, without his saying so in exact words. He wanted the reader to feel the same way about the moon that Emily Dickinson did when she wrote her poem number 122:

> And still within the summers' night
> A something so transporting bright
> I clap my hands to see—
> Then veil my too inspecting face
> Lest such a subtle—shimmering grace
> Flutter too far for me—

GARDENING UNDER THE MOON

Gardening at night is nothing new but until the leisure world of the twentieth century, advice revolved around vegetables and not flowers. A farmer from the sixteenth century wrote:

> Sowe peason and beanes, in the wane of the
>   moone,
> Who soweth them sooner, he soweth too soone,
> That they with the planet may rest and arise,
> And flourish, with bearing most plentiful wise.

The Reverend Timothy Harley, F.R.A.S. in his 1885 book, *Moon Lore*, quotes an old English gardener as saying: "And when the light of the moon waxes warmer, golden-hued plants grow on from the earth during the spring," and "cucumbers and radishes, turnips, leeks, lilies, horseradish, saffron, and other plants, are said to increase during the fullness of the moon; but onions, on the contrary, are much larger and are better nourished during the decline."

Even the growth of mushrooms was supposed to be influenced by the moon above:

> When the moon is at the full,
> Mushrooms you may freely pull;
> But when the moon is on the wane,
> Wait ere you think to pluck again.

And animals, too, as witnessed by M. Martin, Gent. writing about a trip to the New Hebrides of 1698: "The inhabitants of St. Kilda observe that when the April moon goes far in May, the fowls are ten or twelve days later in laying their eggs than ordinarily they used to be."

Percy Bysshe Shelley was more than a poet, he was a political radical of the nineteenth century. He was known to be a professional agitator and while in Dublin, he went out at night in the December of 1812 to talk to the poor laborers who worked the entire day and were forced to garden little vegetable patches under moonlight in order to feed their families.*

"It has come under the author's experience," he wrote, "that some of the workmen on an embankment in North Wales, who, in consequence of the inability of the proprietor to pay them, seldom received their wages, have supported large families by cultivating small spots of sterile ground by moonlight."

Today gardening by moonlight is not by misfortune but by choice. And moonlight gardeners plant their seeds according to the phases of the moon because they believe that the same action that the moon directs toward the tides also applies to the water in the ground. Vegetables and flowers that open to the air should be planted from the new moon to the full moon while root vegetables should be set out during the dark nights of the moon, from full to new. And nothing should be planted on the exact day of the new moon or the full moon.

The Old Farmer's Almanac not only gives directions for planting thirty-two vegetables by

---

*The full moon nearest to the autumnal equinox is called the harvest moon. For several nights it rises shortly after sunset, its light enabling farmers to continue gathering their crops without the aid of artificial light.

moonlight but also advises that flowering bulbs need to be planted by the dark of the moon and all flowers by the light of the new moon.

But planting isn't the only thing to do in moonlight. Recently the newsletter *The Avant Gardener* reported that two German scientists found that weeding by moonlight resulted in fewer weeds during the daytime. Test plots cultivated at night had forty times fewer weeds than those plots cultivated by day. The theory is that the tiny amount of light that a weed seed receives when exposed before it goes under the earth again is enough to stimulate and trigger sprouting.

The Rev. Harley also wrote that: ... [the moon] waits on us like a link-bearer, or lackey; it is our admiring Boswell, living and moving and having its being in the equability it derives from attending its illustrious master."

And shining above, it opens up a whole new world for the evening garden.

THE MOONLIGHT GARDEN

In 1901 Alice Morse Earle wrote a book called *Old-Time Gardens.* It's a wonderful book full of all kinds of chatter about gardens and gardeners written at a time when a garden was an integral part of any home. "I plant a garden like none other," she writes, "not an everyday garden, nor indeed a garden of any day, but a garden for 'brave moonshine,' a garden of twilight opening and midnight bloom, a garden of nocturnal blossoms, a garden of white blossoms, and the sweetest garden in the world."

One of the most unusual gardens she described was the white moonlight garden that belonged to the Hon. Ben. Perley Poore, Indian Hill, at Newburyport, Massachusetts. During Poore's lifetime the garden had extraordinary charms. On the hillsides around the farm, he grew every variety of native tree that could survive a New England winter, then, to carry on the theme of white, there were vast herds of snow-white cows, flocks of white sheep, and all the oxen were white. Adding

white to white, white pigeons circled in the air above white dovecotes, and the farmyard poultry were also all white; one local account reported there were white peacocks on the garden walls, but these reports were discounted.

> Only the white sheep were sometimes seen
> To cross the strips of moon-blanch'd green.

"On every side," wrote Mrs. Earle, "were old terraced walls covered with roses and flowering vines, banked with shrubs, and standing in beds of old-time flowers running over the lovely hillside, was the Garden, and when we entered it, lo! it was a White Garden with edgings of pure and seemly white Candytuft from the forcing beds, and flowers of Spring Snowflake and Star of Bethlehem and Jonquils; and there were white-flowered shrubs of spring, the earliest Spiraeas and Deutzias; the doubled-flowered Cherries and Almonds and old favorites, such as Peter's Wreath (*Spiraea prunifolia*), all white and wonderfully expressive of a simplicity, a purity, a closeness to nature."

Now it's interesting to note that the famous White Garden at Sissinghurst, the creation of Vita Sackville-West and her husband, Nigel Nicolson, saw the light bulb of an idea in December 1939, when a garden pond was drained and Vita thought of planting a white garden there, a plan that was not to see completion until ten years later.

But the American garden was begun in 1833, when it was laid out and planted by the parents of Major Poore, after they returned (it must be admitted) from an extended tour of England, no doubt under the influence of the English flower garden.

Poore's garden featured a magnificant double flower border over seven hundred feet long. A broad, straight path edged with trimmed boxwood ran down through the center with a twelve-foot-wide flower border on each side. Seven hundred feet of double flower border, fourteen hundred feet of flower bed, twelve feet wide.

"It do swallow no end of plants," the gardener is quoted as saying.

The White Garden at Sissinghurst

The guidebook to Sissinghurst (published by The National Trust) has this to say about the White Garden:

This has been described as "the most beautiful garden at Sissinghurst, and indeed of all England." It lies at the foot of the Priest's House, and is divided by neat low hedges of box. All the flowers in this garden are white or grey. Lacy white festoons of strong-growing roses arch over the centre. Later in the year, generous plantings of *Lilium regale* come up through grey artemisia and silvery *Cineraria maritima*. Still later, the great metallic-looking onopordons grow up, and clouds of gypsophila throw a veil around the pencils of a white *Veronica virginica alba*, and a few belated white delphiniums and white eremuri persist. Under the silver willow-leaved pear (*Pyrus salicifolia pendula*) is a lead statue of a virgin by the Yugoslav sculptor, Rosandic, cast from the walnut original in the library; and on the far side an archway overlooks the rich farmlands of the Weald.

The White Garden was planted in 1949–1950. The first plant was the silvery willow-leaved pear that was moved from the Rose Garden. The total cost of the plants used for the garden was exactly £3 since most of the stock came from cuttings and seedlings. Purchased plants were *Crambe cordifolia* and *Gypsophila* 'Bristol Fairy'.

Vita described the garden in an article in the *Observer*:

I hope you will survey a low sea of grey clumps of foliage, pierced here and there with tall white flowers. I visualize the white trumpets of dozens of Regale lilies, grown three years ago from seed, coming up through the grey of southernwood and artemisia and cotton-lavender, with grey-and-white edging plants such as *Dianthus* 'Mrs. Sinkins' and the silvery mats of *Stachys lanata* (*S. byzantina*). . . . There will be white pansies, and white peonies, and white irises with their grey leaves . . . at least I hope there will be all these things. I don't boast in advance about my grey, green, and white garden. It may be a terrible failure. . . .

Of course, it wasn't.

As a final tribute to the White Garden at Sissinghurst and its worldwide reputation, it should be noted that the garden of the Bali Hyatt Hotel at Sanur Beach features a special garden of plants with white flowers or variegated leaves designed as a tropical tribute.

I consider myself to be extremely fortunate in that I stayed overnight at Sissinghurst, and was able to walk the White Garden at dusk, under the light of the moon, and again early in the morning, before the mists had melted on the weald.

Another White Garden

America has been blessed with a number of garden writers who have known of the beauty of evening gardens and the special fascination of white flowers; Alice Morse Earle is one, Neltje Blanchan is another, and Louise Beebe Wilder is a third.

Mrs. Wilder dreamed for years of having a white garden. In the 1918 *Colour in My Garden*, she wrote: "Some day I should like to plant a garden to the night, to be frequented only at dim twilights, by moonlight, or when there is no light save the faint luminousness of white flowers. There should be sombre evergreens for mystery, an ever-playing fountain to break the tenseness, a pool for the moon's quaint artistry, and a seat."

She went on to describe a garden with the wraithlike shad bush, cherry trees to "hang like ghostly balloons among the shadows," white roses, scented pinks, and great white peonies.

Then in 1935 in *What Happens in My Garden* (The Macmillan Company), she again wrote about her dream: "I never have come anywhere near to realizing this dream, never had space enough to be anything so special . . . ," but she did see a white garden of "such stuff as dreams are made on," on an estate in Wales, on the river Ely, not far from ancient Llandaff.

Like Sissinghurst, the garden was enclosed by stone walls of a warm pinkish gray, the curious hue of the stone making a wonderful background for the pale and white flowers. She saw the garden at twilight, next to a gray and cloudy day, the best time to view a white garden and was welcomed by a clematis with white blooms that wound around tall iron gates. "It is impossible to describe its beauty at this dim hour—so soft, so ethereal, so mysterious, half real it seemed," she wrote. "At twilight, of course, it seemed a little unreal, but isn't that true of almost any garden at this hour when the hand of man is less apparent and mysterious agencies seem to have brought it into being?"

The shape of the garden was a large rectangle and at the back was a raised stone pool lined with the palest of sea-blue tiles. From a spout in a frame of carved lilies, a jet of water rose high in the air, swaying in the wind, then falling back with a sigh to the clear waters of the basin. On either side of the pool were tubs filled with white lilies-of-the-Nile.

A four- or five-foot border lay against the enclosure's wall and all the flowers were planted there; the gateway was seven feet wide. The rest of the garden was cut grass, unbroken except for a very old thorn tree that spread its crooked branches and its shadow over a small iron table and a few comfortable garden chairs.

The flowers that bloomed in this garden were phloxes, tall and short; white sweet peas that were supported on trellises at the back of the border; gladioli and dahlias; and a number of different annuals. The borders were edged with stone, and spilling over out onto the lawn were masses of white annual pinks, petunias both frilly and plain, *Phlox drummondii*, verbenas, pale yellow and white California poppies, sweet alyssum, Carpathian harebells, white coralbells, and more.

At dusk the fragrance from the white tobacco, stock, lilies, masses of white heliotrope, tuberoses, and petunias filled the night garden with sweet perfumes.

A *CLAIRE-VOIE* IN THE GARDEN

One of the features of the White Garden at Sissinghurst is called a *claire-voie*. This is a large round hole cut in a hedge of, in this case, clipped cypresses that gives a view to the gardens beyond—in essence a window to another room. It's often found in older French gardens—and a few American gardens as well—where the opening has been located to give a view of the rising moon. In China they have the *di xue*, meaning moon door or literally ground hole. Here, too, these decorative openings not only look out to other parts of the garden but to the moon as it rises in the evening.

The same effect can be achieved by building a latticework wall or a wire fence, then cutting a large hole in the center, and planting it with annual or perennial vines.

Some time ago I found a large wrought-iron circle—the kind, I think, once used to bang with a rod and call volunteers to the local fire department or ranchhands to dinner. I had it welded to an iron post and it now sits as a combination minimalist garden sculpture and a *claire-voie* without a hedge.

SOME WHITE FLOWERS FOR THE MOONLIGHT GARDEN

"Of all colors, white is the prevailing one; and of white flowers a considerably larger proportion smell sweetly than of any other color," wrote Charles Darwin—and little did he realize what he started in the world of gardening. Darwin probably missed the scientific journal that reported the news about the inner workings of the eye, the failure of the color-reading cones to respond to moonlight and only the rods, with their monochromatic sense of place, able to interpret the scene. As mentioned before, to plant the moonlight garden, the gardener must resort to white, off-white, and light yellow flowers.

ALBA AND THE WHITE

Often while thumbing through a knowledgeable garden book or a good nursery catalog, you will find the word *alba* (or *albus*, or *album*, because the word must match the species ending) used in conjunction with a number of white-flowered plants. The word is either added after var. (for variety) or included in single quotes like 'Alba'. *Alba* is Latin for white. It's the root word for a number of English words including an *alb*, a close-fitting white vestment used by participants in the Eucharist; *alba* meaning the white matter in the brain or spinal cord; an *alba* could also be a very old type of verse, usually describing the parting of lovers at dawn, having a refrain that ends with *alba*, in this case the *alba* meaning dawn in Provençal French; finally in old English, rent payable in silver coin was called *alba firma*.

The following list contains a number of white flowers, including annuals, one biennial, bulbs, perennials, shrubs, and small trees. There are thousands more but most of these are usually available from nurseries around the United States.

Annual Whites

The following flowers include true flowers, germinating, blooming, and seeding in one season, and some tropical perennials that are usually treated as annuals, and a few tropicals that should spend the summer in the garden and winter in

the greenhouse. The true annuals do well in ordinary garden soil in full sun. Other requirements are noted in the descriptions. Spent flowers should be removed to promote continuous blooming. Whenever possible, in order to guarantee as long a season of flowers as possible, start all these seeds early in the spring—just make sure you provide enough light to prevent young seedlings from becoming leggy.

Cleome hasslerana 'Helen Campbell', a white-flowered cultivar of the spider flower, should be planted in masses. Cleomes look like blooming shrubbery topped with eight-inch balls of blossoms. The common name refers to the long waving stamens in the flowers. They are breathtaking at twilight and quite fantastic in the light of the moon. The flowers also have an evening scent that is strong with your nose in the flowers but becomes sweet with distance. Stems can reach a height of six feet and bloom begins in August.

Cobaea scandens 'Alba' is the white form of the cup-and-saucer vine, so-called because the large cup-shaped flower sits on five united sepals, the effect being that of a Victorian tea set. In areas where the temperature stays above 40°F, they are tropical perennials and will reach a length of twenty-five feet. In colder climates treat them as annuals since they bloom the first year from seed. The floral scent is not attractive since they are pollinated by bats.

Cosmos bipinnatus 'Purity' has four-inch-wide flowers with many white petals surrounding a yellow center, all on two- to three-foot stems. 'Sonata' is a shorter type on two-foot stems. Plants produce blossoms all summer long and tolerate poor and dry soil but need excellent drainage. Too much nitrogen produces rank foliage and fewer flowers. They make excellent cut flowers.

Digitalis purpurea 'Alba' is the white form of the popular purple foxglove. This is a biennial plant blooming in its second year. As a plant for the evening garden, it's spectacular and far more interesting than the common purple variety.

Plants like partial shade—especially in the South—with well-drained soil.

Helianthus annuus 'Italian White' remains the most perfect sunflower I know. Not tall and imposing like its big yellow relative, these four-inch-wide flowers have creamy white petals surrounding black centers, and in the moonlight garden they look like halos floating in the air. A new cultivar called 'Luna' has petals of sulfur yellow and the flowers glow at twilight.

Impatiens, or jewelweed, is a tropical flower that has been extensively hybridized and each year sees new colors on the market. They are extremely popular because they do well in the shade and also adapt to growing in tubs and pots. 'Bride' is a current white form in the Shady Lady hybrids and the Super Elfin hybrids have two-inch flowers on foot-high plants. Impatiens will bloom all summer and are especially valuable as edging plants, outlining a garden path on even the darkest nights.

Justicia carnea 'Alba', the plume plant or Brazilian-plume, originally came from northern South America and has been an old conservatory plant since Victorian times. Glossy dark green leaves are topped with immense umbels of two-lipped flowers on two-inch tubes. A well-grown plant will be a star in the moonlight garden, the pure white flowers forming a glowing torch. Provide good, moist soil and, during the summer, a spot in partial shade. Plume plants can overwinter in a sunny window as a fine houseplant, then spend every summer in the garden.

Lavatera trimestris, the tree mallow, has a white form called 'Mont Blanc'. The four-inch-wide flowers resemble hollyhocks, and bloom on bushy plants about two feet in height. They make very effective temporary hedges.

Nigella 'Miss Jeckyll Alba' is the white form of love-in-a-mist, a charming annual with flowers that have finely divided petals.

Pelargonium 'Multibloom White', 'White Elite', and 'White Orbit' are three choices of summer geraniums with all-white flowers. These tropical perennial plants can either be set directly in the ground or set about the garden in pots. While geraniums will continue to bloom under adverse circumstances, they really need a good soil laced with humus and some shade from the worst of the noonday sun, and never let the soil completely dry. Just make sure to remove spent flowers. Bring these plants into a cool, sunny room for the winter where they will continue to bloom. You can take cuttings to provide plants for next year's garden.

Phygelius 'Moonraker' (*P. aequalis* × *P. capensis*) originally came from Longwood Gardens. This is a beautiful creamy white form of the famed Cape fuchsia and stands two to three feet high, covered with long and drooping, tubelike flowers ending in six rounded lobes all summer long. They look like they should be moth-pollinated flowers and possibly could be in an American garden, but in their original home of South Africa, the flowers are pollinated by hummingbirds. Treat the plants like pelargoniums and bring them in for the winter but they can be hardy as far north as Philadelphia, if planted against a south-facing wall and mulched well after the first frosts.

Solanum melongena 'Alba', or the white eggplant, is frankly a curiosity. Here the flowers are unimportant; the egg-shaped fruits of glistening white are everything. They are a sure conversation stopper in the moonlight garden.

The last two annuals are white forms of ever-popular garden flowers. *Verbena* 'Armour White' is suitable for either a ground cover or for hanging baskets, while the white forms of the common garden pansy, *Viola* 'Universal White' or 'Accord Clear White', will produce flowers all season long whether used as ground covers or as edging plants along the garden path.

Bulbs with White Flowers

Every year new tulip and daffodil cultivars hit the garden market and many of them feature white flowers. Beds of white tulips are to my mind far more beautiful in a garden than any number of orange, yellow, red, or even purple flowers; 'Purissima', 'Hibernia', and the peony-flowered 'Mount Tacoma' are especially fine. And drifts of any of the various cultivars of white daffodils and narcissus can be far more fetching than any cloud of yellows. To walk out into the early spring garden, under an April moon, and see the stars above that will soon be blocked out by the coming leaves, then to smell the fragrant daffodils, is a marvelous yearly ritual to be awaited with joy—and don't forget the white calla lilies mentioned in Chapter 8.

The following bulbs all have white flowers. They can be planted at various spots around the garden where the moonlight falls.

Colchicum is a genus of bulbous plants (really corms) that are called fall crocuses but are really members of the lily family. They should be naturalized in the garden like daffodils and their only drawbacks are the very large and sometimes coarse leaves that appear in early spring. Many of them come in lavenders and various shades of lilac, but luckily for the moonlight garden, there are a few whites. Their flowers appear anytime from early September on to November, depending on the climate.

Colchicum autumnale 'Album' is hardy to at least −10°F and colder if properly mulched. The pure white flowers stand three inches high. *Colchicum speciosum* 'Album' has the same quality of hardiness but here the pure white chalice-shaped blossoms are five inches high and very beautiful. There is a white form, either a variation of the double-flowered 'Waterlily' or *C. autumnale* 'Alboplenum' but it is extremely rare and I've only seen it in one garden.

Among the white-flowering spring crocuses are *Crocus biflorus* 'Scotch Crocus', white with purple striping: 'Joan of Arc', a large pure white flower; 'Snow Bunting', one of the earliest of spring flowers; and 'Bowles's White', a white flower with a yellow base.

Colchicum autumnale 'Alboplenum' blooms in the autumn garden.

There are a number of autumn-flowering crocuses, including *Crocus hadriaticus* (synonym, *C. sativus* var. *cartwrightianus* 'Albus'), or the white saffron crocus, a rare pure white species with red pistils that blooms throughout Greece. The corms bloom in October and reach a height of four inches.

The various colchicums and crocuses should be planted in areas with full spring sunlight or under deciduous trees. Set them at the correct spacing and soil depth as recommended when you buy them. If you have naturalized these corms in an open lawn, make sure you let the foliage completely ripen and die back before you cut the lawn.

Crinum × *powellii* 'Album' has graced a pot in our moonlight garden for three years. This is a hybrid between *C. bulbispermum* × *C. moorei* produced by E. G. Henderson in 1888. Five to ten wonderfully fragrant four-inch trumpet flowers of pure white open in succession. The strap-shaped leaves are a deep green. These bulbs are hardy as long as the ground doesn't freeze so if mulching gives adequate protection, set these bulbs in good well-drained garden soil that contains plenty of humus. If not, let the foliage die back naturally, and let them overwinter in a warm place.

Among the most beautiful of fall flowers are the hardy cyclamen. They are not hardy north of USDA Zone 6—unless given protection—but they are so fine they deserve the strain of extra effort. The best one to try is *Cyclamen hederifolium* (synonym *C. neapolitanum*) 'Album'. Not only are the flowers close to perfection, the leaves are a shiny green with marbled patches of silver that glisten in the moonlight.

If the hardy cyclamen are unable to withstand your climate, grow them in pots—about an inch wider than the width of the individual corm—using a well-drained, sandy soil. Water them well while plants are in bloom, then let the foliage die back, and store the corms, pot and all, in a warm place until the next growing season.

The snowdrops, the many species of *Galanthus*, bloom in very early spring, often pushing up through the snows of early spring. The flowers are white, sometimes with touches of emerald green. Look for the cultivars 'Giant Snowdrop', with larger than type, pendulous, bell-shaped flowers, or 'Double Snowdrop', a form with doubled petals. They are hardy to USDA Zone 2 and only need a spot with spring sun and well-drained soil to succeed.

Galtonia candicans, or the summer hyacinth, is hardy to USDA Zone 6 (use a mulch at the colder ends of 6), blooming in midsummer. The forty-inch stems carry many pendulous, bell-shaped flowers of pure white with just a touch of green.

They should be planted in bunches so the resultant hundreds of flowers will glisten in the moonlight. Make sure the soil is rich in humus and well drained. These bulbs need full sun.

Lilium auratum, the Chinese or gold-banded lily, has been in our evening gardens since we began and were mentioned in Chapter 2. The nine-inch flowers with recurved petals bloom in late August, each petal banded with a golden stripe. Stems can reach a height of eight inches. *Lilium regale*, the royal lily, will bear as many as eighteen to twenty flowers on six-foot stems. The petals are wine-colored on the outside but open

The pure white flowers of *Galtonia candicans*, the summer hyacinth, sparkle in the garden moonlight.

to reveal shiny white interiors with a yellow throat and orange anthers. And nothing is more beautiful than a well-grown clump of Madonna lilies (*L. candidum*).

There are dozens of other bulbous plants that have white flowers. They include the alba form of the puschkinia (*Puschkinia scilloides*), the white grape hyacinth (*Muscari armeniacum* 'Album'), the star of Bethlehem (*Ornithogalum arabicum*), lily-of-the-valley (*Convallaria majalis*), not to mention white cultivars of the dahlias and the gladiouses. Every year if you search the bulb catalogs, you will find many, many more.

Perennial White Flowers

Entire books have been written on white perennials and most garden perennials have a white form. So the following plants are more unusual choices than the plants normally found in white gardens.

Actaea pachypoda, doll's eyes, are American wildflowers that, when blooming, are little tufts of starry white anthers. In late fall the fertilized flowers turn to white berries, each with one black spot, and they make an arresting contribution to the moonlight garden. Soil should be deep, laced with compost, and doll's eyes need a place shielded from the hot sun. They are hardy in USDA Zones 4 to 8.

Campanula lactiflora 'Alba' bears huge panicles of deeply lobed, bell-shaped flowers of white on four-foot stems; a grove of these blossoms can so reflect the moonlight that they become beacons in the dark. *Campanula persicifolia* 'Fleur de Neige' is a magnificent double white form of the common garden campanula, the willow or peach-leaved bellflower. The nodding flowers are over an inch and a half long. These plants do very well in sun or light shade in good, well-drained garden soil with some humus added. They are hardy from USDA Zones 4 to 8.

Cimicifuga racemosa, the black cohosh or snakeroot, blooms in late summer and sends forth six- to seven-foot stems that bear dozens of tiny white starlike flowers with many white stamens. *Cimicifuga americana* has shorter flowering stems reaching about six feet. Both species are happy in good, moist garden soil with plenty of humus added. Once planted they go on for years without any attention from the gardener. Give snakeroot full sun in the North and partial shade in the South. Plants will seed about and naturalize. They are hardy in USDA Zones 4 to 8.

Clematis montana is a perfectly lovely vine that will turn a garden wall into a cloud of fragrant silvery white four-petaled blossoms. Originally from China, this clematis is only hardy in USDA Zone 6 and south. A well-grown plant can reach a length of twenty-five feet. Since the flowers bloom on last year's ripened stems, remember to prune only after flowering is over in order to allow time to produce plenty of new growth for next year's flowers. Clematises like a cool root run which means the roots like to be shaded from the drying effects of the hot summer sun.

Crambe cordifolia, the colewort, and *C. maritima*, the sea kale, somewhat resemble baby's breath but their clouds of small white flowers suspended over the large dark green leaves look more like swirling ground mists in the moonlight garden. *Cordifolia* reaches a height of six feet and *maritima* of two feet. These plants are not hardy north of USDA Zone 6. They need well-drained, sandy soil in full sun.

Dicentra spectabilis 'Alba' is the white form of the bleeding heart. Originally from Japan, the pink form of this flower has been a garden favorite since Victorian times. The heart-shaped flowers with their one tear are strung out on arching branches and are very effective in the moonlight garden. They bloom from spring into May but by midsummer the plant dies back. In order to hide the gap, plant a *Hosta plantaginea* on either side. Except in far northern gardens, bleeding hearts want partial shade and a moist soil. They are hardy in USDA Zones 4 to 8.

Echinacea purpurea, the American coneflower, is one of the almost perfect perennials in the gardener's collection. The solitary daisylike flowers are often six inches wide, the petals surrounding a spiny center that becomes cone-shaped as the flowers mature. Two fine white forms are available: 'White Lustre', with creamy white flowers and 'White Swan' with pure white rays. Unlike many cultivars, these white forms come true from seed. Provide ordinary, well-drained garden soil in full sun. Remember to remove spent blossoms to prolong bloom from summer until frost. Coneflowers are hardy in USDA Zones 4 to 9.

Eremurus himalaicus, the Himalayan desert candle, is often listed by bulb merchants but it really is a perennial herb with thick, cordlike roots that resemble a black starfish with thin legs. Hundreds of inch-wide white flowers will crowd a stem that can reach a height of seven feet. The flowers, both open and in bud, can cover a stem length of two feet. The two-foot leaves are unimportant and soon fade away after the flowering season is past. Once established in a garden, let them be. They need deep, well-drained soil with plenty of humus with full sun and should be mulched in areas colder than USDA Zone 7. These flowers are spectacular in the moonlight garden.

Helleborus niger, the Christmas rose, and *H. orientalis* 'Alba', the Lenten rose, are evergreen clump-forming plants with attractive and interesting flowers that bloom respectively in late December to early January and early March to mid-April. The Christmas rose has white flowers faintly flushed with pink and the alba form of the Lenten rose is pure white. Both these flowers lend interest at a time when other flowering plants are at a minimum. They like partial shade and well-drained soil and will withstand very dry conditions without any perceptible damage. They are not hardy north of USDA Zone 6. If grown in colder areas, they need protection not only from winter winds but sleet and snow which can damage blossoms. They do not move well so buy containerized plants whenever possible.

Hemerocallis 'Joan Senior' represents the best yet of the daylilies with white petals. It isn't quite white, more of an ivory, but pretty close. The recurved blossoms are six inches wide on twenty-four-inch stems blooming in early summer. Each plant will produce a number of buds. For information on cultivation, see page 91.

Lysimachia clethroides, the gooseneck plant, blooms in July and August. The arched stems bearing clusters of small white blossoms look exactly like their namesake. A large bed of these plants is very effective, and if given proper growing conditions, these plants will soon fill a large space since they are somewhat invasive. Goosenecks do well in full sun or partial shade and like most soil. Hardy to USDA Zone 4.

At first glance *Macleaya cordata* (synonym *Bocconia cordata*), the plume poppy, doesn't look like a candidate for the moonlight garden until you examine the undersides of the large leaves. Light green on top, the undersides are covered with white silvery hairs. When an evening wind gently moves through the garden, the random movements of the upturned leaves reflecting available light make them quite ghostly. The countless small white flowers that bloom in summer have no discernible petals but dozens of white stamens that add to the effect. Give plume poppies full sun and ordinary garden soil in the North or partial shade in the South. They are hardy to USDA Zone 4.

Most gardeners think of poppies in terms of orange and scarlet but the oriental poppy, *Papaver orientale*, has a number of white cultivars, the best being 'Perry's White'. The five-inch flowers, each on a thirty-inch stem, have white satiny petals surrounding a purple center. They are hardy to USDA Zone 4 and need full sun in good, well-drained soil. If gardening in an area with especially hot summers, try 'Sprite', a new cultivar with white flowers edged with pink, about two feet high and blooming over a much longer period than the typical oriental poppy.

Parnassia palustris, the grass of Parnassus, is

The brilliant white, satiny petals of an oriental poppy cultivar, 'Perry's White', glow in the moonlight.

a charming wildflower that blooms late in summer with saucer-shaped waxy white flowers on stems up to one foot high. Plants prefer full sun but will take partial shade in the South, though the soil must be evenly moist at all times. They are hardy to USDA Zone 5.

There are two different kinds of peonies: the herbaceous types are shrubby plants and die down to the ground in the winter, while the tree peonies have branches covered with bark that remain standing in the garden all year long. Both have attractive foliage and both have truly beautiful forms that feature elegant white flowers, most having that subtle, sweet fragrance like no other plant in grandmother's garden.

Paeonia suffruticosa is the Japanese tree peony, a bush that usually reaches a height of five feet with a six-foot spread. For the evening garden try 'Companion of Serenity', with flowers of a delicate pink; 'Gessekai', a ruffled, pure white semidouble; and 'Haku Benryu', bearing snow white, ruffled flowers with centers of pure gold.

The common herbaceous peonies are mostly derived from *Paeonia lactiflora*. There are a number of truly beautiful white cultivars available from today's nurseries. Look for 'Cheddar Regal' with blossoms of pure white with a golden center; 'Top Brass' bearing blossoms of pure white lightly touched with pink and lightly scented; and 'Norma Volz' with large white, fully double flowers just brushed with pink.

Both types bloom in late spring to early summer and prefer an ordinary but well-prepared garden soil with added humus and a place in full sun in the North, but partial shade in the South. The regular peonies are hardy in USDA Zones 4 to 8 while the tree peonies start in USDA Zone 5.

Physostegia virginiana, the obedient plant, is a clump-forming plant that bears three-foot spires of flowers that resemble small snapdragons. They bloom toward the end of summer and are very easy to grow. The usual flowers are pink but two white forms are available: 'Alba', about three feet tall, and 'Summer Snow', about two feet tall. Be-

cause the flowers are joined to the main stem with a slim pedicel that in turn is held by a small leaf or bract, individual flowers will remain where they are pushed by the gardener. Soil should be moist with full sun or partial shade. They are hardy to USDA Zone 4.

Platycodon grandiflorus is called balloon flower, a name referring to the balloon shape of the unopened blossoms. Once open, the flowers are about two inches wide, forming a cup with five pointed lobes. Originally from Japan, the plants bloom over a long season, but get a late start in spring. The first shoots usually poke through the soil when all other plants are up. Three white cultivars are usually available, 'Albus,' 'Snowflake', and 'Mariesii Alba'. Provide full sun to partial shade in good, well-drained garden soil. They are hardy to USDA Zone 4.

Rheum nobile, Sikkim rhubarb, is a plant that will produce a pleasure-palace tower of white for the evening garden. This plant is a sibling to garden rhubarb (*R. rhaponticum*), but all resemblance ends in late summer when this rhubarb comes into bloom. The height in bloom is about five feet and the tall stem is covered with overlapping pale cream-colored bracts that hide insignificant flowers. They come from the Himalayas and are hardy to USDA Zone 6. Give the plants full sun to partial shade in a deeply prepared, well-drained soil with plenty of humus.

Smilacina racemosa, false Solomon's seal, is an American wildflower whose three-foot leafy stems are topped with feathery sprays of white flowers that appear in late spring to early summer. They are elegant when bending over a garden pathway or growing against a bank or wall. Plants prefer partial shade—especially in the South—and moist soil with plenty of humus. They are hardy in USDA Zones 4 to 9.

Trillium grandifolium, among the most beautiful of the American wildflowers, are clump-forming perennials, bearing large, three-petaled white flowers about fifteen inches high; they seem to float above three-part, dark green leaves. Tril-

liums will take early spring sun but after blooming want shade. Good garden soil should be laced
with humus and kept evenly moist. Never pick
trilliums since the three leaves a few inches below
the flower are the only leaves the plant has and
without them the roots are unable to store food
for the following season. They are hardy in USDA
Zones 5 to 9.

Some White-Flowering
Shrubs and Trees

The following trees and shrubs are perfect for the
small scale of a moonlight garden and all have
lovely white flowers. The white forsythia blooms
in very early spring, followed by the shadbush,
the star magnolia, and ending with the white rose
which will continue to bloom until cut back by
a hard freeze.

Abeliophyllum distichum, the white forsythia,
will live through winters that plunge to −25°F,
yet bloom every April, long before the yellow
forsythias are even thinking about opening up.
Although it resembles a forsythia, this plant has
a genus all its own and deservedly so. A native
of central Korea, white forsythia has been growing in American gardens since 1924, but it still
doesn't have the popularity it deserves. The
flower buds appear in late summer, so always do
any pruning in the spring after blossoming is over
for the year. If you start with a good-size con-
tainer-grown plant, it should reach six by four
feet in about three years. Plants want full sun and
any good, well-drained garden soil. They are
hardy in USDA Zones 5 to 9.

Amelanchier canadensis, the shadbush or
Juneberry, is a deciduous tree that blooms in early
spring (in the Northeast when shad come up the
rivers to spawn), covering itself with clusters of
white, long-petaled flowers. With age, the trees
ultimately reach a height of thirty feet and such
a tree bloomed every year just at the edge of the
pine woods in our garden in the Catskills, a fog
of white with flowers that always opened around

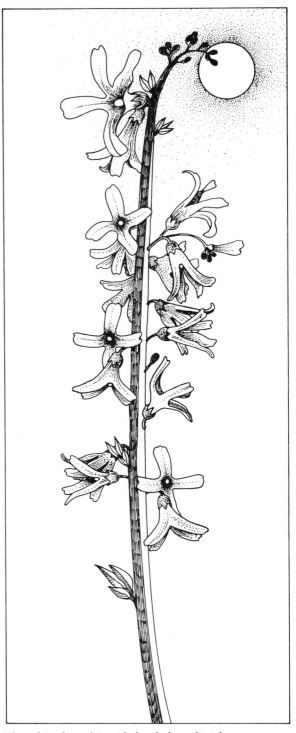

The white forsythia, *Abeliophylum distichum*.

the end of April. It was such a beautiful tree that we moved a seedling to the edge of the formal garden where its bloom echoed that of its relative up the hill. The shadbush can be pruned after flowering to stay as a large shrub or a small tree and is best in well-drained soil—though they will tolerate a wide range of soils. They are hardy to USDA Zone 4.

Camellia japonica, the camellia, is a marvelous shrub for the moonlight garden. We have the beautiful white cultivar 'White Swan'. On extremely cold winter nights, where temperatures plunge to 0°F or below, I must cover the shrub with a blanket but that's a small price to pay for the marvelous flowers. Most camellias are hardy through USDA Zone 7, and work continues on developing more cold-hardy plants. There are three beautiful white cultivars usually available in the United States: 'White by the Gate', 'Frost Queen', and 'Yuki Botan'.

For gardeners in the North, camellias can be grown in tubs and winter in the greenhouse or any sunny place where temperatures stay above freezing. Well-drained neutral to acid soil is needed and they can be pruned after flowering. Without pruning most reach a height of about ten feet. Give them full sun and a protected spot away from harsh winter winds.

Cytisus × *praecox* 'Moonlight' is a spectacular May-flowering shrub that is smothered with pealike blossoms of sulfur yellow. As twilight deepens, the flowers will glow and almost seem luminescent. The leaves are small but the branches are long and whiplike and keep their green color all year long. A well-grown shrub can reach a height of eight feet and will do well in average well-drained soil on the acid side, in full sun. They are hardy in USDA Zones 6 to 8.

Cornus kousa, the Chinese dogwood, is a shrub or small tree that can reach a height of twenty feet. Its spring-blooming flowers are small but they are surrounded by four white bracts (leaves that act like petals). Plant in sun or partial shade (in the South, more shade is necessary), in

good, moist but well-drained garden soil. Trees are hardy to USDA Zone 5. A blooming Chinese dogwood is the best bet for the moonlight garden if a davidia is not practical.

Davidia involucrata, the dove or handkerchief tree, is included in this list only because it is so beautiful in the evening or moonlight garden—unfortunately it is only hardy in USDA Zone 7 and south. Discovered in China in 1869 by Père Davida, a French Catholic missionary, the tree was lost then found again, finally coming to the western world in 1899, brought back by Ernest Henry Wilson, the great plant collector. Said Wilson: "I am convinced that *Davidia involucrata* is the most interesting and most beautiful of all trees which grow in the north temperate regions." The flowers bloom in June, surrounded by two large white bracts that, from a distance, resemble white doves. In the moonlight, davidia in flower looks as though a migration of albino lunar moths has settled on the tree. For all its beauty, the tree is not too fussy about cultivation needing only fertile, well-drained but moist soil and a place in full sun or partial shade.

Hibiscus syriacus 'Diana' is a triploid introduction from the U.S. National Arboretum that produces huge, waxy, pure white flowers, six inches across, that bloom all summer and, unlike others in the genus, stay open all night along. The bush reaches a height of eight feet and produces no seedlings. The spent blossoms fall cleanly to the ground each day. They want full sun in a well-drained soil and, since blossoms appear on new growth, for larger flowers prune back severely in early spring, leaving two to three buds per branch. Space the plants five feet apart for an excellent hedge. Hardy to USDA Zone 5.

Hydrangea anomala subsp. *petiolaris*, the climbing hydrangea, is a beautiful vine, a deciduous climber that has yellow-orange bark which peels much like that of a birch tree and clings to any vertical surface using aerial roots. The dark green leaves are two to four inches wide on long slender petioles. In late spring, the pure white

The star magnolia, *Magnolia tomentosa*, bears many blossoms and is hardy in many northern gardens.

flowers are flat-topped clusters six to ten inches wide looking like typical hydrangea blooms. This particular vine looks best when set against a stone wall. It prefers ordinary moist garden soil with added humus and partial shade but will take full sun in the North. They will not bloom well in dense shade. Hardy to USDA Zone 5.

Hydrangea quercifolia, the oak-leaved hydrangea, will reach a height of eight feet, bearing very attractive leaves that resemble those of an oak. Upright panicles of beautiful and fragrant white flowers appear from July to September, followed by leaves that turn scarlet to burgundy for autumn. These bushes make beautiful backdrops for a bed of flowers or simply as hedge borders. Although catalogs list them as being hardy to USDA Zone 5, that really includes only the southern precincts, and then they need protection from bitter winter winds. Provide ordinary, well-drained garden soil and except in hot and dry areas, full sun or slight shade; some shade is preferred in the South. 'Snow Queen' is remarkable

for the number of blossoms and the magnificent autumn color. Its compact growth reaches a height of seven feet and the same spread in about six years.

Magnolia tomentosa (synonym *M. stellata*) is the hardiest of the magnolias. The first introduction of this shrub came in 1861 when Dr. George Hall of Rhode Island brought them back from Japan. They ultimately reach a height of twenty feet but most stay about ten feet high, making them especially valuable for the small garden. Their many branches bear elliptical green leaves about four inches long. The white flowers bloom in early spring and have anywhere from twelve to forty tepals. A number of cultivars have been introduced featuring larger flowers, many with a faint pink flush. Unlike many magnolias, *M. tomentosa* seedlings will produce flowers in their second year. These shrubs are hardy to USDA Zone 6 but if given a very sheltered spot, they sometimes succeed in the warmer parts of USDA Zone 5. Give them good garden soil and a spot in full sun in the North and partial shade in the South.

Two years ago I noticed that the flowers on our star magnolia had a faint sweet fragrance which carried on into the evening and it was this scent that led to my investigations into the night fragrance of many of the other species of magnolia.

Rhododendron catawbiense, the mountain rhododendron, grows to twenty feet. It is an evergreen shrub, often with age a small tree bearing six-inch-long oval green leaves, glossy above. Clusters of lilac-purple bell-shaped flowers appear in late spring. It is also an American native rhododendron, the parent of many Catawba Hybrids, and valuable because of their hardiness, surviving in USDA Zone 5. It requires a well-drained acidic soil composed of leaf mold combined with sphagnum peat moss well mixed in. Heavy clay soil with added humus and alkaline soils are slow death to all rhododendrons and azaleas. May is the best month for rhododendron displays, but a lot of the dwarfs bloom in April. 'Winter Snow' grows to a height of four feet and bears snow-white blossoms, each blossom lightly marked in the center with a red mark.

There are many hybrids among the rhododendrons. 'Creamy Chiffon' is the result of an unknown cross but the double creamy yellow flowers cover a four-foot bush, hardy to −5°F. Because of the yellow tint in the flowers, they glow at dusk before turning white under the light of the moon.

Other white cultivars include 'Album Novum', a five-foot plant bearing white flowers with just a touch of pink; 'Cyprus', just under three feet with large white flowers; and, just under five feet, 'Ice Cube', bearing white flowers with a hint of yellow at the throat.

Rhododendron obtusum 'Album', the Hiryu azalea, grows to four feet. It's semievergreen but often deciduous in addition to being dimorphic, meaning it has two sets of leaves; one-inch elliptical, dark green leaves are followed in spring by more oval-shaped summer leaves, with a few leaves persisting to the following spring. White flowers bloom in spring. Not hardy north of USDA Zone 6.

Remove the spent blossoms of all rhododendrons to prevent seed formation and channel the plant's efforts into next year's crop of blooms.

Rosa Meidiland (pronounced may-d-land), or landscape roses, originally came from France and are perfect as ground covers and for hedging in a small garden. Since they are reproduced by cuttings and grow on their own roots—unlike many specialized roses—they are hardy throughout the contiguous United States. Because of this root hardiness, they will survive in USDA Zone 4. I can't say enough about the Meidilands: Any ground that grows grass can grow these roses. They require little if any pruning, some have attractive fruits, and most bloom from spring through to fall. Unless noted below, space them three feet apart.

'Alba Meidiland' is a white everblooming ground-cover rose bearing clusters of small white blossoms on a plant that reaches two feet in height with about a four-foot spread. A great plant for carpeting a difficult bank or slope. For a hedge, plant on four-foot centers.

'White Meidiland', bearing a three-inch-wide, pure white double flowers begins to blossom in June and repeats throughout the summer. The plants grow about two feet high and spread to five feet. Leaves are a glossy dark green and the only chore is deadheading to prolong bloom.

Syringa vulgaris, the common lilac, has been gracing American gardens since the middle 1600s, when the first colonists brought them over from Europe and England. While there are a number of white cultivars, the best is still the double white 'Madame Lemoine', and the unopened flowers are excellent for forcing. Lilacs are hardy to USDA Zone 3; in fact, they do poorly in areas with very warm winters. Ordinary garden soil is fine but lilacs must have full sun to really thrive.

Viburnum × *carlcephalum* is mentioned in

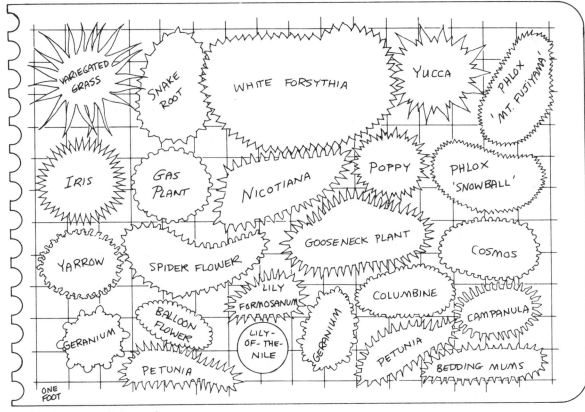

A plan for a moonlight garden.

Chapter 2 as a fragrant plant. I mention it here again to remind the reader of its great value in the moonlight garden, not only for the scented balls of white flowers but because a well-grown specimen makes a perfect place to hang various blooming potted plants over the course of the summer.

A Plan
for a Moonlight Garden

I've pared down the Poore borders to a reasonable rectangle that measures sixteen feet long and eleven feet wide. If you feel happier with a free-form shape, change the layout since the flowers are so beautiful they will adapt to most any pattern you choose. Since spring nights are often damp and chilly, the peak of flowering in this garden is set for later in the year and is at its best under a summer moon.

The largest feature of the bed is a white forsythia (*Abeliophyllum distichum*). If you start with a good-size plant, it should reach six by four feet in about three years, and can easily be pruned if it becomes too large. Blooming occurs in the first few weeks of spring when four-petaled flowers cover the bush and smell sweetly of honey under an April moon. Later in the season the leaves will act as a background for many of the other white flowers.

Another feature that will last throughout the entire season is the variegated miscanthus (*Miscanthus sinensis* 'Variegatus') with its white-edged leaves.

As spring moves along, white columbine (*Aquilegia canadensis* 'Silver Queen') is followed by white Siberian iris (*Iris sibirica* 'Snow Queen'), a fine plant whose grassy foliage looks good all summer, and yucca (*Yucca filamentosa*) with its soft white nodding bells on six-foot stems.

The white gas plant (*Dictamnus albus*) spans the month of June covered with its attractive spikes of unusual flowers, but planning is really needed for this plant dislikes being moved and once in place should be left alone.

By July the white campanula sends forth its bell-shaped flowers (*Campanula persicifoila* 'Grandiflora Alba') and will continue blooming well into August. Then the black snakeroot (*Cimicifuga racemosa*) starts to bloom, its white wands of stars seemingly blurred by an out-of-focus lens, running up and down six-foot stems. Then, too, the gooseneck plant (*Lysimachia clethroides*); the white balloon flower (*Platycodon grandiflorus* 'Album'), the summer phlox (*Phlox paniculata*), either 'Mt. Fujiyama' (sometimes called 'Mt. Fuji') at forty inches or 'Snowball' at thirty—and wait until you see the moths that visit these flowers—and the yarrow (*Achillea ptarmica* 'The Pearl') are all at their best and will continue on into September.

And for late July into August, a pot containing a number of blooming lily-of-the-Nile (*Agapanthus africanus* 'Albus') should be moved about for the best effect, always in full sun. This plant is only hardy south of USDA Zone 8 and should spend winters in a greenhouse, the basement, or a cool window. Use a soil mix of equal parts of loam laced with humus, sharp sand, and shredded peat moss. Keep the mix evenly moist. One cultivar called 'Alice Glouster' is reportedly hardy to USDA Zone 7 but I haven't tried it yet. The flowers are white, blooming in summer.

Then at the end of August and into September, plant the fragrant white blossoms of *Lilium formosanum*, bearing its six-inch flowers on four- to six-foot stems. Although open and fragrant during the day, their perfume is far stronger at night. These bulbs are hardy to USDA Zone 6, sometimes Zone 5 with plenty of mulching. Provide average well-drained garden soil in full sun.

Among the annuals used for the moonlight garden are white geraniums (*Pelargonium* × *hortorum*), white petunias (*Petunia* × *hybrid*), white nicotiana (*Nicotiana alata* 'Grandiflora'), white cosmos (*Cosmos bipinnatus* 'Purity'), white spider flowers (*Cleome hasslerana* 'Alba' or 'Snow Queen'), and for a final round of white for a harvest moon, some white bedding mums (*Chrysanthemum* × *morifolium*).

If you have more room, try adding a white poppy (*Papaver orientale* 'Perry's White'), some thirty inches in height. When it goes dormant in summer, interplant with more cosmos or cleome.

Fireflies flicker in the summer moonlight of an open field.

CHAPTER THIRTEEN

ℱIREFLIES AND GLOWWORMS

All night have the roses heard
The flute, violin, bassoon;
All night has the casement jessamine stirred
To the dancers dancing in tune;
Till a silence fell with the waking bird,
And a hush with the setting moon.

ALFRED, LORD TENNYSON, *Maud*

*W*hen twilight falls in our garden and the edge of the rhododendron thicket is already deeply dark, we sometimes go out to watch the bats. With an effort originally born of instinct, they silently swoop and glide, resembling fluttering bits of brown against the darkening sky. And with every dive another insect enemy is gone; the garden can breathe reasonably free for another day.

Everyone knows most of the visitors to the daytime garden; the birds, bees, and bugs are familiar to all. But the daylight hours have nothing on the nightlife that is found, especially if you look carefully, in the evening garden.

ABOUT THE MOTH

Bees and butterflies, being creatures of the sunlight, are like all good citizens, either heading for the hive or at least a sheltered place under some leaves for the night. (There are a few species of nocturnal bee, and Africanized bees will gather nectar in the moonlight, but most of the bee tribe are day-trippers.) So the majority of the nocturnal and/or night-fragrant plants are visited by moths.

Butterflies and moths are members of the order *Lepidoptera*, a group that includes over 11,230 species. Despite their preponderance on sunny summer afternoons, butterflies account for only some eight hundred of these species—all the rest are moths.

Like those of butterflies, moth wings are covered with scales. If you examine a wing under a hand lens, you will see that it is a transparent membrane stretched over a complex system of veins, or struts, much like the overlapping shingles on the roof of a house. These tiny scales are the powder that is left upon your finger after touching a moth or butterfly. The color of the wings is not from pigment; rather, the individual scales are grooved like the surface of a phonograph record and break up the light that falls

211

upon them into various colors unique to each species. This is the reason why antique Victorian tea trays and various picture mosaics that use butterfly and moth wings in their compositions never lose their colors but remain fast as long as the wings are kept intact and not harmed in any way.

Moths, like butterflies, have a complex life cycle consisting of various metamorphoses that occur between their beginnings as eggs, their hatching into caterpillars, then their succession of molts called pupation, in which the so-called worm is encased in a chitinous coffin that eventually opens to reveal an insect that flies with wings of beauty.

The eyes of a moth are compound and made up of many facets that fit together like the individual mirrors of the great light-collecting telescopes. Each of these facets is like a miniature eye, having its own lens and retina. These units are in turn connected by nerve fibers to the insect's brain. Some moths have dozens of such facets connected to one sense cell, enabling them to see and interpret the dimmest of light.

And if you shine a flashlight on the eyes of a moth, you will see that they sparkle like the reflectors on the back of a bicycle. This is because the retina of the moth's eye has a tapetum, a membrane that reflects light back through the retina, giving it another turn at stimulating the rods. It is the light-gathering power of these eyes that enables moths to fly about in what to us is the dark.

But they also have antennae to guide them through the night; these structures act like the insect's nose. Although located in the same place on the moth's head as on a butterfly's, moth antennae are sometimes simple in outline but usually far more complex. The basic knobs can be set with many different patterns of cilia, or small hairlike projections and many more look like feathers.

These antennae or feelers react to the molecules of scent wafted on the air in much the same way the olfactory nerves in our nose react to odors of various kinds. They are also necessary to the moth's sense of balance for when these antennae are removed, the injured moth appears lost and cannot fly.

Moth Flowers

There are pronounced differences, both visible and olfactory, in the way day-blooming flowers and those that brighten the night attract evening visitors.

Because butterflies do not have a highly developed sense of smell, butterfly flowers are often brightly colored, including many with petals of pure red or pure orange. Their odor is generally light, pleasant, and very agreeable, like a meadow basking in the summer sunlight. The flowers themselves are usually held erect with a pronounced rim for a butterfly (or bee) to land upon; the petals are often marked with dots or lines, guides to the center of the flower. And finally, most of the butterfly flowers stay open both day and night.

Moth flowers are usually white or at best faintly tinted, and often drab and insignificant. The perfume, however, is strong and heavy, often a very sweet and soapy smell. Except for many orchids, most nocturnal flowers are tubelike, their nectar hidden deep within the blossoms, and the petals, when present, are deeply lobed or fringed, easier for a moth to see but hardly proper for a landing strip. And they often close during the heat of the day.

The perfume from these flowers is so strong that it is detected over great distances by the moths that visit and pollinate them. A naturalist named Kerner once marked a hawkmoth with vermillion coloring, and set it down over three hundred feet from a honeysuckle plant (*Lonicera caprifolium*). "When twilight fell," he said, "the hawkmoth began to wave its feelers—they serve as olfactory organs—hither and thither a few times, then stretched its wings and flew like an arrow through the garden towards the honey-suckle." When the observer reached the flowers, he found the vermillion-sprinkled moth fluttering in front of the honeysuckle flowers and sucking nectar.

Moths have very long probosces, or tongues—in fact the longest of any flower-visiting animals. Some sphinx moths have probosces over six inches long that coil up like the mainspring in an old-fashioned watch when the moth is at rest. Using these tongues, they are able to hover in front of a tubelike flower rather than land upon the petals. The hawkmoths are so good at hovering that many gardeners mistake those that are active during the daytime for small humming-birds.

Because of the hovering action of moths, flowers that are pollinated by these creatures are usually found to have their nectar deeply hidden within the flower and their anthers very loosely attached to the filaments. As a result, they easily touch the body of the moth as it hovers in front of them. Many lilies are pollinated by moths and their hinged anthers are readily seen.

Some Representative Moths

Since butterflies are creatures of the sunny afternoon, it should be no surprise that many have quite beautiful common names: the Acadian hair-streak, Propertius's dusky wind, the little wood satyr, and Linda's roadside skipper come to mind. Yet it's with some amazement that I find the same imagination has been applied to naming the various moths. Among the more charming are the blurry chocolate, the delightful bird-dropping moth (so named because when at rest, the wing pattern resembles its namesake), the wayward nymph or sweetfern underwing, the transfigured hydriomena, and the turbulent phosphila. The following are a few of the moths found in the evening garden. During the day, by-the-by, moths are carefully hidden on the undersides of leaves or down in the crannies where tree roots meet

the soil, or hundreds of other hiding places where they are usually safe from daytime predators.

THE SPHINX OR HAWKMOTHS

The sphinx or hawkmoths are usually very large with robust bodies and wings that look like those of a stealth bomber—and they seem to fly almost as fast. The common name of sphinx refers to the resting stance of the caterpillars which is said to resemble the Egyptian Sphinx. The death's-head moth (*Acherontia atropos*) is one of the most famous members of the clan, renowned for the strange and obvious markings of a skull on the back of its thorax.* This moth emigrates from North Africa and southern Europe to the British Isles annually, but it never survives the winter. To add to its weirdness, the death's-head is able to emit a high-pitched squeak when it forces air through its tongue. The skull and squeal inspired Edgar Allen Poe's short story "The Sphinx," in which an American is terrorized by a creeping skull. He wrote: "The Death's-headed Sphinx has occasioned much terror among the vulgar, at times, by the melancholy kind of cry which it utters, and the insignia of death which it wears upon its corslet." Poe, however, took some poetic license with his choice of the death's-head as they are not to be found in America.

But we do have some attractive (and less threatening) American moths in this group. The pink-spotted hawkmoth (*Agrius cingulatus*) can have a four-inch wingspread, the hindwings gray shading to pink at the base and the abdomen sporting pink crossbars. The caterpillars feed on jimsonweed, pawpaws, sweet potatoes, tomatoes, and a number of morning glories. Many of the caterpillars of the sphinx moths are called hornworms because of the spinelike projection on their back end. The caterpillars pupate in the

*The death's-head moths used in the movie *Silence of the Lambs*, were really tomato hornworms harvested in North Carolina with an abstract skull affixed to their backs.

ground and sometimes the gardener will find the pupa, easily recognized as a member of this group because of the handlelike affair that contains the very long proboscis. One of the favorite flowers of this moth is the common garden phlox.

The hummingbird clearwing (*Hemaris thysbe*) is the day-flying moth that many gardeners mistake for a hummingbird. Its wingspan is over two inches and its wings vibrate with a buzzing sound while it hovers at flowers drinking nectar. Their bodies are brown, sometimes banded with black, and both the fore- and hindwings have large transparent areas. The caterpillars eat hawthorns, honeysuckles, and snowberries. This is a widespread moth, its ranges extending from Canada and Nova Scotia southward to Florida and westward to the Mississippi. But western gardeners have one of their own called the Thetis clearwing (*Haemorrhagia thetis*).

THE SILKWORM AND ROYAL MOTHS

There are three giant silkworm moths that are among the most beautiful of nocturnal creatures. The first one I ever saw was an ailanthus silkmoth (*Samia cynthia*) and that was when, believe it or not, we lived in midtown Manhattan. The wingspan is four inches and the olive-brown wings are tinted with pink and have white markings. Their primary food when caterpillars are the leaves of the Chinese tree-of-heaven (*Ailanthus altissima*), and, like many New Yorkers, we had one in our backyard just off Ninth Street. One summer night I found an almost perfect specimen of this fantastically beautiful moth.

They were first introduced into Philadelphia in 1861 from Europe, the Europeans having gotten them from China a few years earlier. Some investors interested in silk futures imported the moth in the hope that they would provide a good grade of silk. Coarse silk can be produced from the cocoons of this moth, but it takes a great deal of hand labor to produce it. In this country, where mechanization is the rule, no way was ever found to unwind the silk automatically. Their exact pattern of distribution is not known, but they are found from Massachusetts to Georgia and west to Indiana. These moths fly by day and are not attracted to lights.

The cecropia or robin moth (*Hyalophora cecropia*), common throughout the United states east of the Mississippi, is extremely beautiful. The wings are over five inches across, the forewings having an abstract pattern of various shades of brown with wavy diagonal lines like imaginary waves on a velvet beach. There are large black eyes at the tip of each wing. The hindwings have the same moirélike pattern and a white thumbnail in the middle of a sea of brown. The moths emerge from their cocoons in late spring or early summer. The caterpillars feed on willows, maples, and lilacs. Adult moths will fly to lights but they are sometimes found out and about during the daylight hours. In the western part of the country there is the Columbian silk moth (*H. columbia*) and the ceanothus silk moth (*H. rubra*).

The luna moth (*Actias luna*) is probably the most beautiful of all. The wings are over four inches wide and colored a pale pastel green with large "owl's eyes" on each wing and the hindwings have a long tail. For all their beauty, they are amazingly common throughout the East, ranging from Canada to Florida and westward to Texas. The caterpillar feeds on beeches, hazelnuts, willows, and cherries.

Io moths (*Automeris io*) are another amazingly common species for all their beauty as adults. They are smaller moths, with wingspans less than three inches. Both sexes are easily recognized by the white-centered, black-and-blue bull's-eye on the hindwing. The forewing of the female is a bright reddish brown while the male's is yellow. The caterpillars eat just about any leaf they can find. Their green bodies are covered with clusters of spines that are mildly poisonous if they penetrate the skin and so should be avoided, if possible.

THE ISABELLA TIGER MOTH

Many gardeners might be unaware of the adult form of the Isabella tiger moth (*Pyrrharctia isabella*), but most know the caterpillar, famous as the wooly bear, with its furry coat of reddish brown, capped with black at either end. Wooly bears eat both perennials and trees, concentrating on asters, clover, corn, sunflowers, birches, elms, and maples. They are often seen in the fall as they crawl along looking for a safe place to spend the winter. When disturbed they curl up and feign death. Folklore claims that winters can be predicted by the amount of black on a wooly bear's body. Unfortunately, a wooly bear can be found to back up any opinion since the color differences are due to age, not psychic ability. As they grow older, the black disappears and reddish brown becomes the prominent color. The moth itself is less than an inch in width and dark orange in color.

THE MOTH AND THE FLAME

I have a favorite garden book in my library called *The Gardener's Week-End Book* by Eleanour Rohde and Eric Parker. There is a section called "Garden Moths" and it describes a number of English species, the only Atlantic crossover being the hummingbird hawkmoth. This chapter is headed by a charming pen-and-ink drawing of three moths flying into a candle's flame.

Moths will fly to many different kinds of light, not just a burning candle. Coleman-type gas lanterns, streetlights—both mercury vapor and white—flashlights, black-light fluorescents, and a plain match will each attract their share of moths—and other insects, too. Perhaps the tapetums in their retinas are overloaded by the in-

tensity of the artificial light where, according to nature, there shouldn't be any light. But why then don't moths attempt to fly to the moon? Still they come to the light, whether electric or candle, and nobody seems to know why they do—

'Tis placid midnight, stars are keeping
    Their meek and silent course in heaven;
Save pale recluse, for knowledge seeking,
    All mortal things to sleep are given.

But see! a wandering Night-moth enters,
    Allured by taper gleaming bright;
Awhile keeps hovering round, then ventures
    On Goethe's mystic page to light.
With awe she views the candle blazing;
    A universe of fire it seems
To moth-*savante* with rapture gazing,
    Or Fount whence Live and Motion streams.

What passions in her small heart whirling,
    Hopes boundless, adoration, dread;
At length her tiny pinions twirling,
    She darts, and—puff!—the moth is dead.

        —THOMAS CARLYLE,
        The Tragedy of the Night Moth

FIREFLIES AND GLOWWORMS

We always know when summer has truly arrived in the garden for the fireflies start to flash their mating lights. Their activity varies according to the arrival of summer in your area of the country but usually in May, June, or July every bush and cranny twinkles with the firefly version of the Morse code.

Although most people call them lightning bugs or fireflies, both common names are incorrect since these glowing Tinker Bells are really beetles, belonging to the Lampyridae family. Nearly all are luminous and in some species not only the adults of both sexes but all stages in the life cycle

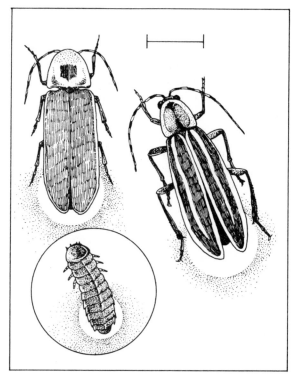

The pyralis firefly, *Photinus pyralis*, at left and the Pennsylvania firefly, *Photuris pennsylvanicus* at right. The inset shows a firefly larvae or glowworm.

luciferin. The result is the cool green glow of cold light, light, literally, that produces no heat. Since nature rarely wastes anything, eventually the oxyluciferin is changed back to luciferin and again produces cold light as a product. Only ten percent of the energy reaction produces heat and ninety percent is cold light. By comparison, electric lights emit five percent light and ninety-five percent heat.

At one time scientists would buy collected lightning bugs, snipping off their tails in order to obtain enough luciferin and luciferase for laboratory work. But today, the chemicals are produced through genetic engineering, with bacteria manufacturing the luciferin needed for research. Yet after years of study, and knowing why this cold light is produced, nobody knows exactly how.

There has always been an argument about the meaning of these flashing signals but today biologists know that each species has its own code of flashes and uses them to attract mates in the darkness of the night. Within a few weeks after mating, the females lay their eggs in the ground, then the adults die.

Firefly eggs glow too. While the eggs develop, the growing larvae light up inside the eggs. After hatching, they become glowworms and do what they do best: eat slugs and snails and other insect larvae. If you thought ladybugs and praying mantises were carnivorous, they have nothing on these tiny killing machines. Hollow and sharp hooklike mandibles inject an anesthetic into the victim, thus paralyzing it before it becomes food.

After spending the summer eating, the glowworms dig small tunnels and overwinter in deep sleep. With the warming of spring, they emerge to eat again, then pupate, and finally reemerge as a new firefly population, ready to start the cycle again.

The glowworm glow is another mystery of nature. Why do the eggs and larvae glow? Is the answer merely the conservation of nature—since

are luminous, even though its purpose is for courtship.

Each beetle has its own light organ located at the tip of its abdomen. These lamps look like miniature flashlight bulbs; they have a flattened side that faces the world consisting of a transparent window while the inside back of the lamp is lined with a reflecting material much like the tapetum of the nocturnal eye. Every one of these light-producing organs contains over seven thousand cells, packed with minuscule granules of chemicals that include a complex organic compound called luciferin (named for Lucifer, the Devil, originally known as the brightest of the angels). These light organs also contain an enzyme called luciferase, and when these two chemicals meet in the presence of oxygen, magnesium ions, and adenosine triphosphate, they form oxy-

they eventually must glow to perpetuate the species, why not get the machinery refined at an early stage?

The pyralis firefly, *Photinus pyralis*, lives east of the Rocky Mountains. The beetles are up to a half inch in length and both sexes have a flashing yellow light. The females do not fly. The flash of this species is easily recognized: it's always visible as the male beetle flies into the sky on an inclined path; when he reaches the apex of his flight pattern, the flash diminishes in brightness.

Photinus scintillans is another species of the photinus firefly and is quite common at dusk. Here the flying male signals to the stationary female with short, yellow flashes of light at intervals of five to six seconds.

The Pennsylvania firefly, *Photuris pennsylvanicus*, ranges from the Atlantic Coast to Texas, and north to Manitoba. Here the light is greenish, and both sexes produce a flash at about two- to three-second intervals after complete darkness has fallen.

In the southwestern United States the so-called fire beetles are found in subtropical lowlands. They belong to the genus *Pyrophorus* and have three luminous organs on their abdomens. While these insects are under one inch in length, there are tropical species up to two inches long that are worn as luminous decorations by partygoers, and rumor has it that the light from one beetle is bright enough to allow the owner to read the local newspaper.

Other Glowworms

The European glowworm is the wingless female of *Lampyris noctiluca* and is very famous both in legend and literature. This is the insect described in Thomas Hardy's *The Return of the Native*. Here three men, Wildeve, Christian, and Venn, are playing an outdoor game of dice when their lantern is extinguished by a death-head's moth.

As their eyes grew accustomed to the darkness they perceived faint greenish points of light among the grass and fern. These lights dotted the hillside like stars of low magnitude.

"Ah—glow-worms," said Wildeve. "Wait a minute. We can continue the game."

Venn sat still, and his companion went hither and thither till he had gathered thirteen glow-worms—as many as he could find in a space of four or five minutes—upon a foxglove leaf which he pulled for the purpose. The reddleman vented a low humorous laugh when he saw his adversary return with these. "Determined to go on, then?" he said dryly.

"I always am!" said Wildeve angrily. And shaking the glow-worms from the leaf he ranged them with a trembling hand in a circle on the stone, leaving a space in the middle for the descent of the dice-box, over which the thirteen tiny lamps threw a pale phosphoric shine. The game was again renewed. It happened to be that season of the year at which glow-worms put forth their greatest brilliancy, and the light they yielded was more than ample for the purpose, since it is possible on such nights to read the hand-writing of a letter by the light of two or three.

KATYDIDS AND CRICKETS

Katydids are large green insects closely related to the meadow grasshoppers that live in trees, the males singing only in the evening and on into the night: "Katy did, Katy did, she did," and another song comes from another nearby tree: "Katy did, Katy didn't, she did." The females can also sing in a quieter fashion but rarely do. Both insects continually wave long silken antennae above their two- to three-inch flattened bodies. There are those who say that distance lends enchantment to the katydid's song, since the sound can be quite rasping at close quarters. There are a number of species throughout the United States but the most

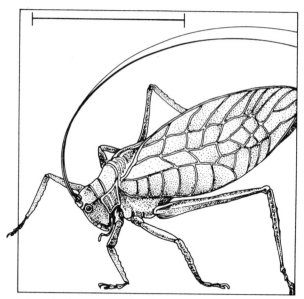

Pterophylla camellifolia, the common green katydid of the United States.

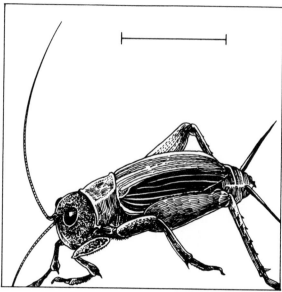

Gryllus pennsylvanicus, the common American field cricket.

common is *Pterophylla camellifolia*. They produce their songs by rubbing a file located on one wing over a scraper on the other. Once they begin to call, they continue to do so until the final killing frosts.

Many crickets are found around the world. In China, crickets are considered good luck and are housed in charming little cricket cages made of bamboo. But the time-honored hero of Dickens's *Cricket on the Hearth* is the European house cricket, *Acheta domestica*, while the common American field cricket is *Gryllus pennsylvanicus*. Older nature books often gave instructions on how to keep *Gryllus* crickets as pets using a lantern globe set on soil in a flower pot as a good cage. The captives were fed on lettuce, moist bread, and, in what sounds like an ominous suggestion, to lessen cannibalism, some bone meal.

Both the house and field crickets begin to sing in early summer but there are so many other evening noises then that crickets are rarely heard until their progressively persistent cries reach their peak when the afternoon shadows of autumn lengthen in the garden. Like the katydids, crickets sing late into the night, their song the result of rubbing their wings together; only males can sing.

Other crickets important to the evening garden are the tree crickets. There are many species and all are excellent singers but only the males give forth with song. Some live on trees and shrubs while others live within grass and weed thickets. The former usually sing only at night while the second sing both day and night with the song usually being a long trill, though occasionally they will make a short chirp.

The snowy tree cricket, *Oecanthus fultoni*, is first heard in September, his song coming from trees and shrubs in and around the garden. This song is notable for two reasons. First, because they rub their wings faster in warmer weather, you can use the song to tell the temperature. Count the number of chirps made in fifteen seconds and add forty. The result is the approximate temperature in degrees Fahrenheit.

The second gift is stranger. The snowy tree cricket seems to be the only insect that knows he belongs to an insect orchestra.

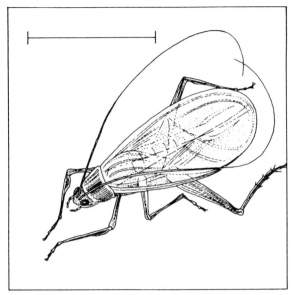

Oecanthus fultoni, the snowy tree cricket.

A metaphid jumping spider belongs to the genus *Metaphidippus* and has the best eyesight in the spider world.

"If you listen on a September evening," wrote Anna Botsford Comstock in the wonderful 1903 book, *Ways of the Six-Footed*, "you will hear the first player begin; soon another will join, but not in harmony at first. For some time there may be a see-saw of accented and unaccented notes; but after a while the two will be in unison; perhaps not, however, until many more players have joined the concert. . . . Sometimes an injudicious player joins the chorus at the wrong beat, but he soon discovers his error and rectifies it."

Jumping Spiders

Most gardeners would probably gloss over any discussion of spiders in the evening garden, but I have a soft spot in my heart for one special member of the spider tribe.

This is the jumping spider, a gregarious creature that frequents the garden both day and night. If caught in the rays of a flashlight, at least six of his eight eyes immediately shine like marcasite in old Victorian jewelry. It is the only spider I know of that is able to see a human being and will actually play hide-and-seek with your finger; I suppose the spider looks at me like giant prey but whatever the reason for its behavior, it is amusing.

John Crompton, in his 1950 book, *The Spider*, told the story of a night in a Hong Kong hotel when he was plagued by three mosquitoes. Finally he turned the light on and watched as one mosquito flew to the nearest wall where it paused to rest. As he watched, a small dark object crept out from a nearby corner, and with all the stealth of a jungle guerrilla, crept closer and closer to the seemingly unknowing victim until the spider leapt upon his prey. Mr. Crompton then finished off the other two.

There are other spiders that frequent the night air but they do not have the charm of the jumping spiders; for that reason I think it's best to think of them as out of sight, out of mind.

Mosquitoes

The mosquito life cycle lasts from ten days to a few weeks, depending on the species. Female mosquitoes live two weeks to several months, and most species will lay several clutches of eggs a season. It's the females who bite. They need a blood meal before they can produce eggs. Males do not bite, merely feeding upon plant sap.

The eggs are laid in pools of standing water. The eggs hatch into water-dwelling larvae, tiny wormlike creatures known as wrigglers, wriggling to the surface for air. Any water that stands for over a week in warm weather is a potential breeding ground. And they do not need much water. Look around the yard and garden for empty jars and cans, birdbaths that are not filled weekly, leaf-clogged gutters, and garden pools without fish.

When dealing with mosquitoes the first thing to remember is that those stupid electronic bug zappers do not work with them. They attract moths and other night-flyers, few (if any) of which are a danger or bother to you.

Mosquitoes love warm, moist, moving bodies and revel in carbon dioxide, the byproduct of

A little brown bat flies across the moon.

breathing. Because we exhale more carbon dioxide during or after exercise or hard work, mosquitoes are a special pest at those times. Mosquitoes also favor dark, nonreflective clothing and, unfortunately, the female hormone, estrogen, is another great attraction.

Citronella candles are somewhat effective in the open air and there are now a number of fairly effective but harmless insect repellents to send mosquitoes on their way. Most experts suggest the repellents be applied directly to the skin or clothing.

Finally, pyrethrum-based products are available in spray form and mosquitoes are killed by pyrethrum.

BATS

The full moon is shining down on the evening garden. It's a warm night in July and the overhead sky is purple-black, studded with stars. There is

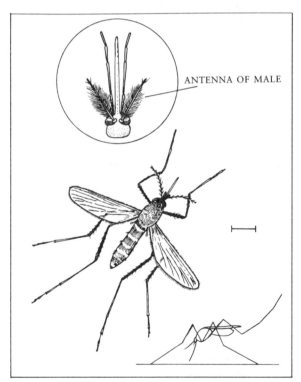

A female mosquito (*Calex* spp.) showing biting posture. The plumed antennae of a male are shown in inset.

ANTENNA OF MALE

still an orange glow in the west and we can see the black silhouettes of little brown bats, zipping in great circles as they catch insects on the fly. Their greatest activity is during the first half of the night, the time when there are more flying insects to devour.

While most people fear bats, even believing the old poem about bats getting under hats and sticking to your hair, today there is a glimmer of hope on the PR horizon, since Dracula appears to have given way to Batman. Finally, the "caped crusader," with his bat signal and his batmobile, has presented bats as a symbol of truth, justice, and the American way.

Bats will not get under your hat. They can, in fact, avoid a wire as fine as a human hair. By emitting high-pitched clicks or little bursts of sound that produce faint echoes which are heard by the sensitive ears of the bat, it is able to fly around your hat. Regardless of what some people say, the clicks are ultrasonic, far too high a frequency to be heard by a human ear.

And most bats are not ugly, especially when their wings are outstretched. They are simply mice with wings, the wings being a membrane stretched like a drum's skin over the skeletal parts of their forearms.

Bats as Pollinators

An amazing number of the world's nocturnal and night-fragrant plants are pollinated by bats, or their eventual seeds are spread about by bats that are attracted to their tempting fruits. Although a number of cactuses are bat-pollinated, including the great saguaro cactus of the American Southwest, the majority of these plants are tropical.

Bat flowers are characterized by blooming mostly at night, and, like moth-pollinated flowers, predominantly have a white or cream color. These flowers have a strong odor at night, often reminiscent of fermentation. They also bear a large quantity of nectar and pollen. Finally, bat flowers are often positioned away from the plant's foliage since flower-pollinating bats have a less developed sonar system than most of the other bat varieties.

There are approximately two hundred species of *Heliconia*, tropical plants related to the banana and best known in the flower trade as lobster-claws or false birds-of-paradise. Most of these flowers are pollinated by hummingbirds, but one, *H. solomonensis*, has relatively inconspicuous green inflorescense and flowers, and bright orange fruits, and is bat-pollinated.

W. John Kress is the Associate Curator of Botany at the National Museum of Natural History and, with Fred Barry, has co-authored a book called *Heliconia: An Identification Guide* (Smithsonian Institution Press, 1991). In 1983, he carried out investigations dealing with this bat-pollinated species.

"The bats hang head-down from the top of the bract," said Dr. Kress, "using the claws on its feet and after checking the inflorescence, crawl to the nearest open flower. When an open flower is found, the bat hangs with its wings folded crouched close to the flower and thrusts its snout into the open perianth, lapping up the nectar at the base of the flower tube. Bats usually remain at the flower for thirty seconds before looking for another open bloom."

Among the plants pollinated by bats are bananas, the sausage trees (*Kigelia* spp.), various members of the genus *Bombax*, and the durian tree (*Durio zibethinus*) of Southeast Asia.

Elizabeth Erdman is an American conservationist and a champion of the bat. She is out to tell the world what many people know but many more do not: that the bat is a valuable predator, harmless to people, having a relatively low incidence of rabies—more people are killed by lightning strikes or bee stings than bat rabies. In thirty years, only ten people in the United States and Canada have contracted rabies from bats. Like everything else, there is reason for keeping the public afraid of bats: the lucrative pest control industry.

If you do find a bat that does not try to avoid your presence, do not pick it up or handle it, as it is likely to be injured or ill. Call a local veterinarian for advice.

"Bats are nature's way of keeping our insect population in check," says Ms. Erdman. "They are the only major predator of night-flying insects in the world. Incredible as it may seem, some bats consume half their body weight in insects in one night, and they may consume half of that, or one quarter of their body weight, in as little time as thirty minutes. Bats have been known to travel up to fifty miles in one night to get their fill, returning home to roost during the day."

Miss Erdman and Bat Conservation International (BCI) warn everyone that the bat is in danger and her facts are backed up by the United States Department of Interior. According to their publications, bats are being killed by people, insecticides, and habitat destruction at an alarming rate.

"People are needlessly afraid of bats," she said. "This is primarily due to the legend of Dracula and the rumors of bats attacking people. But bats are really gentle, warm-blooded mammals that keep to themselves and are an integral part of our ecological system and vital to natural insect control."

My wife and I both believe her. So in our old garden we installed a bat box fifteen feet above the ground in the white pine tree that stood between the garden's edge and the nearby woods. We used plans from BCI to build the bat home and it was occupied by the first bat family by mid-May.

OWLS, TREE FROGS, AND FLYING SQUIRRELS

Lots of other animals are out at night. Skunks, for example, opossums, mice and voles, cats, even deer forage in the dark. But these animals are usually wary of human beings and you'll never know they're there.

But owls often will who, who, who in the evening garden and you should welcome them on every occasion. Thanks to reasonably keen eyes and astounding hearing, owls can locate prey in absolute darkness. Whether great horned owls, hoot owls, or barn owls, they are formidable killing machines, raptors replacing the daytime hawk.

In between the calls of the owl, you can hear the marvelous sounds of the tree frogs. Their high-pitched voices are a long and reedy tremolo that is especially compelling on warm summer evenings or in that quickening hush before the breaking of an afternoon thunderstorm.

Tree frogs are tiny things, no more than two inches long. Their scientific name is *Hyla versicolor*, the species name referring to their various colors of light gray or green or brown. The first tree frog I ever found was less than an inch and a half in length, of a light gray color, and blended perfectly with the bark of a white ash sapling. I

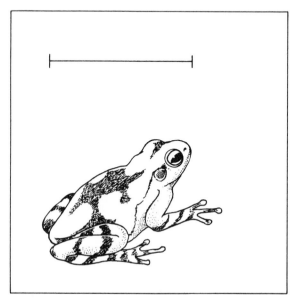

Hyla versicolor is one of the American tree frogs.

found this midget vocalist by following the sound of his voice. They all have sticky pads on their toes and can climb a vertical surface with ease.

You begin to notice tree frogs in May when they start to trill in the afternoon and keep it up well into the evening. They lay their eggs on plant stems in nearby ponds, and within seven weeks, the little frogs are half an inch long and ready to leave the water.

Finally, if you are very, very lucky, you might see one of the most beautiful and delightful of the night's creatures, the flying squirrel. There are two species, the northern flying squirrel, *Glaucomys sabrinus*, and the southern flying squirrel, *G. volans*.

These animals are very small, their heads and bodies no longer than six inches, with a four-inch flattened tail. Their fur is very thick, olive-brown above and white below. There is a rippling fold of loose, furred skin running along their sides from wrist to ankle. When these little squirrels wish to go from tree to tree, they leap into the air, spread the loose skin like a kind of wing, and can glide up to a hundred feet. They make birdlike tweets and a group can be heard to twitter.

Their eyes are very large, glowing red from the tapetum behind the retina, but even with red eyes, they're still cute. These little animals make excellent pets, although even in captivity they never change their nocturnal habits, being lethargic and sleepy by day and rambunctious by night. They have been known to live in attics but do not make the mess or noise that red squirrels can. They have been known to live thirteen years.

CHAPTER FOURTEEN

ℒIGHTING FOR THE EVENING GARDEN

If Caesar can hide the sun with a blanket,
or put the moon in his pocket,
we will pay him tribute for light.

WILLIAM SHAKESPEARE, *Cymbeline*

By day or by night the garden is an extension of the home and like the home it should strike a delicate balance between art and nature. The charm of walking through a purely wild landscape is in direct proportion to the effort of the walk: if the path is clear and well-marked, the walk becomes a welcome adventure, but if the thorns and branches are interlocked before you, the fun quickly dulls and everything becomes an unwanted struggle.

The same is true of the evening garden. If the pathways are well marked or lighted, whether the night is in summer or winter, once outside, you have walked from one room of your house into another.

I've walked many evenings in the garden and even the whip of winded snow or the piercing cold of sleet has not dulled my sense of enjoyment.

Since the light of the moon isn't available every evening, the next step in creating the evening gar-den is to provide enough light to mimic the moon or otherwise bathe the garden path with a gentle glow so the night visitor can enjoy the sights, sounds, and fragrances without tripping or stubbing a toe against a low rock wall.

One of the most beautiful evening gardens I ever saw was in the middle of the Lower East Side in Manhattan. Here in a backyard surrounded by buildings and fences, where daylight was too weak to support anything except some starved ivy, the owners found some marvelous antique garden furniture, and with the careful placement of candles and artificial lighting, turned what would have been a miserable effort at a living garden into a wonderful place for summer nights.

To understand the power of light at night, visit a son et lumière or a sound and light show. There is an especially fine example of this showmanship at the sixteenth-century French château Chenonceau in the Loire Valley. Here brilliantly designed light fixtures and floodlights illuminate specific parts of the château. Renaissance dance music floats out over the summer night from strategically placed loudspeakers, sparkling lights move from one end of the garden to another, and voices read from letters written by Catherine de Médicis or Henry II of France, for this château was the home of Catherine after the death of Henry and the banishment of Henry's mistress Diane de Poitiers. The brochures explain the historical connections and one paragraph ends with ". . . as soon as night invades nature again, we will discreetly take our leave, so that nymphs and birds may reclaim their domain."

This is what an evening garden can be.

LIGHTING THE GARDEN AT NIGHT

Almost in answer to the evening gardener's prayer, low-voltage lighting has become available to the mass market and ceased to be a luxury item. Even local hardware stores are known to stock complete sets of garden-lighting kits that will last more than a few seasons. The following pages are an attempt to present just a small sample of what is happening in the world of night-lighting.

Low-voltage lighting uses a special step-down transformer that reduces the regular—and dangerous—household current of 120 volts to a safe 12 volts. And it's truly safe. Even if you grasp a bare wire or cut through a cable with a chain saw, you will not get a shock! You need not worry about children or pets being electrocuted or dangerously burned since the cables can be buried in the garden using an ordinary garden trowel. While not the thing for large gardens, low-voltage lighting is perfect for the small homeowner and the small garden.

The costs are reasonable, too. We've had a system of outdoor lights in each of our gardens over the past six years and I doubt if the average three hours of light a night have raised our electric bill more than a few dollars a month.

If you have a very large garden or a big front yard, however, you might consider the installation of an extended 120-volt system where low-voltage sets are plugged into various outlets along the line. Already there are questions about where to put the lighting and how much you will need.

Making a Plan

With any gardening endeavor, the place to start is with pen and paper. As Amy Lowell wrote in "Planning the Garden,"

> Bring pencils, fine pointed,
> For our writing must be infinitesimal;
> And bring sheets of paper
> To spread before us.
> Now draw the plan of our garden beds,
> And outline the borders and the paths
> Correctly.

This needn't be a complicated map—or artistic. It just helps the gardener to arrive at the starting gate with some idea of what's coming down the pike.

Indicate the position of your house, garage, and other permanent features including the driveway, walkways, garden paths, utility lines, pools, ponds, and terraces, and be sure to include any especially attractive parts of your landscape, like a large tree or clumps of trees, or any rocks or boulders. Now place a piece of tracing paper over your base map and make your future notes on the tracing paper.

Go out into the evening garden and decide what you would like to illuminate. There are many options to consider. Are you interested in the security offered by night-lighting? Is there one part of the walkway up to the front door that could use illumination? Is there a grand old tree in the middle of the front lawn that could almost become a living outdoor sculpture if lit either from below or above?

Your final plan should indicate the location of power sources, the fixtures, and all the connecting lines. Generally small areas of your garden that will be easily lit by what is generally called mood lighting will be adequately handled by a 12-volt system. Larger areas that need intense light or if you wish for big scale lighting with pronounced dramatic effects, you will probably need the 120-volt system. In our garden we used both systems: The gentler parts of the garden are wired with 12-volt lights while the trees and shrubbery are lit with 120-volt lamps.

In addition to the aesthetic values of outdoor lighting, there is the value of security. At the same time your garden and grounds are bathed in the glow of carefully placed lamps, so are trespassers.

A few tips:

1. When designing your illuminated landscape, remember your neighbors. Be sure that your lights are never aimed at someone else's property.

2. Plan ahead. If you hire an electrician to install one outdoor outlet, think a few years down the line. While he or she is there for one job, it's always cheaper to put in another outlet, just in case.

3. When thinking dramatic, don't get too grandiose. Lights burn out, so don't put a light where you will need the local fire department to change a bulb.

4. Put controls like timers and switches in an accessible place. Although our timer is on an outdoor circuit, the line runs out of the inside circuit breaker, so, if need be, I can turn the system off from inside the house.

5. Keep bright outdoor lights away from windows or outdoor eating areas because they will attract some insects.

6. When lighting an object, try to use more than one light. One light makes an object appear flat while two lights lend dimension.

7. Install an automatic timer for your light system. This will ensure that your lights will go on every evening whether you remember or not and it will also make sure the lights are turned off, thus saving wear and tear and electricity.

8. Remember that less is more. Unless a particular lamp is designed to be ornamental, most night-lighting fixtures should be inconspicuous, blending into the garden by day, not taking it over.

8. Experiment. Using a long extension cord, try your lights in various parts of the garden before deciding on their final placement. And don't be afraid to break rules of design. You might have a garden where such rules do not apply.

The Intensity of Light

It's important at this point to know that there are various levels of light intensity. Recognizing them will enable you to read a manufacturer's claims with an open eye.

Light is measured in levels of brightness called footcandles, a footcandle being the amount of light cast on a white surface by one candle, one foot away, in an otherwise dark room.

The lowest light is *dim light*. The best example of dim is the light cast by a full moon. This is about one tenth of a footcandle.

Medium-bright light varies between one half to seven or eight footcandles. Most individual low-voltage garden fixtures equal one footcandle, while those fixtures in the 120-volt range can go up to five.

Bright light is equal to eight footcandles or more. A comfortable light for reading is fifty footcandles and the level of most stores and offices is over one hundred footcandles. While some trees or areas in an evening garden could be illuminated to the brightness of twenty footcandles, most areas would be best at five or below.

Lighting Techniques

DOWNLIGHTING OR AREA LIGHTING. If lights are placed high up in trees, pointed down at the ground, they are able to cast a wide path of light, easily illuminating your lawn or garden and opening up these areas for evening enter-

Above: Downlighting or area lighting.

Above right: Uplighting.

Lower right: Moonlighting.

tainment while doing double duty as nighttime security. When lamps are positioned closer to the ground, they can highlight flower beds, pathways, or steps.

UPLIGHTING. There's a gardener down the street from our house who has a large maple tree in his front yard. The tree is some sixty feet high, a complex tangle of trunks, stems, and branches. Phil installed a floodlight where the trunk begins to branch out and aimed it at the canopy above. The result is a shimmering mass of leaves during the summer and a starkly beautiful sculpture during the winter. This is a perfect example of uplighting.

MOONLIGHTING. We have some very stately oaks in our backyard that are between fifty to sixty feet high. I have some floodlights placed high up in these trees and the effect at night is the same as walking through bright moonlight, only in this case the colors of the flower beds and lawn are easily visible. When the lights are high

Silhouetting.

Shadowing.

up in a tree or mounted near the top of a two- or three-story house, the effect can mimic pools of moonlight. Moonlighting is especially beautiful in the winter with snow on the ground.

ACCENT OR SPOT LIGHTING. Lights are often used to focus a beam of brighter light on focal points in the garden, including favorite specimen plants, small trees, or garden sculpture. Accent lighting is easy to overdo, making your garden into a sound and light show (without the sound), and instead of the eye drifting slowly over the scene it will be pulled from light to light, so caution is advised when planning your design.

DIFFUSED LIGHTING. Here specially designed fixtures cover light bulbs with frosted glass or plastic panels that diffuse the light, thus casting relatively low levels of light on flower beds or walkways. This is an especially valuable approach for many seating areas on patios and terraces.

SILHOUETTING. This is a beautiful effect achieved by placing lights below sight level, in front of a wall or other vertical surface so that the wall is washed with soft light. A shrub, bush, or sculpture in front of that wall will create the same effect as mountains against a twilight sky.

SHADOWING. This is much like silhouetting except the light is placed in front of an object so that its shadow will fall on the wall or screen behind it. Shadowing can create a markedly beautiful scene, especially when soft winds move the leaves and branches of plants like bamboos or palms.

GRAZING. Here lights are placed close to a house or garden wall and the light falling at a slant across stone, brick, or even shingles brings out the special quality of the textures. Grazing works for wall sculptures and other wall decorations.

CROSS-LIGHTING. Illuminating one tree, a grove of trees, a sculpture, or even a large stone from two or more sides gives a special three-dimensional feeling to a scene. Cross-lighting works best with floods and other lamps equipped with diffusers. If the lights are installed in trees, let the beams cross high overhead rather than close to the ground.

PATH LIGHTING. When there are long pathways in a garden or steps from one level to another, small lights can illuminate these walks both for beauty and safety.

STEP LIGHTS. A number of lighting styles are available to light steps in the garden. It's easy to feel your way along a garden path in the dead of night but try memorizing steps! Rather than chance a fall, place some lights wherever the level of the garden changes.

FAIRY LIGHTS. Many are the evenings I wish I had stock in one of the fairy light companies. Every outdoor cafe and restaurant now features fairy lights that literally cover trees. These lights show us the way to theater seats, frame windows and doorways, and bring a dramatic flair to the facades of hotels, most of which are so poorly designed that if it weren't for fairy lights twinkling up the elevators, nobody would ever come inside. If kept within bounds, clear fairy lights can be quite charming in a small garden when draped in a casual manner over a small tree or rhododendron.

POOL AND FOUNTAIN LIGHTING. Special underwater lights are available that can create very dramatic effects in swimming pools or sparkling fountains, or small waterfalls as they splash over rocks in the garden.

As with the garden proper, both low-voltage and regular 120-volt lighting systems are available. But remember when working with water, special precautions must be taken. For safety's sake if you use 120-volt systems, be sure your electrician installs a special ground fault interrupter (GFI) in the system. A GFI is a safety device that interrupts a circuit in about one fortieth of a second if it detects any current leaks, thus pre-venting the danger of shock. They are often required by local electrical codes for many outdoor circuits, and here is one case of better safe than sorry.

Special kits with Hagen lights are available for water gardens. They include tightly sealed and especially bright lights, lens filters to give special color effects to the water, transformers, and cables. Very easy to install, these self-contained lighting units can be placed at the pool's bottom, plugged into a special extension cord that includes a GFI, and then be plugged into a regular 120-volt outlet.

One thing to remember about lighting pools or ponds—don't use downlighting directly on the water's surface since it will act like a mirror and interrupt any reflections of nearby rocks or other garden highlights; lights are better if placed under the water, but only if the water is clear. Cloudy water is accentuated by lights. Just take a flashlight and shine it down in your pool; the beam will light every particle, the result being a pool of haze.

But a large water lily is with its leaves spread out upon a garden pool, lit from below with a Hagen light will leave visitors stunned by the beauty of it all.

The 12-volt and 120-volt Systems

The installation of low-voltage systems is well within the working grasp of most gardeners but remember when installing 120-volt systems that electricity is dangerous and most residential areas have either electrical codes or building codes or both that you must follow. Unless you know exactly what you are doing, hire a professional to install the 120-volt part of your system.

You will need an outdoor 120-volt convenience outlet on the side of your house or at a convenient spot at the garden's edge or close to your terrace. Once this is installed—preferably by a local electrician who knows the housing and building codes in your area—the rest of the job can be done by you.

Basic outdoor 12-volt lighting kits usually contain a transformer—with more expensive models featuring a timer—plus fifty or a hundred feet of insulated copper cable, and four or six lights. They are available for less than a hundred dollars, but like everything else, you get what you pay for. Try to avoid the cheap plastic sets in discount centers because the plastic quickly becomes brittle when left to the action of weather. If your garden budget won't cover six or so of the more expensive outdoor lights, buy one light whenever you can; you'll be happier in the long run.

If installing a 12-volt system, permits are rarely required by local building codes. But if using a 120-volt system, get a copy of your local electrical code. It will contain specifications on the types of conduit and cable needed and how deep it must be buried. AND NEVER WORK ON A LIVE CIRCUIT NO MATTER HOW MUCH YOU THINK YOU KNOW!

HOW MANY LIGHTS?

Both the 120-volt and 12-volt systems have limitations. In a 120-volt system, the number of lights you can have on any one circuit is a function of the amount of current available, the length and thickness of the wire run, and the total number of watts required to operate your choice of fixtures. Assume that you have tapped into an existing line that has a 15-amp fuse or circuit breaker. This means the line can support a maximum of 1,500 watts. Now add up the total watts already on the line. For example if you have a number of 75-watt indoor lights on the line and you sometimes plug in a vacuum cleaner, or a fan in the summer, the total used is about 800 watts. That leaves 700 free watts, so you could safely add an outdoor system of at least 500 watts. From here on in, you should check with an electrician who will tell you the size and length of wire you can use for installation.

There are usually three different capacity transformers offered with the 12-volt system. The basic 108-watt transformer will support six 18-watt fixtures on a one-hundred foot cable (a total of 108 watts). A 250-watt transformer will support ten or more fixtures but their total number of watts must not exceed 250. For example, you could run two hundred-foot cables, each with five fixtures. You could mix four 18-watt and one 50-watt lights on one side and one 18-watt and two 50-watt lights on the second cable for 170 watts on each cable, making a total of 240 watts. It is very important that the load on each cable is balanced: If there are 100 watts on the first cable there must be 100 watts on the second. And because there are voltage drops on cables longer than one hundred feet, that is the maximum run you should use. A 500-watt system allows more lights with the total at 500 watts or less. For additional information, check the specifications supplied with the lighting kit you purchase.

One final thing about transformers. There are waterproof transformers and dry transformers, the second type needing an absolutely dry place for installation. When used outdoors, both must be plugged into a raintight outdoor outlet AND NEVER USE AN EXTENSION CORD!

Lamp Types and Fixture Styles

Today's outdoor lighting fixtures use a number of modern bulbs. They include the time-honored incandescent lamps that most indoor lamps use and other forms of incandescents including reflector bulbs (like car headlights) and outdoor reflector bulbs, chiefly a reflector called PAR (short for parabolic aluminized reflector); U-shaped fluorescent tubes that are specially designed to be used in the evening garden, giving a great deal of light with a small amount of electricity; low-voltage lamps designed for use with a 12-volt circuit; and quartz incandescent and quartz-halogen lamps that operate at higher temperatures but give a consistently brighter light.

NIGHT LIGHTS

Ten years ago if you wanted fixtures for the evening garden there were Malibu lights from California and little else. Today there are dozens of companies and hundreds of designs. Some are very ugly and very expensive, some are very ugly and very cheap but there are a few that have the right combination of aesthetics and practicality. I have ignored night lights that look like they were designed for nineteenth-century barrooms. I've also voted no to lights in the shape of mushrooms or that have animal silhouettes on their faces. I've also neglected lights that call themselves high-tech or contemporary, and eschewed any lights that use rippled pieces of shiny Plexiglas, designed to ape crystal chandeliers for the backyard.

And speaking of shiny surfaces, keep in mind that all those polished fixtures you see in the showroom will quickly lose their sheen out in the great outdoors. Wind, rain, snow, and acid dew, in fact weather in general, will take its toll. The best metals for fixtures are copper, bronze, or heavy aluminum; the first two acquire a patina as they age and the third can be painted—and repainted—any number of colors.

One of the best series of designs that I've found in low-voltage fixtures is produced by the Lite-Nite Company. Their fixtures are made of copper with brass fittings and all feature excellent designs available in three finishes, natural copper, verdigris, and polished copper. The natural copper is best since it will age to a dark brown or green patina. The fixtures are small in scale and easily blend into the garden setting. Additional glare shields are available, as is a photo control that will operate lighting systems from dawn to dusk.

For black fixtures of excellent design, Luma Lighting Industries produce a number of attractive fixtures featuring a black polyester powder coating that is extremely durable.

Since late last winter, a fluorescent floodlight from Kelsey-Kane in Florida has helped to light up my garden. It is hidden from garden view by a clump of ferns but shines up on our star magnolia and in turn on a larger dogwood tree with a trunk wrapped in English ivy. Not only were the trees beautiful in spring flower, and in summer leaf, but now in early winter, with their bare branches dotted here and there with lichens, their beauty remains.

These floodlights hold two fluorescent bulbs but are ballasted separately so the gardener can pull out one lamp and burn the other, the one light burning just 17 watts. The fixtures have a huge beam spread and that spread can be adjusted with internal glare guards.

There are color filters for these lamps, an option that, at first, I wasn't too excited about. The instructions recommend using a warm white bulb (2,700K) on most trees and plants, since a pure white light causes foliage to look washed out. Then you can add either a green or amber filter that covers half of the fixture. The gold accentuates the browns in tree trunks while the green highlights foliage—and it really works. Blue is recomended for snow in winter gardens and in Florida some of the more tropical plants are said to look better with a pink filter. A three-sided glare guard is also available for when the lights are placed close to windows.

When ground mounting a fixture under a tree, the best effect is had by placing it very close to the trunk. As mentioned before, uplighting creates a more three-dimensional look while front lighting has a tendency to flatten the scene. The company also recommends sealing all openings to the electrical junction box and lighting fixture with silicone to thwart ants and other insects from finding a new home.

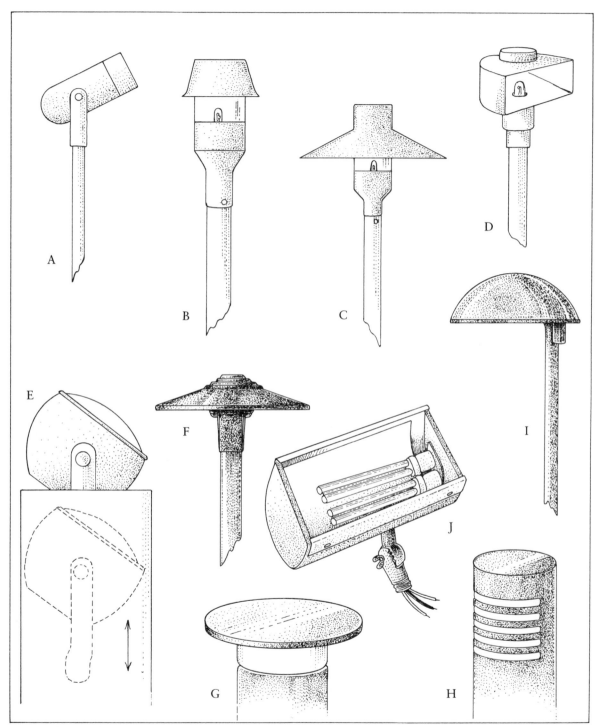

Various designs for night light fixtures. A-E are made of copper and brass by the Lite-Nite Company; F-I are made by Luma Lighting and feature a black polyester powder coating; J is a fluorescent floodlight made by Kelsey-Kane.

SOLAR LIGHTS

A new line of outdoor lighting is on the market. These fixtures use solar energy to charge their batteries so no wiring connections are needed. Although styles differ, each unit has a small panel on top which catches daylight and charges the battery. Then at night, the light can burn for several hours before requiring another charge the next day.

More expensive lamps even have infrared detectors that keep the lights off until needed. This is an especially important feature, since these solar units do not carry enough power to charge a light for all-night use.

While adequate for a very small garden, these solar lights are not very powerful and until the technology improves, the gardener's best bet is to invest in low-voltage lighting.

MAKING YOUR OWN FIXTURES

The ubiquitous clay flowerpot with the drainage hole in the bottom makes an excellent night-light; use a 25-watt bulb in a commercial rubber socket. Or if you have an old metal watering can that has seen better days, cut a hole in the side and set a flood light in a commercial holder that comes complete with a spike for fixing in the ground. The same trick would work with a plastic watering can.

One of the best quick garden lights I ever made used a simple fluorescent light fixture of the type made to fit under kitchen cabinets. The fixture was installed underneath an old wooden garden bench and reflected light on a line of small potted plants that sat beneath.

Finally, use a short piece of a clay drainage tile to make an uplighter using a PAR reflector bulb set in an adjustable holder.

Other Lights for the Night

John Singer Sargent's painting *Carnation, Lily, Lily, Rose* (1885–86) shows two young girls dressed in white standing in the midst of a darkening flower garden festooned with lilies, roses, and carnations, carefully taking tapers and lighting large paper Japanese lanterns for the evening festivities.

Lighting the evening garden need not be limited to electrical systems. Take *luminarias*, or "little lights," for example. These festive outdoor lights had their beginnings back in the 1600s when Mexican villages along the Rio Grande would build small bonfires from criss-crossed piñon boughs. They were lit on Christmas Eve to show the way for the Christ Child. Then in the early 1800s, the paper bag made its appearance, brought by Yankee traders who traveled along the Santa Fe Trail. Now, rather than a bonfire, a regular brown paper bag was filled with two or three inches of sand, and a candle or votive light was set in place. Today they are the principal feature of holiday lighting at Christmastime and ready-made electric luminarias are available featuring brown or white plastic sleeves and 7-watt bulbs.

The common concrete Japanese lanterns available at the larger garden centers are usually reasonable imitations of Japanese stone lanterns. Japanese tea ceremonies were often held in the evening and these beautiful carved stone lanterns provided the light needed for the guests to wend their way along garden pathways. There were *tachi-gata*, or pedestal lanterns; *oki-gata*, small lanterns that were placed at the edge of a pond; and *yukimi-gata*, or snow-viewing lanterns.

Many garden suppliers stock Shoji lanterns, like the screens, made of cedar framing and glazed with weatherproofed and nonflamable fiberglass paper.

Votive candles set within small clay pots make festive lighting for the evening garden. Or look for garden flares, special coated candles that will burn up to three hours. Even plain white plumber's candles from the hardware store when set in small clay saucers, can brighten up your night.

The Winter Garden at Night

Our first garden in upstate New York suffered through at least five months of possible sleet and snow, the winter season beginning shortly after Thanksgiving and often continuing to mid-April. But the garden was not a total loss. In addition to the low-voltage lighting visible from the dining room—including a Japanese snow lantern on the edge of the rock wall surrounding the scree bed— I installed a number of 150-watt PAR reflectors set two feet above the tops of the library windows and three more above the window wall in the dining room. I put two more high up under the eaves on the side of the house. When winter winds blew and icy flakes swirled through the branches of twin white pines outside the library window, snowstorms were a sight to see. Out in the garden, beyond the dining room's glass doors, bare and twisted twigs of a Harry Lauder's walking stick (*Corylus avellana* 'Contorta') shared space with the whiplike branches of a weeping birch (*Betula pendula* 'Tristis'), as both glittered with hoarfrost. Just to their left were the brilliant red stems of a Siberian dogwood (*Cornus alba* 'Siberica') poking up through a crusted snow that sparkled like a million diamonds from the garden lights. The only light in our dining room was an antique crystal chandelier that held six candles surrounding an ancient kerosene lamp. Right after New Year's, we began to wish for winter's passing, but looking out at the evening garden helped the time to pass with a small share of grace.

Sculpture in the Evening Garden

There is one more thing of great value in the evening garden and that is sculpture. In addition to the various 12-volt fixtures that were mentioned above, out in the old rose garden there is

a three-foot diameter black iron armillary sphere, its pedestal surrounded by a boxwood hedge— the sphere will be lit when I have time to run the wires from the house. On the wall of the terrace at the rear of the house sits a black Persian cat from the Boston Museum. His base is lost in a tangle of ivy and he's lit from the side by a small spotlight. There he sits, winter and summer, and it's especially interesting when one of the real cats chooses to sit beside him.

Finally, in the middle of the scree bed surrounded by ornamental grasses and dwarf conifers, is our newest addition, a gargoyle. About two feet behind him is a low wall that is washed with light by two hidden diffusers, leaving the gargoyle in silhouette.

Gargoyles have an old and distinguished history. They were used as decorative spouts projecting from buildings to throw out rainwater gathered by gutters along a roof. The most famous are the High Gothic grotesques leaning out from the parapets and cornices of Notre Dame in Paris. But hundreds of feet above the streets of Manhattan, just below the top of the Chrysler Building, four gargoyles also look out over the city, while here in Asheville one of the taller buildings in town has its own stone gargoyles looking out for spirits of the night.

A Plan for a Terraced Evening Garden

The following garden is planned for an area around a terrace, either close to or attached to a home or apartment. There are two reasons for this location: First, a source of electricity is needed for the outdoor lighting and, second, it's much nicer to sit on stone or gravel to watch the fireflies than on dew-bespotted grass. Nights are romantic, but they are often damp, especially in the Northeast.

The terrace shown in the plan measures ten by fifteen feet and is decorated with tropical night-bloomers that can happily summer outside but must come in for the winter in most of the United

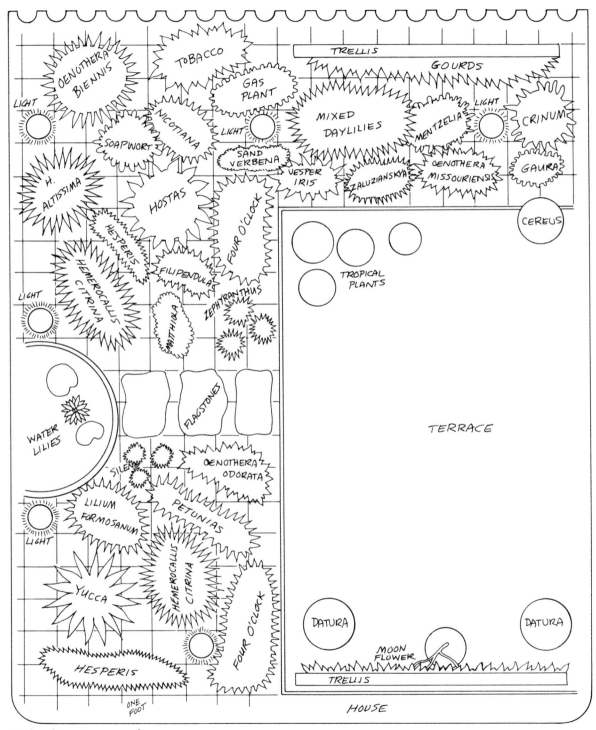

A plan for a terrace garden.

States. This terrace garden includes a few decorative pots that hold moonflowers that twine up a wooden trellis, night-blooming cereus, angel's trumpet, some *Gladiolus tristis*, and night jessamine. If you are short on night-blooming tropicals to scatter around the terrace, remember that a potted palm or three or four large ferns are more effective at night, bathed in the glow of various low-voltage fixtures, than they ever were during the day.

Around the terrace are annuals for night fragrance, another trellis bearing white-flowering gourds, and many other flowers of the night. A fieldstone pathway leads to the rest of the backyard, where low-voltage lighting illuminates the trees beyond the garden—and provides for easier walking when there is no moon.

If you decide to install a small pond, think about using some of the special underwater lights. These are especially effective and cast a romantic glow over the entire garden. But also be aware that pond water must be kept clean. To be sure, install a filter to keep everything bright and sparkling.

Finally, nothing is more beautiful than the sound of a splashing fountain or running water in the evening garden. A fan fountain will provide a six-foot spray that will sparkle like a moving chandelier. A lily bubbler allows water to bubble up and spill over the sculptured lead petals and pads. Or try a dome fountain. This consists of a slender stainless steel tube that releases the water in an unbroken sphere ready to cascade down upon the water lily leaves. Another simple fountain shoots a stream of water to four feet where it arches and splashes back on the pond's surface. Even if your installation is nothing but a hose that releases a stream of water that gurgles in and around the roots of a nearby tree, there will be magic in the night.

❧ SOURCES ❧

Sources for Plants

Bromeliads

Tropiflora
3530 Tallevast Road
Sarasota, FL 34243
(813) 351-2267

Bulbs

Bio-Quest International
P.O. Box 5752
Santa Barbara, CA 93150
(805) 969-4072

McClure & Zimmerman
P.O. Box 368, 108 W. Winnebago
Friesland, WI 53935
(414) 326-4220

Cactuses

Greenlife Gardens
101 County Line Road
Griffin, GA 30223
(404) 228-3669

Rainbow Gardens
1444 E. Taylor Street
Vista, CA 92084
(619) 758-4290

Carnivorous Plants

Carolina Exotic Gardens
Route 5, Box 283-A
Greenville, NC 27834
(919) 758-2600

Peter Pauls Nurseries
RD #2
Canandaigua, NY 14424
(716) 394-7397

Daylilies

Daylily Discounters
Route 2 Box 24
Alachua, FL 32615
(904) 462-1539

Fragrant Plants

Companion Plants
7247 N. Coolville Ridge Road
Athens, OH 47501
(614) 592-4643

Sandy Mush Herb Nursery
Route 2, Surrett Cove Road
Leicester, NC 28748
(704) 683-2014

Lilies

B & D Lilies
330 P Stret
Port Townsend, WA 98368
(206) 385-1738

Magnolias

Greer Gardens
1280 Goodpasture Island Road
Eugene, OR 97401
(503) 686-8266

Louisiana Nursery
Route 7, Box 43
Opelousas, LA 70570
(318) 948-3696

Magnolia Nursery & Display Garden
12615 Roberts Road
Chunchula, AL 36521
(205) 675-4696

Orchids

The Angraecum House
P.O. Box 976
Grass Valley, CA 95945
(916) 273-9426

Jones & Scully
18955 S.W. 168 Street
Miami, FL 33187
(305) 238-7000

Orchids by Hausermann
2N 134 Addison Road
Villa Park, IL 60181
(708) 543-6855

Perennials

Coastal Gardens & Nursery
4611 Socastee Boulevard
Myrtle Beach, SC 29575
(803) 293-2000

Forestfarm
990 Tetherah Road
Williams, OR 97544
(503) 846-6963

Holbrook Farm and Nursery
Route 2, Box 223 B
Fletcher, NC 28732
(704) 891-7790

Lamb Nurseries
East 101 Sharp Avenue
Spokane, WA 99202
(509) 328-7956

Niche Gardens
1111 Dawson Road
Chapel Hill, NC 27516
(919) 967-0078

Andre Viette
Route 1, Box 16
Fishersville, VA 22939
(703) 943-2315

Seeds

The Banana Tree
715 Northampton Street
Easton, PA 18042
(215) 253-9589

The Fragrant Path
P.O. Box 328
Fort Calhoun, NE 68023

Chiltern Seeds
Bortree Stile, Ulverston
Cumbria LA12 7PB, England
(0229) 581137

Plants of the Southwest
930 Baca Street
Sante Fe, NM 87501
(505) 983-1548

Societies
(some with Seed Exchanges)

Alpine Garden Society
AGS Centre, Avon Bank
Pershore, Worcestershire
WR10
3JP, England
0386-552657

American Horticultural Society
7931 E. Boulevard Drive
Alexandria, VA 22308
(800) 777-7931

The American Orchid Society
6000 S. Olive Avenue
West Palm Beach, FL 33405

American Rock Garden Society
221 West 9th Street
Hastings, NM 55033
(612) 437-4390

Arizona Native Plant Society
P.O. Box 41206
Tuscon, AZ 85717

Bat Conservation International
P.O. Box 162603
Austin, TX 78716
(512) 327-9721

The Hardy Plant Society
710 Hemlock Road
Media, PA 19063
(215) 566-0861

The Hoya Society International
P.O. Box 54271
Atlanta, GA 30308

The International Geranium Society
4610 Druid Street
Los Angeles, CA 90032

The Royal Horticultural Society
80 Vincent Square
London SW1P 2PE, England

Scottish Rock Garden Society
21 Merchiston Park
Edinburgh EH10 4PW, Scotland
031-229-8138

Tropical Flowering Tree Society
Fairchild Tropical Garden
10901 Old Cutler Road
Miami, FL 33156
(305) 248-0818

Tropical Plants

Berry's Tropical Plants
6450 SW 81 Street
Miami, FL 33143
(305) 667-4036

John Brudy Exotics
3411 Westfield Drive
Brandon, FL 33511
(813) 684-4302

Glasshouse Works
Church Street, P.O. Box 97
Stewart, OH 45778
(614) 662-2142

Kartuz Greenhouses
1408 Sunset Drive
Vista, CA 92083
(619) 941-3613

Logee's Greenhouses
55 North Street
Danielson, CT 06239
(203) 774-8038

Stallings Exotic Nursery
910 Encinitas Boulevard
Encinitas, CA 92024
(619) 753-3079

Water Lilies

Lilypons Water Gardens
6800 Lilypons Road, P.O. Box 10
Buckeystown, MD 21717
(301) 428-0686

Wildflowers

We-Du Nurseries
Route 5, Box 724
Marion, NC 28752
(704) 738-8300

Sources for Tools and Supplies

General Garden Tools, Pots, etc.

The Walt Nicke Company
P.O. Box 433, 36 McLeod Avenue
Topsfield, MA 01983
(508) 887-3388

Mellingers, Inc.
2310 W. South Range Road
North Lima, OH 44452
(216) 549-9861

Sources for Electrical Outdoor Lighting

Lite-Nite Company
819 Pickens, Suite 1
Marietta, GA 30067
(404) 514-0951

Luma Lighting
P.O. Box 4069
Orange, CA 92613
(714) 282-1116

Lumière Design & Manufacturing, Inc.
31360 Via Colinas #101
Westlake Village, CA 91362
(818) 991-2211

Luminarias, Lanterns, Candles, and Torches

The Shop
208 West San Francisco Street
Santa Fe, NM 97501
(800) 525-5764

Pottery Barn
P.O. Box 7044
San Francisco, CA 94120
(800) 922-9934

Sculpture

Museum of Fine Arts, Boston
Catalog Sales Department
P.O. Box 1044
Boston, MA 02120
(800) 225-5592

Design Toscano
7 E. Campbell Street
Arlington Heights, IL 60005
(800) 525-0733

Gazing Globes

Milaeger's Gardens
4838 Douglas Avenue
Racine, WI 53402
(414) 639-2371

Barr, Claude A. *Jewels of the Plains*. Minneapolis: University of Minnesota Press, 1983. One of the best books ever written about wildflowers of the Great Plains.

Benson, Lyman. *The Cacti of Arizona*. Phoenix: The University of Arizona Press, 1950.

Bisset, Peter. *The Book of Water Gardening*. New York: A. T. De La Mare Printing and Publishing Co., Ltd., 1907. Although many plant cultivars have changed, the growing advice is still excellent.

Blanchan, Neltje. *The American Flower Garden*. New York: Doubleday, Page & Company, 1909. Not only is this a good garden book of the time but the binding on the original publication is magnificent.

———. *Nature's Garden*. New York: Doubleday, Page & Co., 1904. Full of wonders about wildflowers, how they grow and survive, and the bees and moths that flit from blossom to blossom.

Britton, N. L. and J. N. Rose. *The Cactaceae*. Washington, D.C.: Carnegie Institution of Washington, 1937. Reprint, New York: Dover Publications, 1963. The most complete book ever compiled on cactuses.

Church, Arthur Harry, M.A., D.Sc. *Types of Floral Mechanism*. Oxford: The Clarendon Press, 1908. Diagrams and descriptions of how flowers are pollinated.

Compton, John. *The Spider*. London: Collins, 1950. Some of the finest natural-history writing ever attempted.

Comstock, Anna Botsford. *Ways of the Six-Footed*. Boston: Ginn & Company, 1903. The fascinating world of insects.

Conard, Henry S. and Henri Hus. *Water-lilies and How to Grow Them*. New York: Doubleday, Page & Company, 1907. Covers all aspects of the Amazon water lily.

Davis, Ben Arthur. *Daylilies and How to Grow Them*. Atlanta: Tupper & Love, 1954. Especially valuable for gardeners in the South.

Dictionary of Gardening. The Royal Horticultural Society. 4 vols. and supplement. Oxford: Clarendon, 1965. Next to *Hortus Third*, these volumes are the most used in my library.

Earle, Alice Morse. *Old Time Gardens*. New York: The Macmillan Company, 1901. The definitive story of the Hon. Ben. Perley Poore's moonlight garden. My copy of this book was once in the library of Richardson Wright.

Faegri, K. and L. Van der Pijl. *The Principles of Pollination Ecology*. New York: Pergamon Press, 1971. Describes all the insects that pollinate flowers.

Fairchild, David. *The World Was My Garden*. New York: Charles Scribner's Sons, 1938. The world of plants just before Japan invaded the Islands of the Pacific.

Genders, Roy. *Perfume in the Garden*. London: The Garden Book Club, n.d. A marvelous, chatty book full of information on scented flowers.

Gleason, Henry A. *The New Britton and Brown Illustrated Flora of the Northeastern United States and Adjacent Canada*. New York: Hafner Publishing Company, Inc., 1963. An update of the original Britton and Brown with many new plants.

Graf, Alfred Byrd. *Exotic Plant Manual*. East Rutherford, New Jersey: Roehrs, 1970. Contains 4,200 black-and-white photos along with complete cultural tips on both indoor and outdoor plants.

Hill, Jason. *The Contemplative Gardener*. London: Faber and Faber, 1939. One of the few books to mention color theory in the evening garden.

Hill, Lewis and Nancy Hill. *Daylilies: The Perfect Perennial*. Pownal, Vermont: Storey Communications, Inc., 1991. An excellent source for daylily cultivation.

Hillerman, Fred. E. and Arthur W. Holst. *An Introduction to the Cultivated Angraecoid Orchids.* Portland, Oregon: Timber Press, 1986. The definitive book on these night-fragrant orchids.

Holland, W. J. *The Moth Book.* New York: Doubleday, Page & Co., 1903; Reprint, New York: Dover Books, 1968. A literate look at the lives of moths, the kind of book on nature that is no longer written or perhaps could be written in today's world.

Hortus Third. Revised by the staff of the L. H. Bailey Hortorium. New York: Macmillan Publishing Co., Inc., 1976. Flawed but still one of the best American references around.

King, Ronald. *The Temple of Flora by Robert Thornton.* Boston: New York Graphic Society, 1981. The whole story of Thornton's floral plates with only two mistakes: the drops falling from the Aloe in Plate XII are nectar, not water, and the Dragon Arum in Plate XXII is the second pressing, not the first.

Knuth, Dr. Paul. *Handbook of Flower Pollination.* Oxford: The Clarendon Press, 1906. Insect pollinators featuring bees, bats, and moths.

Loewer, Peter. *Gardens by Design.* Emmaus, Pennsylvania: Rodale Press, 1986. Twelve garden designs, including one for a night garden.

MacDougal, Jan. *Charleston in Bloom.* Charleston, South Carolina: Oak Manor Press, 1990. An excellent tour to Charleston houses and gardens.

Mathew, Brian. *The Iris.* New York: Universe Books, 1981. Covers both common and rare plants.

Mee, Margaret. *In Search of Flowers of the Amazon Forests.* Edited by Tony Morrison. Woodbridge, Suffolk, England: Nonesuch Expeditions, 1988. A trip down South American rivers in search of jungle plants including night-blooming cactuses.

Menninger, Edwin A., D.Sc. *Flowering Vines of the World.* New York: Hearthside Press, Inc., 1970. The definitive book on vines.

Menzel, Donald H. and Jay M. Pasachoff. *A Field Guide to the Stars and Planets.* Boston: Houghton Mifflin Company, 1983. A literate and well-illustrated guide to the heavens.

Morley, Brian D. and Barbara Everard. *Wild Flowers of the World.* New York: Crescent Books, 1970. Much information on tropical plants along with superb illustrations.

Morton, Julia F. *Exotic Plants for House and Garden.*

New York: Golden Press, 1977. A Golden Guide that covers a number of nocturnal tropical plants.

Munson, R. W., Jr. *Hemerocallis, the Daylily.* Portland, Oregon: Timber Press, 1989.

Nichols, Beverly. *Sunlight on the Lawn.* New York: E. P. Dutton & Co., 1957. Nichols wrote some of the best gardening books in the English language. This is one of them.

Northen, Rebecca Tyson. *Home Orchid Growing.* New York: Prentice Hall Press, 1990. The best all-around guide to growing orchids.

Padilla, Victoria. *Bromeliads.* New York: Crown Publishers, 1973. The definitive book on collecting and growing bromeliads.

Parkinson, John. *A Garden of Pleasant Flowers (Paradisi in Sole: Paradisus Terrestris).* New York: Dover Publications, Inc., 1976.

Percival, Mary. *Floral Biology.* London: Pergamon Press, 1965. Fascinating information on floral structure and agents of pollination.

Phillips, Roger. *Mushrooms of North America.* Boston: Little, Brown and Co., 1991. An up-to-date and well-photographed book on mushrooms.

Powell, Claire. *The Meaning of Flowers.* New York: Shambhala, 1979. Many references to the language of flowers.

Rohde, Eleanour Sinclair and Eric Parker. *The Gardener's Week-End Book.* London: Seeley Service & Co. Ltd., 1939. Practical gardening knowledge and wonderful bits of reading.

Rickett, Harold William. *Wildflowers of The United States: The Northeastern States.* New York: McGraw-Hill Book Company, 1966. An excellent reference.

———. *Wildflowers of the United States: The Southeastern States.* New York: McGraw-Hill Book Company, 1966.

The Royal Horticultural Society Dictionary of Gardening. Oxford: The Clarendon Press, 1974. For listings of rare species and interesting facts, this can't be beat.

Schultz, Ellen D. *Texas Wild Flowers.* Chicago: Laidlaw Brothers, 1928. Many facts on both common and rare Texas wildflowers.

Scott-James, Anne. *Sissinghurst, The Making of a Garden.* London: Michael Joseph, 1974. The definitive book on the design and development of the Nicolsons' garden.

Spellenberg, Richard. *The Audubon Society Field Guide to North American Wildflowers, Western Region*. New York: Alfred A. Knopf, Inc., 1979. One of the best all-around guides to western wildflowers.

Stout, A. B., *Daylilies, The Wild Species and Garden Clones, Both Old and New, of the Genus Hemerocallis*. New York: The Macmillan Company, 1934; Reprint, Millwood, New York: Sagapress, Inc., 1986. Still the best book on the history of the daylily.

Taylor, Norman. *Fragrance in the Garden*. New York, D. Van Nostrand Company, Inc., 1953. Little-known facts on fragrance in the garden.

———. *The Practical Encyclopedia of Gardening*. New York: Halcyon House, 1936. The best of the Taylor encyclopedias.

Thoreau, Henry D., *Journal*. Edited by Bradford Torrey and Francis H. Allen. New York: Dover Publications, 1962. All fourteen volumes bound as two.

Wells, B. W. The Natural Gardens of North Carolina. Chapel Hill: University of North Carolina Press, 1932.

Wilder, Louise Beebe. *Adventures in My Garden and Rock Garden*. New York: Doubleday, Page & Company, 1923. Entertaining and delightful.

———. *Adventures with Hardy Bulbs*. New York: The Macmillan Company, 1936; Reprint, New York: Dover Books, 1974; Reprint, New York: Collier Books, 1990. The basic book about bulbs.

———. *Colour in My Garden*. New York: Doubleday & Page & Co., 1918; Reprint, New York: Atlantic Monthly Press, 1990. Probably the finest American book ever written on using flower color in the garden.

———. *The Fragrant Garden*. New York: The Macmillan Company, 1932. Reprint, New York: Dover Books, 1974. Reprint, New York, Collier Books, 1990. The basic book on fragrance in the garden.

———. *What Happens in My Garden*. New York: The Macmillan Company, 1935. Reprint, New York: Collier Books, 1991. Much information on evening primroses.

Wright, Richardson. *The Story of Gardening*. New York: Dodd, Mead & Company, 1934. Everything about gardens from Babylonia to agricultural experiment stations.

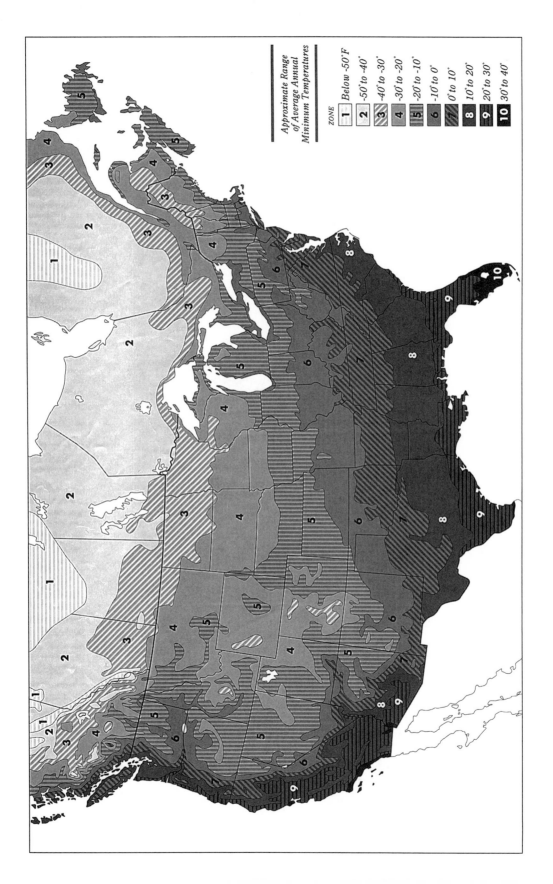

Approximate Range
of Average Annual
Minimum Temperatures

ZONE
1 Below -50°F
2 -50° to -40°
3 -40° to -30°
4 -30° to -20°
5 -20° to -10°
6 -10° to 0°
7 0° to 10°
8 10° to 20°
9 20° to 30°
10 30° to 40°

Numerals in *italics* indicate illustrations.